Equal Shares

The Real Utopias Project

Series editor: Erik Olin Wright

The Real Utopias Project embraces a tension between dreams and practice. It is founded on the belief that what is pragmatically possible is not fixed independently of our imaginations, but is itself shaped by our visions. The fulfillment of such a belief involves 'real utopias': utopian ideals that are grounded in the real potentials for redesigning social institutions.

In its attempt at sustaining and deepening serious discussion of radical alternatives to existing social practices, the Real Utopias Project examines various basic institutions – property rights and the market, secondary associations, the family, the welfare state, among others – and focuses on specific proposals for their fundamental redesign. The books in the series are the result of workshop conferences, at which groups of scholars are invited to respond to provocative manuscripts.

Equal Shares
Making Market Socialism Work
The Real Utopias Project
Volume II

◆

JOHN E. ROEMER

with contributions by
Richard Arneson, Fred Block, Harry Brighouse,
Michael Burawoy, Joshua Cohen, Nancy Folbre,
Andrew Levine, Meike Meurs, Louis Putterman, Joel Rogers,
Debra Satz, Julius Sensat, William Simon, Frank Thompson,
Thomas Weisskopf, Erik Olin Wright

Edited and introduced by Erik Olin Wright

VERSO
London • New York

First published by Verso 1996
© this collection Verso 1996
© in individual contributions the contributors
All rights reserved

Verso
UK: 6 Meard Street, London W1V 3HR
USA: 180 Varick Street, New York NY 10014–4606

Verso is the imprint of New Left Books

ISBN 1–85984–933–4
ISBN 1–85984–053–1 (pbk)

British Library Cataloguing in Publication Data
A catalogue record for this book is available from the British Library

Library of Congress Cataloging-in-Publication Data
A catalog record for this book is available from the Library of Congress

Typeset by Keystroke, Jacaranda Lodge, Wolverhampton
Printed by Biddles Ltd, Guildford and King's Lynn

Contents

Acknowledgments

We would gratefully like to thank the Wisconsin Alumni Research Foundation and the Anonymous Fund of the University of Wisconsin for providing generous funding for the conference that led to this volume. We would also like to thank the A. E. Havens Center for covering many of the incidental costs involved in turning the conference papers into a book and the staff of the Center for making the practical arrangements for the conference.

Earlier versions of a number of papers included in this volume were previously published in a special issue of *Politics and Society*, copyright Sage Publications, Inc. 1994, and are reproduced here with permission. They are:

Chapter 1: John Roemer, 'A Future for Socialism', *Politics and Society* 22:4 (December, 1994), pp. 451–78.

Chapter 2: William H. Simon, 'Inequality and Alienation in the Socialist Capital Market', ibid., pp. 479–88.

Chapter 3: Nancy Folbre, 'Roemer's market Socialism: a Feminist Critique', ibid., pp. 595–606.

Chapter 6: Joshua Cohen and Joel Rogers, 'My Utopia or Yours: comments on *A Future for Socialism*', ibid., pp. 507–22.

Chapter 7: Mieke Meurs, 'Market Socialism as a Culture of Cooperation', ibid., pp. 523–34.

Chapter 8: Erik Olin Wright, 'Political Power, Democracy and Coupon Socialism', ibid., pp. 535–49.

Chapter 9: Louis Putterman, 'Comments on a *Future for Socialism*', ibid., pp. 489–506.

Chapter 12: Harry Brighouse, 'Transitional and Utopian Market Socialism', ibid., pp. 569–84.

Chapter 13: Richard J. Arneson, 'What do Socialists Want?', ibid., pp. 549–68.

Chapter 15: Michael Burawoy, 'Why Coupon Socialism Never Stood a Chance in Russia: the Political Conditions of Economic Transition', ibid., pp. 585–94.

Preface
The Real Utopias Project

Erik Olin Wright

'Real Utopia' seems like a contradiction in terms. Utopias are fantasies, morally inspired designs for social life unconstrained by realistic considerations of human psychology and social feasibility. Realists eschew such fantasies. What is needed are hard-nosed proposals for pragmatically improving our institutions. Instead of indulging in utopian dreams we must accommodate to practical realities.

The Real Utopias Project embraces this tension between dreams and practice. It is founded on the belief that what is pragmatically possible is not fixed independently of our imaginations, but is itself shaped by our visions. Self-fulfilling prophecies are powerful forces in history, and while it may be polyannish to say 'where there is a will there is a way', it is certainly true that without 'will' many 'ways' become impossible. Nurturing clear-sighted understandings of what it would take to create social institutions free of oppression is part of creating a political will for radical social changes to reduce oppression. A vital belief in a utopian destination may be necessary to motivate people to leave on the journey from the status quo in the first place, even though the actual destination may fall short of the utopian ideal. Yet, vague utopian fantasies may lead us astray, encouraging us to embark on trips that have no real destinations at all, or worse still, which lead us over some unforeseen abyss. Along with 'where there is a will there is a way', the human struggle for emancipation confronts 'the road to hell is paved with good intentions'. What we need, then, are 'real utopias': utopian ideals that are grounded in the real potentials of humanity, utopian destinations that have pragmatically accessible waystations, utopian designs of institutions that can inform our practical tasks of muddling through in a world of imperfect conditions for social change. These are the goals of the Real Utopias Project.

The Real Utopias Project is an attempt at sustaining and deepening serious discussion of radical alternatives to existing institutions. The objective is to focus on specific proposals for the fundamental redesign of basic social institutions rather than on either vague, abstract formulations of grand designs, or on small reforms of existing practices. In practical terms, the Real Utopias Project consists of a series of workshop conferences, each revolving around a manuscript that lays out the basic outlines of a radical institutional proposal. The essays presented at these conferences are then revised for the books in the Real Utopias Project.

Introduction

Erik Olin Wright

For a hundred and fifty years, struggles for radical egalitarian alternatives to capitalism have been waged under the banner of 'socialism'. While the precise meaning of this idea has always been the subject of intense debate, radical egalitarians have usually believed that an economy based on private ownership of the principle means of production and the overriding search for profit maximization could be supplanted by one organized around the satisfaction of human needs through some kind of public or social ownership. Even among those social democratic reformers whose political efforts were directed mainly towards ameliorating conditions in the existing society, rather than working for a rupture with capitalist institutions, socialism still served as a visionary backdrop which kept radical egalitarian values alive.

Since the mid-1980s this vision has increasingly seemed to many people to be a fantasy. This is perhaps ironic. One might have anticipated that the demise of the command economies in the USSR and elsewhere would have emancipated the idea of socialism from the liabilities of Soviet authoritarianism. After all, for decades democratic socialists in the West had been denouncing the undemocratic practices in the Soviet Union and arguing that socialism should be understood as the extension of radical democracy to the economy, rather than bureaucratic control of production. At long last, one might have thought, the ideal of democratic socialism could gain credibility.

That is not what has happened. With the end of authoritarian state socialism, the idea of socialism itself has lost credibility. Capitalism increasingly seems to many people of the Left as the only viable possibility. For all of its deep and tragic flaws, the empirical example of the Soviet Union at least demonstrated to people that some alternative to capitalism was possible; capitalism was not the only game in town. Democratic socialists could then plausibly argue that the flaws in the command economies could be remedied with serious demo-cratic reconstruction. Without the practical example of even a flawed, but still radical alternative to capitalism, capitalism assumes ever more strongly the character of a 'natural' system, incapable of radical transformation.

In this context, the Left is in vital need of bold and creative new thinking on the question of the institutional conditions for radical egalitarian alternatives to capitalism. Whether or not in the end such alternatives are properly described as 'socialism' is not really important; the crucial issue is forging well-grounded ideals of how such egalitarian values can be translated into a politics of radical institutional innovation.

This volume in the Real Utopias Project series is devoted to an examination of one such proposal: John Roemer's innovative and provocative model for how institutions could be designed so as to make 'market socialism' a sustainable – and desirable – way of organizing an economy. To many people the expression 'market socialism' is an oxymoron: either the markets have to be massively curtailed for socialist principles to mean anything or the socialism has to be deeply corrupted to enable markets to work properly. John Roemer, in his 1994 book, A Future for Socialism (Harvard University Press), challenges this view by elaborating a relatively simple device which, he believes, will enable an economy both to have well-functioning markets and to remain faithful to the egalitarian ideals of socialism.

How does Roemer propose to accomplish this? In a nutshell, his proposal involves creating two kinds of money in a society: commodity money, used to purchase commodities for consumption, and share money, also referred to as 'coupons', used to purchase ownership rights in firms. These two kinds of money are non-convertible: you cannot legally trade coupons for dollars. Coupons are distributed to the population in an egalitarian manner. Citizens, upon reaching the age of majority, are given their per capita share of the total coupon value of the productive property in the economy. With these coupons they can then buy shares from which they derive certain ownership rights, including dividends from the profits of firms and the right to vote for at least some of the people on the boards of directors of firms. There is thus a stock market, but the stocks can only be purchased with coupons, not dollars. Shares and coupons are not transferable. You cannot give your shares away, but must sell them at the market coupon rate, and you cannot give your coupons away. At death, all shares and unspent coupons revert to the state for redistribution. The non-transferability and non-convertibility of coupons prevents ownership from becoming concentrated: the rich (in dollars) cannot buy out the poor. Since stocks are sold for coupons, not dollars, firms cannot directly raise capital by selling stocks. Financial capital is raised through credit markets organized by state banks and through various schemes by which the state converts the coupons acquired by firms when they issue stock into dollars. This involvement of the state allows for a significant degree of 'planning the market'. The result of this scheme, Roemer argues, is relatively freely functioning market mechanisms along with a sustainable egalitarian distribution of property rights, a roughly equal distribution of profits, and a significant planning capacity of the state over broad investment priorities; in other words, market socialism.

In May 1994, the Havens Center for the Study of Social Structure and Social Change at the University of Wisconsin, held a two-day workshop conference on Roemer's book. This volume in the Real Utopias Project begins with a summary of the core ideas of Roemer's proposal. This is followed by the revised versions of the conference papers which critically examine various aspects of Roemer's model and its normative and practical implications.

PART I

A Proposal for Market Socialism

═══════ 1 ═══════

A Future for Socialism
John E. Roemer

1 Introduction

The demise of the Communist system in the Soviet Union and Eastern Europe has caused many to believe that socialism cannot exist, either in the present world or as an ideal. I shall argue that it can, but that it requires some revision of standard views of what constitutes socialism. If one thought socialism were coextensive with the Soviet model, then clearly it would be dead. I shall defend the idea of market socialism.[1]

The term 'market socialism' comes to us from what has been called the socialist calculation debate of the 1930s, in which the two principal protagonists were Oscar Lange and Friederich Hayek. Lange argued that what economists now call neoclassical price theory showed the possibility of combining central planning and the market; while Hayek retorted that planning would subvert at its heart the mechanism which is the source of capitalism's vitality. Hayek's criticisms of Lange's market socialism, and more recently those of Janos Kornai, are for the most part on the mark. But the experiences of capitalism, as well as of socialism, since 1945, suggest ways of reformulating the concept of market socialism in response to the Hayekian critique of its intellectual ancestor. This reformulation is my task.

Economic theory does not yet enable us to write a complete balance sheet of the benefits and costs of the market mechanism. During the 1930s, when Lange and Hayek wrote about market socialism, the Soviet Union was undergoing rapid industrialization. There was, apparently, full employment in that country, while workers and machines were massively idle in the industrialized capitalist world. Hayek therefore wrote from a defensive position, while Lange may well have felt that his proposal was fine-tuning for

7

a socialist system that was, inevitably, the face of the future. Today, the tables are turned. Yet both the pro-socialists of the 1930s and the pro-capitalists of today jump too quickly to conclusions, for we understand fully the effects of markets only in very special circumstances.

Economic theory can explain how, if all economic actors are small relative to the market and cannot individually affect prices, if externalities are absent, and if there is a sufficient number of insurance and financial markets, the equilibrium in a market economy will engender an allocation of resources that is Pareto efficient – that is, efficient in the sense that no other allocation of resources exists which could render everyone simultaneously better off. But this kind of static efficiency may be relatively unimportant compared to the dynamic efficiency with which markets are often credited – that they produce innovations in technology and commodities more effectively than any other economic mechanism could. Although we seem to have much evidence of market dynamism, we have no adequate economic theory of it; nor do we have a controlled experiment which would permit a skeptical scientist confidently to assert that markets are superior to planning in this dynamic sense. The real-life experiments are severely polluted, from a scientific viewpoint: the most dynamic economies of the 1960s onwards (Japan and the East Asian tigers) have used markets with a good dose of planning, and the Communist economies not only had planning and the absence of markets but also political dictatorship, a background condition an experimental designer would like to be able to alter.

The social scientist must, therefore, be more agnostic about the effects of the market than are elementary economics textbooks and the popular press. Indeed, contemporary economic theory has come to see markets as operating within the essential context of non-market institutions, most notably: firms; contract law; the interlinking institutions between economic institutions and other actors, such as between the firm and its stockholders; and the state. Large capitalist firms are centrally planned organizations (in which internal transactions are not mediated by a price system), usually run by managers hired to represent the interests of shareholders. This they do imperfectly, as their own interests do not typically coincide with the interests of shareholders. Contract law is an essential supplement to the market: long-term contracts are, indeed, instruments which render it costly for parties to them to return to the market during the life of the contract. Furthermore, in different capitalist economies different kinds of non-market institutions have evolved. We do have somewhat of a real-life experiment which can help in evaluating alternative economic mechanisms. Germany and Japan, for example, have very different institutions through which owners of firms monitor their managements from those in the United States and the United Kingdom.

In short, the market does not perform its good deeds unaided; it is supported by a myriad cast of institutional characters which have evolved painstakingly over time, and in a variety of ways, in various market economies. My central argument is that these institutional solutions to the design problems of capitalism also suggest how the design problems of socialism may be solved in a market setting.

To see why this may be so, I will first quickly, and necessarily inadequately, summarize the theory of income distribution of Hayek, more generally, of the Austrian school of economics. According to this view, the distribution of income in a market economy is, in the long run, determined by the relative scarcity of various factors of production, principally human talents, including entrepreneurial talent. Property rights should, in the long run, be viewed as themselves derivative of talent. Firms are indeed just the means through which entrepreneurs capitalize their talent; in turn, it is profits from firms which enable their owners to purchase real estate and other natural resources, so that, in the long run, natural resources, too, are owned by talented people or their descendants. Furthermore, any attempt to interfere with the operation of markets – that is, with the institution that maximizes the freedom to compete in the economic sphere – will only reduce overall welfare, as it will inevitably result in conditions which inhibit entrepreneurs from bringing their talents fully into play.

Were this 'naturalistic' view correct, egalitarians would have little remedy for inequality other than education, serving to develop the talents of as many as possible, and perhaps inheritance taxes. What I believe the institutional view of capitalism that I have outlined shows, however, is that the advanced capitalist economy is in large part the product of large, complex institutions, whose operation depends upon the combined efforts of many 'ordinary' people – ordinary in the sense that their talents are not of the rare variety that the Hayekian view envisions, but result from training and education. The wealth of society is not due primarily to rugged and rare individuals, but is reproducible, according to blueprints which are quite well understood. The market is necessary to implement competition and to economize on information, but not so much to cultivate the inspiration of rare geniuses.

A particular way in which the modern view of capitalism suggests a future for socialism is in its understanding of the firm as a nexus of principal–agent relationships. It is not correct to characterize modern capitalist firms as instruments by which entrepreneurs capitalize their talents. The profits of firms are distributed to many owners, who have no direct control over decisions which affect profitability, and who are in large part not responsible for firms' successes or failures. Firms are run by hired agents of their owners: this suggests that hired agents could as well run firms in a socialist economy, one in which profits would be distributed even more diffusely than they are in the large capitalist corporation. Indeed the mechanisms that have evolved (or been designed) under capitalism that enable owners to control management can be transported to a socialist framework.

In contrast to the 'thin' Hayekian and neoclassical views, which see markets as a minimal structure organizing competition among talented individuals, the modern 'thick' view sees markets as operating within the context of complex, man-made institutions, through which all individual contributions become pasteurized and refined. These two views of the market are, I suggest, substantially different, and the latter 'thick' view, unlike the former, is amenable to the coexistence of markets and socialism. Income distribution, in particular, is more malleable under the thick view; the door is opened to reducing inequality substantially, short of massive education, as the realloca-tion of profits will, if properly done, have little or no deleterious effect on economic efficiency.

In what follows, I will try to flesh out these vague claims.

2 What Socialists Want

I believe socialists want:

1. equality of opportunity for self-realization and welfare;
2. equality of opportunity for political influence; and
3. equality of social status.

By self-realization, I mean the development and application of one's talents in a direction that gives meaning to one's life. This is a specifically Marxian conception of human flourishing,[2] and is to be distinguished, for instance, from John Rawls's notion of fulfillment of a plan of life, which might consist in enjoying one's family and friends, or eating fine meals, or counting blades of grass.[3] These activities do not count as self-realization, this being a process of self-transformation that requires struggle in a way that eating a fine meal does not. One does, however, derive welfare from enjoying one's family and eating fine meals, and so I do attribute value to these activities in the socialist's reckoning, for (1) requires equality of opportunity for self-realization and welfare.[4]

That equality of *opportunity* for self-realization and welfare is the goal, rather than equality of self-realization and welfare, requires comment. Were equality of welfare the goal rather than equality of opportunity for welfare, then society would be mandated to provide huge resource endowments to those who adopt terribly expensive and unrealistic goals. Suppose I, a poor athlete, come to believe that my life has been worthless unless I reach the top of Mount Everest on foot. This may require a large amount of money, to hire sufficient Sherpas and other support services to make that journey possible. Equality of opportunity for welfare, on the other hand, puts some responsibility on me for choosing welfare-inducing goals that are reasonable. It is certainly tricky to decide what allocation of resources will give all people an equal opportunity for welfare or self-realization, but I hope the principle is clear from this example. What distinguishes socialists or leftists from conservatives is, in large part, the view of how deeply one must go in order to equalize opportunities. Conservatives believe in going not very deeply: if there is no discrimination in hiring and everyone has access to education through a public school system or vouchers, then the conservative standard of equality of opportunity is met. Socialists believe that those guarantees only touch the surface. Equality of opportunity requires special compensation or subsidy for children who have grown up in homes without access to privilege. Most generally, equality of opportunity requires that people be compensated for handicaps they suffer, induced by factors over which they have no control.[5]

Suppose that we have clarified what each of (1), (2) and (3) mean (I will not here attempt to offer any explication of (2) and (3)). The statements of (1), (2) and (3) are still inaccurate. For instance, what socialists really want is not equality of opportunity for self-realization, but equality of such at a high level. So (1) should be restated as: socialists want an organization of society which equalizes the opportunity for self-realization at a level that is no lower than any other organization of society could achieve as an equal level. In other words, (1) says we should maximize, over all possible organizations of society, the level of opportunity for self-realization which can be achieved as an equal level for all. Desideratum (2) calls on us to choose that organization of society which maximizes the degree of equality for opportunity for political influence; a similar statement holds for (3). It is, however, impossible to maximize three objectives at once. That is, the kind of social organization that maximizes the equal level of opportunity for self-realization may well induce highly unequal levels of political influence.[6]

There are two responses to this problem. The first says: there is a form of society in which all three objectives are equalized simultaneously, when 'the free development of each becomes the condition for the free development of all', or some such thing. I think this is an unsubstantiated and utopian claim. The second response says that one must admit the possibility of trade-offs among the three objectives. This, in fact, is what most of us do. For instance, a lively debate has taken place in the socialist movement on the question: 'Which is primary, democracy or equality?' Is equality of opportunity for political influence more important that equality of opportunity for self-realization and welfare? Socialists have different answers to this question. For example, Western socialists assign more importance to equality of opportunity for political influence than most Soviet socialists did. Some socialists did not support the Sandinistas because of the lack of press freedom and democracy in Nicaragua.

I will not offer here any particular preference order over the three equalisanda. I shall be concerned only with investigating the possibility of equalizing income without any unacceptable loss in efficiency. Indeed, I believe raising the income of the poor is the most important single step to improving their opportunities for self-realization and welfare.

3 Public Ownership

I believe that socialists have made a fetish of public ownership: public ownership has been viewed as the *sine qua non* of socialism, which is based on a false inference. What socialists want are the three equalities enumerated above; they should be open-minded about what kinds of property relations in productive assets would bring about those equalities. There is an infinite gradation of possible property rights between full, unregulated private ownership of firms (which exists almost nowhere) and complete control of a firm by a government organ. The link between state ownership and the three equalities is tenuous, and I think one does much better to drop the concept from the socialist constitution. Socialists should advocate those property relations in productive assets that will bring about a society that ranks highest according to their preferences over the three equalities. One cannot honestly say, at this point in history, that one knows what those property rights must be.

I view the choice of property rights over firms and other resources to be an entirely instrumental matter. The history of socialism on the question is, very crudely, as follows. Private property, characteristic of capitalism, was abolished and replaced, under the Bolsheviks, by state property. For complex reasons (including bureaucratic ossification and class interest), this form remained dominant for seventy years. The property form of the labor-managed firm remained peripheral in the socialist movement. The widest variety of property forms became visible in modern capitalism, not socialism: non-profit firms, limited liability corporations, partnerships, sole proprietorships, public firms, social democratic property,[7] labor-managed firms, and other forms of social-republican property.[8] The property forms which will best further the socialist goals may involve direct popular control or state control of the means of production in only a distant way.

By market socialism, I shall mean any of a variety of economic arrangements in which most goods, including labor, are distributed through the price system and the profits of firms, perhaps managed by workers or not, are distributed quite equally among the population. By what mechanism profits can be so distributed, without unacceptable costs in efficiency, is the central question.

From a somewhat more abstract viewpoint, the choice of property relations in firms and land should be optimized over two desiderata: their effect on the distribution of income and their effect on efficiency. With respect to efficiency, we can be more specific: property relations should engender competition and innovation, and should shelter firms from certain kinds of inefficient government interference. Private ownership of firms *sometimes* accomplishes these objectives. It engenders competition when ownership is not too highly concentrated in an industry, and it prevents inefficient political interference when constitutional provisions that prevent such interference are enforced. Private ownership gives certain persons the incentive to demand constitutional enforcement of these property rights and hence of government non-interference. But it is worthwhile noting that, even in the United States, private ownership of firms is not a foolproof institution in respect of preventing government interference. In 1950, President Truman seized the big steel firms in order to force them to increase production of armaments for the Korean War. This action was, in the end, overturned by the courts. I mention this example to encourage us to think more generally about a property relation as an instrument with certain properties. The experience of the twentieth century may suggest that only two alternatives exist with regard to firms: state ownership and private ownership. In principle, there might well exist institutions other than private ownership of firms which would engender competition and prevent inefficient government interference just as well as private ownership does, while having better distributional properties. Surely the failure of the property relation at the other end of the spectrum from private ownership to perform these tasks well should not settle the question.

4 Why the Centrally Planned Economies Failed

The failure of the Soviet-type economies was due to the conjunction of three of their characteristics: (1) the allocation of most goods by an administrative apparatus under which producers were not forced to compete with each other; (2) direct control of firms by political units; and (3) non-competitive, non-democratic politics. Noting this, however, does not explain the failures, for we must uncover the mechanism through which these characteristics induced economic failure. In some of my recent work, I have written that principal–agent problems were the source of failure of the Soviet-type economies.[9] I now believe that the true story is more complex. In this section I shall first outline the argument of Soviet-type failures based on principal–agent problems, then offer some critical remarks on it, and finally modify the argument.

The contour of the argument is that the three characteristics I just listed conspired to prevent the solution of principal–agent problems which, in capitalist democracies, are successfully solved. Communist societies faced three principal–agent problems: (i) the manager–worker relationship in the factory or the collective farm; (ii) the planner–manager relationship; and (iii) the public–planner relationship. Managers must try to get workers to carry out their production plans; planners must try to get managers to carry out the planning bureau's plan; and the planners, in a socialist regime, are supposed to be agents doing the best they can for their collective principal, the public.

The initial, utopian view of the Bolsheviks, and later of the Maoists in China, was that economic incentives were unnecessary to solve these principal–agent problems, and that a socialist society would instead rely upon the transformation of persons into what used to be called 'socialist man'. In Mao's language, all should learn to 'serve the people', and not to take those actions which maximize personal security or comfort. If this transformation had occurred, the agency problems would have been greatly mitigated. In the event, most people could not motivate themselves for a lifetime by serving only the public good; people responded to their immediate situations much as they do in capitalist societies, by trying to look after their material interests a good proportion of the time.

To be more specific, the *manager–worker agency problem* festered for two reasons: workers had little motivation to work hard if it was virtually impossible to fire them, and there was little incentive to earn more because so few goods were available to buy. Much of the consumption bundle, including housing, was provided directly by the firm and not through the market.

The *manager–planner relationship* became one where the planners, or politicians, depended on the firms in their regions for income, and so, rather than carrying out plans proposed by the planning bureau, firm managers entered into bargaining relationships with politicians. An instance of this relationship was the 'soft budget constraint': political authorities extended loans and tax exemptions to firms that, from the viewpoint of economic efficiency, should not have been extended. This was done in part because, not officially recognizing the existence of unemployment, the system had no mechanism for retraining and rehiring laid-off workers. The path of least resistance for government and planning bureaucrats often consisted in continuing to finance a firm that should have been allowed to die.

The third agency problem, between the planners and the public, was supposed to be solved, in theory, by the vanguard role of the Communist Party: 'From the masses to the masses' was Mao's theory of the party as agent of the people. But Mao was wrong; political competition is required to empower the public, and this was thoroughly squashed by Communist parties throughout the world holding state power.

What are the analogous principal–agent problems in a capitalist economy, and how are they addressed? The worker–manager problem remains essentially the same; it is solved by using both the carrot and the stick. Arguably, the carrot works better. For instance, job ladders within the firm, with wages increasing as one moves up the ladder, are constructed to give workers an incentive to build a career in the firm. This is a type of 'efficiency wage' theory, in which a firm pays a worker more than the worker is willing to accept (or, to be somewhat imprecise, more than the market requires) to bind her to the job. Much of modern industrial relations is concerned with ways of solving the manager–worker agency problem. In addition, workers depend almost entirely on their wage income to purchase goods, unlike in the Soviet economies.

Under capitalism, the analog of the planner–manager agency problem is the *stockholder–manager agency problem*. Managers are supposed to undertake policies which are in the best interest of the stockholders (that is, which maximize profits, or the value of the firm). It is often not in the best personal interest of the manager to do so: he may not want to liquidate an unprofitable branch of the firm; he may be reluctant to distribute profits as dividends to shareholders, preferring to keep them to finance projects internally, and thus to avoid the scrutiny that a bank would insist upon before approving a loan; he may purchase corporate jets for executive travel, and make other lavish expenditures that are not in the stockholders' interest. Different capitalist economies have undertaken quite different strategies to solve this agency problem. It is believed by many finance economists that the stock market and the takeover process are the institutions that force managers to operate firms in the interests of shareholders. If profits decline because of bad management, the stock price of the firm falls, and the firm becomes an attractive target for a takeover. This, it is argued, is the main disciplinary device that induces managers to act in the interests of shareholders.

Japan and Germany, however, have quite different ways of creating efficient management. The stock market has been relatively unimportant in Japanese corporate finance. Firms are largely financed by bank loans, and stockholders have little say in corporate decisions. Japanese firms are organized into groups called *keiretsu*, each of which is associated with a main bank that is responsible for organizing loan consortia for the firms in its group. The bank is in large part responsible for monitoring the firm's management. The bank even protects its firms from takeovers. A bank has an interest in running a tight ship so that its *keiretsu* is an attractive one for new firms to join, for if it disciplines unprofitable firms it can easily arrange loan consortia for its *keiretsu*'s members. In Germany, there is also bank-centric monitoring, and takeovers are virtually non-existent.

What is the analog of the public–planner agency problem under capitalism? It must be the *public–stockholder agency problem*, except neither capitalist property relations nor culture require the stockholder to be an agent of the public. At this point, the theory of capitalism invokes Adam Smith: stockholders, that is to say firm owners, are directed to undertake those actions which are in the public interest as if by an invisible hand. But the invisible hand only works well under a stringent set of conditions. In practice, modern capitalist societies have developed other institutions where the invisible hand fails: anti-trust law; regulation of various kinds; indicative planning; taxation and public expenditures; and so on.

The argument, then, seeks to establish that a combination of markets and political democracy solves capitalism's three principal–agent problems better than dictatorship and administrative allocation solve the three analogous problems in Soviet-type economies.

The skepticism I now have about the validity of this argument concerns the growth in Soviet economies in the post-war period until 1970. Indeed, earlier Western criticisms of these political economies were of a markedly different nature from their attacks of the 1980s. In the earlier period, Western critics argued that, *despite* its economic success, Communism was bad for human welfare because of the lack of political freedom.

If, indeed, it is true that for about twenty years in the post-war period, and certainly during the 1930s in the Soviet Union, economic growth was respectable in the Communist economies, then we cannot simply invoke principal–agent problems as an explanation of the failure of those economies in the 1980s. At least, the principal–agent argument is not sufficiently fine-grained, for some characteristic of these economies that changed between 1960 and 1985 must be brought into play. I conjecture that one important change concerned the dependence of the improvement in economic welfare on techno-logical change. In the post-war period, economic welfare could improve rapidly without technological innovation, since these economies were in large part devastated by the war, and rebuilding them increased economic welfare substantially, even without technological innova-tion. By the 1980s, or perhaps earlier, growth in economic welfare depended much more on the ability of an economy to innovate. At this, the Soviet-type economies failed dismally, and it is misleading to characterize this failure as due to principal–agent problems, except in the tautological sense that the public was not being well served by its agents, the planners and managers, if the latter were not succeeding in introducing technological change.

To state the issue somewhat differently, it is false to say that sufficient technological change did not occur because some agent was not carrying out some principal's orders. No one gave such orders. The correct statement is that, without the competition that is provided by markets, both domestic and international, no business enterprise is forced to innovate, and without such forcing, innovation, at least at the rate that market economies engender, does not occur. Perhaps even the 'forcing' view puts too much emphasis on the incentive issue. It might just have been extremely difficult to innovate in the Soviet-type economies, because, for instance, information about commodities on the technological frontier was very hard to come by, because the best engineers and scientists were recruited by the defense sector, and because the *Weltanschauung* of the system belittled the kind of consumer gratification that is catered to by capitalist enterprise. This contrasts with the principal–agent explanation, which emphasizes the view that managers and workers did not work hard because of a failure of incentive due to the economic mechanism.

The question becomes, then, whether an economic mechanism can be designed under which technological innovation will take place, but in which a characteristically capitalistic distribution of income does not come about. More specifically, can competition between business enterprises, leading to innovation, be induced without a regime of private property in firms? For, at this point, we have no observations of innovation as a generic multi-sectoral phenomenon in an economy except when it is induced by competition.

5 Public Bads and the Distribution of Profits

One might object that a market socialism whose focus is the equal distribution of profits will not amount to much, for profits only account for fifteen to thirty per cent of national income, and they may account under market socialism for less than that, because some revenue that takes the form of corporate profits in a capitalist system would there take the form of interest payments to banks and their depositors. I believe, however, that the partial equalization of income that takes place in these systems is only part of the story.

Classical arguments against capitalism note not only its bad distributional properties, but its generation of what in modern economic parlance are called 'public bads'. Public bads are often created by free rider problems: it may be in the interest of each individual to perform a certain action, treating the behavior of others as given, but the collective result is a situation that is worse for everyone than if all had abstained from the action.

There is a class of public bads having the property of being inputs into or joint products of production. Pollution is the prototypical example: it is a joint product of many production processes, and has a negative effect on people's welfare. The essential property of public bads in this class is that their presence increases the profits of firms and indeed the wages of workers. Other examples are wars which increase profits, for example, by lowering the price of imported inputs used by firms; noxious advertising, for instance, by cigarette companies; investment in firms doing business in a South Africa under apartheid; and fast assembly line speeds, or, more generally, the lack of enforcement of labor legislation, and legislation applying to occupational safety and health. All these practices increase profits, and often wages as well, yet also directly reduce the welfare of the population.

It has also been argued that a highly unequal distribution of wealth is itself a public bad, as it creates a kind of society that decreases the welfare of all – most obviously, through the crime that it generates, and less proximately, through the lack of community that it engenders.

The level of public bads in a democratic political economy is an outcome of the political process, where different actors attempt to implement their economic interests. In a capitalist economy, there is a small class of wealthy individuals who receive large amounts of income as their share of firms' profits, and it is generally in their interest to have high levels of the profit-increasing public bads. The positive effect from the public bad on the income of members of this class more than compensates them for the direct negative welfare effect.[10] Individuals who stand to gain from them actively fight, through political activity, for high levels of these profit-inducing public bads. The virtue of the market-socialist proposals is that there would exist no small, powerful class of individuals deriving large incomes from profits, hence no class would have such an interest in fighting for large levels of public bads.

I do not make the blanket statement that, if no class exists which derives large incomes from corporate profits, then low levels of public bads will be forthcoming. One must examine carefully the general equilibrium effects of a market-socialist mechanism that precludes the formation of such a class. I have done some preliminary work on this, which I summarize in section 7 below.

6 A Market Socialist Economy with a Stock Market

In this section, I briefly outline one model of a market-socialist economy. There are four 'corporate' actors among whom financial transactions will take place. The first is the *adult citizenry*. The second is the sector of '*public firms*', but as we shall see, these are not owned directly by the state. In a thorough-going market-socialist economy, all large firms (roughly equivalent to the corporate sector in an advanced capitalist country) would belong to this sector. The third is a set of *mutual funds*. The fourth is the *state treasury*.

Every adult citizen would receive from the state treasury an equal endowment of *coupons*, that can be used only to purchase shares of mutual funds. *Only* coupons can be used to purchase shares of mutual funds, not money. Only mutual funds can purchase shares of public firms, using coupons. Prices of corporate shares and mutual funds are, hence, denominated in coupons; they will oscillate depending on the supply of and demand for shares. Citizens are free to sell their mutual-fund shares for coupons, and to reinvest the coupons in other mutual funds. Finally, firms may exchange coupons with the state treasury for investment funds, and may purchase coupons from the treasury with money. This is the only point at which coupons exchange for money. These investment funds play the role of equity in the firm.

A share of a firm entitles the owning mutual fund to a share of the firm's profits, and a share of a mutual fund entitles the owning citizen to a share of the mutual fund's revenues. When a citizen dies, his mutual-fund shares must be sold, and the coupon revenues are returned to the state treasury. The treasury, in turn, issues coupon endowments to citizens reaching the age of majority.

Firms' investment funds come from two sources: bank loans (or corporate bonds financed by banks) and the state treasury, through coupon exchange. Citizens deposit savings in banks. The supply and demand for loans determines the interest rate, and the supply of coupons and the demand for state investment funds determines the rate at which coupons exchange for investment funds at the treasury. The treasury's funds are raised by taxation of the citizenry (or, perhaps some combination of corporate and personal taxes).

Thus, the coupon system is meant to endow each adult citizen with a stream of income during his lifetime, his transient property right in the nation's 'public' firms. Only during his lifetime does a citizen have an entitlement to the profits of firms. Because shares can be purchased only with coupons, and coupons cannot be sold by citizens for money, rich citizens will not generally own more shares than poor citizens, except in so far as they are better informed about investment opportunities. This effect is mollified by the requirement to purchase mutual funds, not the shares of individual firms. Of course, some citizens will end up holding relatively valuable portfolios of mutual funds, but those cannot be bequeathed to children. *Inter vivos* gifts of mutual funds shares are prohibited.

Mutual funds are used as (mandatory) intermediaries between citizens and firms for two reasons: the first is paternalistic, to protect citizens from squandering their coupon endowments on poor investments. The second reason is somewhat more subtle. Since a citizen cannot pass down her shareholdings to her child, nor can she sell shares for money, were citizens able to purchase (coupon) shares directly from firms, there would be a tendency for some firms to emerge as 'cash cows'. These firms would sell off their assets, and distribute the proceeds to shareholders as dividends. During this process, the (coupon) value of the firm's shares would decrease to zero, but by that time the shareholders would have capitalized their share holdings, thus avoiding the 100 per cent death tax on coupon holdings. Such cash cows might as well constitute an inefficient use of resources. Now, in principle, the same thing could happen with unregulated mutual funds: some funds could specialize in holding portfolios of cash cows. One easy way to prevent this occurrence is to regulate mutual funds by requiring that each have a balanced age distribution of owners. To keep the age distribution balanced would require the mutual firm not to purchase only cash cows.

The existence of both equity and debt finance will allow firms to choose a desired degree of leverage. Were no equity available (but all financing were to be through banks), the interest rate would arguably be higher than it is in a 'comparable' capitalist economy, since debtors would be subject to more risk. There is also an element of wealth redistribution in the institution of firm equity, as designed, for it may be assumed that the taxes which raise funds for the treasury are progressive, while all citizens become initially equal owners of the capital stock through the coupon system.

In equilibrium, the total number of coupons is equal to the total coupon value of equity in the public sector because no firm will desire to hold coupons (absenting transaction costs). Since the total coupon value of stock held by citizens is also equal to the total number of coupons, we have the identity that the total value of stock is equal to aggregate equity of firms in the public sector.

Banks will play a special role in the economy as the primary monitors of firms, as will be described in section 8. Banks will also be public firms in the coupon sector: their shares will be purchasable by mutual funds as well.

As I have indicated, the intention of the coupon mechanism is to distribute the profits of firms quite equally among the adult citizenry. In the next two sections, I study the effect of the coupon system on the welfare of different income strata of the population, due to the effect of equalizing the distribution of profits on the level of public bads as well as the claim that the coupon system will induce the kind of competition and innovation characteristic of capitalist firms.[11]

7 Contrasting Welfare Effects of the Coupon Economy and an Egalitarian Capitalist Economy[12]

The model I shall describe in this section is not intended to be a complete description of a market-socialist economy. A number of matters are ignored, such as investment planning by the state and the monitoring of firms. The purpose of the present model is to analyze one question only, the difference in the level of welfare of citizens that would come about as a consequence of different ways of defining property rights in firms, when profit-inducing public bads exist.

I shall describe an economic environment upon which two possible politico-economic mechanisms shall be alternatively imposed, one capitalist, the other market-socialist (coupon). The problem is to compute the welfare of the population at the equilibrium induced by each mechanism. The environment is described as follows. There is only one good produced, which all people like to consume. There is also a public bad, to be thought of as pollution. One may think of this public bad as an input in each firm's production function, even if, in actuality, it is a joint product of the firm's production process. The level of the public bad that the firm is allowed to 'emit' in part determines its production – the higher the permissible level of pollution, the greater the firm's production at a given level of the other input, which is the good itself. Thus firms produce a good using 'inputs' of pollution and the good.

There are many citizens, of whom a small percentage are initially rich, and a large percentage have initially a middle or low level of wealth. Initially, that is, the rich own a large amount of the good; the middle a smaller amount; and the poor an even smaller amount. All citizens have the same preferences over consumption of the good, at various times, and of the public bad: utility is increasing in consumption of the good, and decreasing in consumption of the bad. The bad is public because all citizens must consume the same amount of it, namely, the amount emitted by firms. There may be many firms in the economy. There are also banks, which accept deposits and make loans.

There are three relevant dates at which things happen in the economy, call them 0, 1 and 2. Consumption of the good occurs at dates 0 and 2, and production and consumption of the public bad occur at date 2. Thus, a person's utility function has the form $u(x_0, x_2, z)$, where x_0 is consumption of the good at date 0, x_2 is consumption at date 2, and z is consumption of the public bad at date 2. There is uncertainty in the economy, which takes the following form. There are various possible *states of the world* that may occur at date 2. These states are brought about by events that should be thought of as occurring outside the model. What is relevant is that the production function of each firm depends upon the state of the world. Thus, the state of the world might be the weather, and the weather might affect the production of firms, which in this case are farms. Or investors may be uncertain about the technological change that will have taken place by date 2. At date 0, all citizens are supposed to know the probabilities with which the various states will occur at date 2. At date 0, each citizen owns, as well as some amount of the good which characterizes her as rich or poor, an equal per capita share of every firm in the economy. At date 0, each citizen shall have to make consumption and investment decisions, whose precise nature depends upon the economic mechanism that shall be imposed. At date 1, citizens vote to determine the level of pollution that firms shall be allowed to emit. At date 2, one of the states of the world occurs, following which production takes place, with each firm emitting the amount of pollution that has been determined by vote at date 1. Output of the firms is distributed to citizens, and consumed by them, according to the investment decisions they have made at date 0. A pictorial representation of the dated nature of events in the economy is presented in figure 1.

Let us now impose a capitalist economic mechanism on this economic environment. There is a stock market at date 0. People initially each own equal shares of all firms, but they can now trade these shares, where the price of a share is denominated in units of the good. (The issues of cash cows, and hence mutual funds, are ignored in this section.) Thus, at date 0, a person can purchase a portfolio of stock, using her endowment of stock and her endowment of the good in trade. She also chooses how much of her endowment to consume at date 0, and how much to put in the bank at the going interest rate. (She may, alternatively, borrow from the bank.) She also must contribute to the firm a share of its total investment (which is its input of the good) equal to the share of its stock she has purchased.[13] After elections take place and the amount of the public bad is determined at date 1, and after the state of the world is revealed and production takes place at date 2, the citizen receives a share of output from each firm equal to the share of its stock she has purchased, and also receives

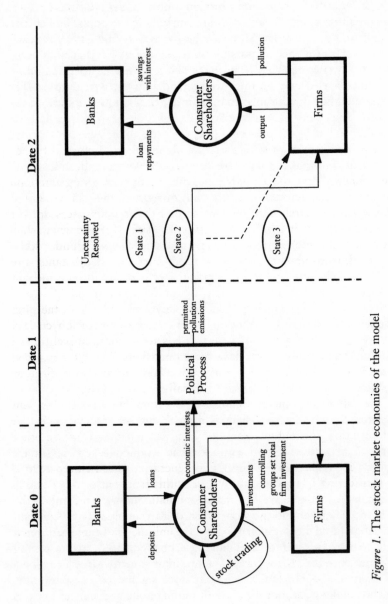

Figure 1. The stock market economies of the model

her principal plus interest from the deposit she made in the bank at date 0 (or, alternatively, pays principal plus interest on the loan she took). Thus, if, at date 0, citizens can predict the outcome of the vote at date 1, and they face prices for stock of each firm and an interest rate, then they can choose a portfolio and consumption plan that maximizes their expected utility, the expectation being taken over the various states of the world that may occur at date 2. This optimal choice will be the same for every poor person and the same for every rich person, but it will, of course, differ among the types of people.

How does a firm choose its level of investment, the amount of input it shall use in production at date 2? At the equilibrium level of investment for each firm, citizens will purchase its stock in varying amounts. The board of directors of the firm will comprise representatives of the three types of shareholders, but with votes that are not necessarily in proportion to their ownership shares. The firm's investment choice must be that which is chosen by the board of directors, under some rule for how the board solves its political problem. For instance, the investment choice might be that which is optimal for the median shareholder on the board.

Finally, we must stipulate how people vote at date 1 on the level of the public bad. Given the investment and consumption choices that people have made at date 0, each has some optimal level for the amount of the public bad. (In this economy with just three types, there is one optimal level of the public bad for the poor, one for the middle, and one for the rich.) Recall that increasing the amount of the public bad increases the output firms can produce at date 2, given their investment choices, and because of this, increases the consumption of the good of each citizen at date 2; but, on the other hand, increasing the level of the public bad also decreases utility directly for each citizen. There is, in general, for each citizen type, a level of the public bad which optimizes this trade-off.

A simple theory of voting would stipulate that the outcome of the election will be the level of the public bad preferred by the median voter, or in this case, preferred by the middle income voters, who will, for the parameters I shall choose, be the median voters. I shall assume, somewhat more realistically, that the political process is sufficiently complex that all three income classes have some impact on the determination of the level of the public bad. As a short-cut to providing a fully fledged theory of this process, I shall simply stipulate that the outcome of the election maximizes some weighted average of the utilities of the poor, the middle and the rich, and shall fix the weights used in this average as a characteristic of the political process.[14]

We are now prepared to state the concept of capitalist politico-economic equilibrium (CPEE). A CPEE is a set of stock prices for each firm's stock and an interest rate at date 0, a portfolio and consumption choice for each citizen at date 0, an amount of investment for each firm, and an amount of the public bad, such that:

1. at that level of the public bad, at those prices and interest rate, and given the investment choice of each firm, the consumption and portfolio choice of each citizen at date 0 maximizes her expected utility;
2. given the portfolio choices of each citizen and the level of the public bad, the board chooses a level of investment for the firm by an internal political process that I shall not describe precisely here;
3. the level of the public bad is the outcome of the political process at date 1 (that is, maximizes the appropriate weighted average of the utilities of the rich, the middle, and the poor), given the portfolio choices of each individual;
4. total bank deposits made and total bank loans extended are equal at date 0.

Under suitable restrictions on the preferences of agents and the production functions of firms, a CPEE exists, and we can calculate it for specific choices of those functions.

Next, I describe the coupon politico-economic mechanism. It is the same as the capitalist mechanism but for one feature: one cannot purchase stock with the good, but only with coupons. This may be thought of in the following way. Each citizen begins with an endowment of the good, as before, and, say, one thousand coupons. The prices of the firms' stocks are announced in coupons only. It is illegal to trade coupons for the good; one can only purchase stock of a firm with coupons, and can only sell it for coupons. Thus, each consumer has two budget constraints, one in terms of the good, and one in terms of coupons. The coupon budget constraint states that a person cannot purchase shares valued in excess of one thousand coupons. The good budget constraint states that total consumption at date 0 plus deposits at date 0 plus amount of the good dedicated to the investment of firms in one's chosen portfolio cannot exceed one's initial endowment of the good.

All else is the same as in the description of the CPEE. We can now define a market-socialist politico-economic equilibrium (MSPEE) as consisting of a set of stock prices for each firm's stock, denominated now in coupons, and an interest rate at date 0, a portfolio and consumption choice for each citizen at date 0, an amount of investment for each firm, and an amount of the public bad, such that conditions (1) through (4), spelled out in the definition of the CPEE, are satisfied. The only difference is that here prices of stock are denominated in coupons, not in units of the good. Under suitable conditions on preferences and production functions, a MSPEE exists, and, for specific choices of those functions, it can be calculated.

Thus one can, in principle, calculate the expected utilities of the rich, the middle, and the poor in the equilibria of the two politico-economic mechanisms. I shall report some of those calculations in a moment. But first, let me conjecture, qualitatively, some of the differences that one might expect in politico-economic choices under the two mechanisms. What one should expect to happen in the capitalist mechanism is that the poor, and to a lesser extent the middle, will sell a good deal of their initial endowment of firm shares to the rich, who shall pay for them with the good, which the poor and middle shall consume at date 0. This will concentrate the ownership of stock in the hands of the rich, with two effects: first, they shall comprise the controlling group in most firms, and hence the firms' investment choices will be in their interest; secondly, they shall have a greater interest than the poor and middle in a high level of the public bad, as they own such large fractions of the stock of firms. In the coupon economy, however, the rich are precluded from buying controlling shares of all firms; shares can only be purchased with coupons and all citizens have the same initial endowment of coupons. One should expect, then, that at equilibrium the middle and poor will control most firms, as they own the majority of coupons in society. Thus, the firms will choose their levels of investments in the interest of the middle and the poor. Furthermore, the rich will derive only a fairly small fraction of their date-two consumption from the profits of firms, and will not, therefore, desire as high a level of the public bad as they did in the capitalist economy.

All this is conjecture, for the general equilibrium effects can be complicated. The only way to be sure what the welfare effects are in equilibrium is to prove a theorem, or to make some calculations. I have no general theorems at this time, but I report the results of some calculations in table 1.

Table 1 presents results from calculating the market-socialist and capitalist politico-economic equilibria for this economic environment,[15] for values of λ running between 0 and 1, where λ is the weight assigned to the utility of the rich and $(1-\lambda)/2$ is the weight assigned to

Table 1 Coupon and Capitalist Equilibria for Various Political Influence Weights

| | Coupon Equilibria | | | | | | | Capitalist Equilibria | | | | | |
λ	$(1-\lambda)/2$	I	z	U_p	U_m	U_r	λ	$(1-\lambda)/2$	I	z	U_p	U_m	U_r
0	0.50	1375	0.568	2.729	3.561	12.853	0	0.50	1384	0.679	2.727	3.558	12.927
0.04	0.48	1384	0.595	2.729	3.563	12.886	0.04	0.48	1410	0.663	2.725	3.563	13.019
0.08	0.46	1392	0.623	2.729	3.565	12.916	0.08	0.46	1433	0.748	2.720	3.563	13.100
0.12	0.44	1401	0.651	2.728	3.566	12.946	0.12	0.44	1454	0.836	2.711	3.560	13.172
0.16	0.42	1409	0.679	2.727	3.567	12.974	0.16	0.42	1473	0.924	2.699	3.552	13.235
0.20	0.40	1416	0.707	2.725	3.567	13.001	0.20	0.40	1491	1.014	2.684	3.542	13.291
0.24	0.38	1424	0.736	2.723	3.567	13.026	0.24	0.38	1508	1.105	2.667	3.530	13.340
0.28	0.36	1431	0.764	2.721	3.566	13.051	0.28	0.36	1523	1.198	2.648	3.515	13.384
0.32	0.34	1438	0.793	2.718	3.565	13.075	0.32	0.34	1537	1.291	2.627	3.498	13.424
0.36	0.32	1445	0.822	2.715	3.564	13.097	0.36	0.32	1551	1.386	2.604	3.479	13.458
0.40	0.30	1451	0.851	2.712	3.562	13.119	0.40	0.30	1564	1.481	2.580	3.458	13.489
0.44	0.28	1458	0.880	2.708	3.560	13.140	0.44	0.28	1576	1.578	2.554	3.435	13.516
0.48	0.26	1464	0.909	2.704	3.558	13.160	0.48	0.26	1587	1.676	2.527	3.412	13.539
0.52	0.24	1470	0.939	2.699	3.555	13.179	0.52	0.24	1598	1.774	2.498	3.386	13.560
0.56	0.22	1476	0.968	2.695	3.552	13.198	0.56	0.22	1609	1.873	2.469	3.360	13.577
0.60	0.20	1482	0.998	2.690	3.548	13.215	0.60	0.20	1619	1.974	2.438	3.332	13.592

λ = political weight of rich; $(1-\lambda/2)$ = political weight of middle and poor; I = investment; z = public bad; u_j = utility of class j, j = p.m.r.

the utility of the poor and of the middle in the determination of the political outcome, the level of the public bad. Three aspects of the equilibria are reported: the level of the public bad, the utilities of the two types, and the firm's level of investment. First, note that the poor and middle-income classes are better off in the coupon economy than in the capitalist economy, for all values of λ, and the rich are worse off in the coupon economy. Secondly, note that the level of the public bad is consistently lower in the coupon economy – so the coupon economy is a green economy. The difference is quite substantial. At $\lambda = 0.24$, which might not be an unreasonable value, the level of 'pollution' is 50 per cent higher in the capitalist economy. Thirdly, note that the level of investment is consistently higher in the capitalist economy.

To summarize, the market-socialist mechanism prevents a free-rider problem from occurring that afflicts the poor and the middle under capitalism. In the capitalist economy, it is individually optimal for each poor and middle-class individual to sell a lot of her shares of the firm to the rich, which creates a class of rich individuals who control firms and whose income depends on profits. The rich come to control firms, and through their influence on the political process, a high level of the public bad ensues. Under market socialism, the poor and the middle are precluded from liquidating their shares. They therefore remain the dominant shareholders and also turn out to be a force for lowering the level of the public bad. The net effect of these changes is not easy to predict in theory, but we have seen that, at least in one example, the poor and the middle end up better off in the market-socialist regime, and that regime is greener, to boot.

A final comment on these results is in order. One advantage of having a coupon stock market in real life would be to prevent the poor from selling their shares prematurely to the rich, something one fears might happen if, let us say, firms in a formerly Communist economy were denationalized by distributing shares to all citizens, after which a fully liberalized stock market were opened. Such premature liquidation of one's stock cannot occur in the coupon economy, since liquidation cannot occur. More specifically, this phenomenon could happen in the capitalist politico-economic mechanism if the poor had poorer information than the rich about the probabilities with which the various states of the world occur at date 2. It is important to mention that this does not happen in the model whose equilibria are reported in table 1: there, all agents are equally knowledgeable and rational. So, in real life, one might expect that the difference between the utility of the poor under the two mechanisms would be even greater than it is in table 1.

8 The Efficiency of Firms and the Rights of Capital Under Market Socialism[16]

I said earlier that the issue for market socialism was whether a politico-economic mechanism could be created under which firms would behave competitively (in particular, in which they would innovate) and be sheltered from inefficient government interference. As Hayek[17] pointed out, and as Kornai[18] ramified Hayek's point with the theory of the soft-budget constraint, when the state controls firms, firm managers are to a large extent absolved of responsibility with regard to errors in judgment. More generally, inefficient practices will not be weeded out as they are in a competitive market environment. The model I have just presented does not address this issue at all. That model's purpose was to examine the general equilibrium welfare effects of the different financing mechanisms, under the assumption that the firm manager is a perfect agent of the firm's controlling group. Indeed, technological innovation was not an issue. The purpose of this section is to argue that there are institutions that would force firms to behave competitively in the coupon economy.

I intend that firms in the coupon economy be organized around a fairly small number of main banks, as in the Japanese *keiretsu*. A main bank would be primarily responsible for putting together loan consortia to finance the operations of the firms in its group; it would, correlatively, be responsible for monitoring these firms. The coupon stock market serves all three functions of a capitalist stock market: the movement in the coupon price of a firm's stock is a *signal* useful to banks and mutual funds which shall monitor the firms; it allows mutual funds *to construct portfolios with varying attributes*, (for example, vis-à-vis risk). It also permits firms to *raise capital*, by exchanging coupons for investment funds from the treasury. If the coupon price of a firm's stock falls or, more often, before that happens, the main bank would investigate how well the firm is being managed. It has an incentive to monitor the firms in its group effectively, because, by so doing, it keeps its firms profitable, and thereby able to pay back their loans. This gives the bank a good reputation, making it easier for it to continue to raise money to finance the operations of firms in its group. It may also be desirable to allow or require banks to purchase shares of firms in their *keiretsu*, as an incentive for their monitoring function.

But why should the bank perform its monitoring job well? Who, that is, would monitor the monitors? The principal question is whether the banks would operate with sufficient independence of the state, making decisions about firms using economic and not political criteria. I and my colleague P. Bardhan do not believe that we have a definitive solution to the problem, although we view the following features of the economy as ones which would induce banks to do their job properly.[19] First, in the present proposal, banks would not be owned by the government, but by mutual funds and, finally, citizens. Bank managers would be hired on a managerial labor market, by a board of directors. Secondly, the reputational concerns of the main banks' managers should act as an antidote to susceptibility to political pressure. In Japan, even though banks have been closely regulated by the Ministry of Finance, managers exhibit keenness to preserve their reputation as good monitors, and banks compete in seeking the position of main bank for well-run firms. The managerial labor market will not forget if a bank manager forgives bad loans or non-performing firms too often. Thirdly, incentive features would be a part of the salary structure of bank management. Fourthly, the doors of international product competition must be kept open, which would act as a check on laxity of the institutional monitors. Fifthly, as Raj Sah and Martin Weitzman have suggested,[20] there should be well-publicized pre-commitments by banks before large investment projects begin, that promise liquidation should their performance at pre-specified dates not exceed pre-specified levels. The public nature of these pre-commitments would preclude the soft-budget constraint problems that Eric Maskin and Mathias Dewatripont have studied,[21] in which it is in the interest of public banks to renegotiate loans on poorly performing projects. Finally, banks may perhaps own shares in the firms they monitor. To the extent that bankers' salaries are linked to the banks' profitability, this would further induce them to monitor firms well.

Many have argued, including Colin Mayer and his co-authors in Europe and Michael Porter in the United States,[22] that a system in which banks monitor firms is preferable to the takeover process as the mechanism guaranteeing firm performance in capitalist economies;[23] there seems ample reason to believe that a similar mechanism can be adapted to a market-socialist economy.

If banks monitor firms aggressively, if firms must depend on banks and the accumulation of coupons for finance, and if the doors to international trade are open, firms will innovate. Under capitalism, innovations are designed in the R&D departments of large firms, and also enter the economy through the formation of new, small firms. In the coupon economy, I envisage that many small private firms would form; those that grow would eventually be bought by large firms in the 'public' sector, as happens under capitalism. Alternatively, the government might purchase the firm and auction it in the public sector. Perhaps joining the public sector would be a prerequisite to receiving loans from the main banks, or loans at preferential interest rates. I am undecided whether all firms that reach a given size should be nationalized in one of these ways, or if private large firms should continue to coexist with firms in the coupon sector, for the sake of competition, and perhaps, of incentive.

I must emphasize that I envisage the coupon proposal as a desirable model of market socialism only when the economy can support sophisticated financial institutions and regulation. (For economies at low levels of development, the Bardhan *keiretsu* model is, I believe, superior.[24]) Without a monitoring organ like the US Securities and Exchange Commission, it would be difficult to control black-market transactions in which wealthy citizens purchased coupons from poor citizens with cash. Recall that one wishes to prevent such transactions in order to preserve the good effects on the level of the public bads consequent upon having a somewhat egalitarian distribution of profit income. With a national accounting system in which all coupon and stock transactions are registered, this would be possible. Contracts in which one citizen agreed effectively to transfer ownership of her coupon portfolio (or its stream of income) to another would not be enforceable in courts. It would, however, probably still be possible to arrange enforceable contracts of this type through the use of a financial intermediary in another country. This kind of behavior would probably have to be regulated.

9 Socialism and Democracy

Almost all Western socialists today are democrats; some, such as Samuel Bowles and Herbert Gintis, are interested in socialism in large part only in so far as it is instrumental for bringing about democracy.[25] I have defined what socialists want as including equal opportunity for political influence and I shall here be conventional in assuming that democracy is a pre-condition for such equality, although this assumption is by no means obviously true. It may be more accurate to say that serious disagreements exist with respect to what form of democracy can deliver the desired equality.[26]

The insistence on democracy has important implications for the socialism of the future, which will involve a change in the language we use to describe it. In a democracy, socialism will be represented by one or several political parties, competing for power with other political parties, some of which will be 'bourgeois'. It may be the case, sometimes, that a regime could be described as socialist for many years, despite the occasional victories of bourgeois parties. We can say that the Scandinavian countries have remained social-democratic despite such occasional victories.

But the situation of the Sandinistas may be another pattern. A socialist party comes to power. For various reasons (its own errors, pressure from US imperialism) it loses the elections some years later, to be replaced by a bourgeois party or coalition that undoes a number of its accomplishments. Then perhaps some years later the socialists again win the elections. In this case, we must transform our language from 'countries being socialist' to 'socialist parties being in power'. Perhaps the Sandinistas would not have made some of the errors they did had they thought of themselves as being a socialist party in power, rather than thinking of Nicaragua as a socialist country.

Nevertheless, a regime of market socialism might well be characterized by its constitution, which would limit the permissible degree of accumulation of private property in productive assets, and perhaps explicitly describe other kinds of property that are (constitutionally) protected. One justification for a supermajoritarian requirement to reverse such provisions is that property relations will not engender long-term planning and, in particular, investment, if they are thought to be easily reversible; another is that large social costs would be sustained in any change in property relations.

I think it is incontrovertible that a key reform necessary to achieve the three desiderata of socialists is massively improved education for the children of the poor and working class. Only through education can the difference in opportunities faced by them and the children of the well-off be eradicated; only when skills become less unequally distributed, because of education, will wage differentials narrow significantly. To devote the required amount of resources to this kind of education will require a massive change in outlook of the citizenry of every large, heterogeneous country. Majorities will have to overcome their racism, but more than that, they will have to be won to the position, as John Donne (Devotion 17, 1623) wrote, that 'No man is an island entire of itself. Every man is a piece of the continent, a part of the main . . .'. Thus, the implementation of a thoroughgoing socialism in a democracy will take a long time, if it must await such a feeling of community among people.

But I think that a number of the ills of capitalism would probably be cured more quickly, without the prerequisite of this feeling of community, because of the changed economic interests people would have under market-socialist property relations. I have outlined how the level of various public bads in a democratic society is the outcome of a political struggle in which different classes fight for their interests. If interests change, then so, in general, will the equilibrium level of public bads. Let me take as an example the Persian Gulf War of 1991. A case can be made that that war was fought to keep the price of oil low, and that the main interests that wanted the price of oil kept low were firms using oil as an input. Of course, consumers want a low price of oil, too; the question is, who was willing to go to war in January 1991 to keep the price of oil low and who would have been content to apply a boycott for another year? As late as December 15, 1990, surveys taken in the United States showed that the great majority of people were opposed to starting a war. One can take this as evidence that they were willing to trade off the possibility of a somewhat higher price for oil and a somewhat higher rate of unemployment for not going to war. Yet President Bush decided to go to war, and he probably had support from 'important people' in doing so. These important people were ones who derive huge amounts of wealth from profits of firms; for them, the fall in profits that would ensue from higher oil prices made the alternative of war a preferable one. Now suppose, in a market-socialist economy, no one received more than roughly a per capita share of total profits. A rise in the price of oil would, of course, hurt profits and wages, but, arguably, no class of 'important people' would have such an overwhelming interest in keeping oil prices low. Almost everyone might prefer to take the chance of higher oil prices to avoid having to fight a war.

If many of the ills of capitalism are public bads of this kind – bads that increase profits – then, even if the preference orderings (for non-economists, 'values') of individuals do not change, a change in the distribution of profit income would change the level of public bads that is engendered by a democratic process. We have seen this effect in the simulations of section 7. I think that, to some extent, racism and sexism are public bads of this kind. An old Marxist argument maintains that divisions among the working class (created, for example, by racism and sexism) strengthen the bosses in the struggle against labor. To the extent that this is the case, capitalism may develop mechanisms to foment racism and sexism, for example, by the treatment of minorities and women in the capitalist media. Were profits equally distributed in the population, the public-bad argument of section 5 implies that such capitalist-inspired fomenting of divisions in the working class would be reduced. I do not ignore the fact that people themselves have racist and sexist ideas, and so one cannot expect changes overnight with respect to these practices. But the change in property relations would dissolve one powerful class interest in the maintenance of discrimination.

A fundamental left-wing criticism of capitalist democracy has been that, as long as capital is in the hands of a small, wealthy class, politics must conform to the needs of that class. Under the coupon system I have outlined, the 'structural power of capital' over society would be broken.

It would be comforting to argue that, once a mechanism for redistributing profits, or for transforming firms into labor-managed ones, had been put in place, then a feeling of such community would develop that the well-to-do would be willing to sacrifice income in order to fund the kind of educational system necessary to raise massively the opportunities of the many. I do not think this is a realistic expectation. I do think, however, that preferences change and that, if the income distribution becomes more egalitarian due to market-socialist property relations, and if the levels of public bads do fall, then preferences will also change in an egalitarian direction. My point is that institutions can be changed more rapidly than preferences.

Nevertheless, I remain agnostic on the question of the birth of the so-called socialist person, and prefer to put my faith in the design of institutions that will engender good results with ordinary people. With such agnosticism, are there nevertheless grounds for believing that market socialism would eventually increase the support for large increases in publicly supported education? Perhaps. Again, I will invoke the public-bad argument. To a degree, education of the working class is a profit-increasing public good, and to this degree, it is rational for capitalists to support its financing. It is almost certainly the case that publicly supported education in the United States is at present below this degree and, indeed, significant sections of the capitalist class support increased educational funding: US workers would be more productive and could more easily acquire profit-enhancing skills if they could read detailed instruction manuals, as Japanese workers can.[27] What may well be the case, however, is that the optimal degree of working-class education for capitalists is less than the socially optimal degree. After a point, increased public education may have a net negative effect on profits (when the profit taxes needed to finance the marginal educational increment for the working class are more than the profits the increment induces), while it continues to have a large positive marginal effect as a non-profit-inducing public good, via its effect on social culture (in which I include everything from improved television programming to public civility). It is this additional educational increment which, according to the public-bad argument made in section 5 a society in which profits are equally distributed is more likely to support through its political process.[28]

I have not thus far addressed what is the largest injustice in the world: the massive inequality between nations, conveniently described as North–South inequality. Furthermore, in the next fifty years, it may well be this inequality which becomes the focus of politics, as the South industrializes, and demands large transfers from the North to enable it to do so without destroying the global commons. I have no doubt that such transfers are required by justice, for where one is born is a morally arbitrary personal feature, and equality of opportunity mandates compensation to those born into societies with low standards of living. The question is whether a market-socialist society would be more prone to support such transfers than a capitalist one.

The practices of the Scandinavian countries suggest perhaps the answer is yes; foreign aid is a larger fraction of national income in Norway and Sweden than in any other country, and this appears to be due to the socialist-person effect.[29] The social-democratic parties in Scandinavia have advocated relatively large development aid on grounds of solidarity. Furthermore, many people in industrialized countries advocated divestment of corporate stock in South Africa: a case where people were willing to sacrifice a small amount of income (in the form of slightly higher wages, profits and pensions that were possible with South African investment) for the sake of the freedom of people in a distant land. It is therefore not absurd to suggest that the low welfare of people in the South is a (profit-inducing) public bad, as far as many people in the North are concerned, and as such, foreign aid might well increase with a redistribution of profits.

10 Conclusion

Democracy is the best political mechanism that we know of for rendering the state an agent of the people. It is not foolproof and there are many versions of democracy, in respect of the relationships between branches of government, the ways in which representatives are chosen, and the role of a constitution. Democracy and the use of markets, both of which I advocate, limit the feasible extent of income redistribution. In particular, since labor markets are necessary, there will be wage differentials and perhaps efficiency requires about the degree of wage differentiation we see in capitalist economies – at least for a large interval of the wage distribution. Because citizens must choose tax systems, and because people tend to believe they deserve what they earn on the labor market, the degree of redistribution of wage income is necessarily limited. There is another element that determines the degree of democratically accessible redistribution through taxes on labor income: the capacity for empathy with other citizens. We have seen the highest degree of redistribution in the Nordic countries. It is not a coincidence, in my view, that these countries are small, and are linguistically, ethnically, racially and religiously homogeneous. I doubt that large, heterogeneous societies will, in our lifetimes, vote to redistribute income as much through the tax system as the Nordic societies have. I would argue likewise in regard to redistribution through inheritance taxes; such redistribution is sharply limited in democratic, heterogeneous societies. From a philosophical viewpoint, I advocate a great deal of redistribution through taxation, but I think it would be utopian to base a blueprint for socialism on that category of instrument.

I believe, however, that there is a substantial degree of freedom in income distribution (in democratic market economies) due to the property relation a society can choose for ownership of its firms. Hayekians assert that a society is, indeed, not free to choose that relation either, on peril of rapid degeneration of its technological vitality. I believe that that assertion is false. It is, ironically, proved to be so by the relative success of large capitalist corporate enterprise. For the Hayekian arguments which deduce the inefficiency of public ownership should apply not only to state-owned firms, but to firms like General Motors, with 700,000 employees, approximately one-third of whom are in some managerial capacity. The agency problems between owners and operators in these firms are severe, yet capitalism has devised several quite different ways of solving them (principally represented by the American, German and Japanese versions). There are, I believe, property relations for firms that can harness these techniques, and would implement a substantially more equal distribution of firm revenue among the population than capitalism does.

When Zhou Enlai was asked to comment on the consequences of the French revolution, he replied, 'It's too soon to tell'. I have argued that the prudent social scientist should likewise remain agnostic about what appears to be capitalism's trouncing defeat of socialism in the late twentieth century.

Notes

1. This chapter summarizes the main ideas of *A Future for Socialism*, Cambridge, MA: Harvard University Press 1994. The description of the coupon economy, in section 6, differs from that in the book, and also from that in an earlier published article with the same title (in *Egalitarian Perspectives: Essays in Philosophical Economics*, New York: Cambridge University Press 1994). The amendments presented here to the coupon proposal are due to suggestions made by participants in the Madison conference of May 1994; they are acknowledged more specifically below. I have, however, made no attempt to incorporate here the many other good suggestions and criticisms of conference participants, to be found in this volume. I am grateful to all of them.

2. For a discussion of self-realization in Marx, see J. Elster, *Making Sense of Marx*, New York: Cambridge University Press 1985, pp. 82–92. For a more general discussion, see 'Self-Realization in Work and Politics: The Marxist Conception of the Good Life', *Social Philosophy & Policy* 3 (1986), pp. 97–126.

3. See John Rawls, *A Theory of Justice*, Cambridge, MA: Harvard University Press 1971, p. 426.

4. C. B. MacPherson defines democracy as equal self-realization among citizens in *Democratic Theory*, Oxford: Clarendon 1973, p. 4.

5. For an elaboration of the idea of equality of opportunity for welfare, see Richard Arneson, 'Equality and Equal Opportunity for Welfare', *Philosophical Studies* 56 (1989), pp. 77–93; John Roemer, 'A Pragmatic Theory of Responsibility for the Egalitarian Planner', *Philosophy and Public Affairs* 22 (1993), pp. 146–66.

6. I ignore a fine point here, the distinction between equality and 'maximin'. With respect to opportunity for self-realization and welfare, I advocate choosing those social institutions which maximize the opportunity for their achievement for those who will have the minimum such opportunity. It is not obvious, however, whether one should advocate 'maximin' opportunity for political influence or equalize political influence at a maximum level, because political influence should probably be defined largely, though not entirely, in relative terms. Social status is a good similar to political influence in this respect: if everyone has equal social status, is it meaningful to speak about the level of that status?

7. By which I mean private property subject to taxation and regulation of various kinds.

8. For a definition and discussion of social-republican property, see William Simon, 'Social-Republican Property', *UCLA Law Review* (1991), pp. 1335–413.

9. See John E. Roemer, 'Can There Be Socialism after Communism?', *Politics & Society* 20 (1992), pp. 261–76.

10. This is so even if the rich cannot escape exposure to the public bad, as indeed they often can.

11. Several elements of the coupon economy as described here have been amended from my original presentation of it in *A Future for Socialism*, Cambridge, MA: Harvard University Press 1994, due to suggestions made by participants at the Madison conference. I am grateful to William Simon for suggesting that coupons be exchangeable by firms for investment funds, and to Louis Putterman for suggesting the age-profile regulation of mutual funds as a way of precluding the cash cow phenomenon.

12. This section is based on John E. Roemer, 'Limited Privatization in the Presence of Public Bads', in J. E. Roemer, ed., *Property Relations, Incentives, and Welfare*, New York: Macmillan, in press.

13. In this section, citizens supply investment funds directly to firms. The issues of leverage and different forms of firm financing are not modeled here.

14. I have proposed and studied elsewhere models in which the rich can influence the outcome of elections in which they are in a small minority, through campaign spending and electoral propaganda. See John E. Roemer, 'The Strategic Role of Party Ideology When Voters Are Uncertain about How the Economy Works', *American Political Science Review* 88 (1994), pp. 327–35.

15   The utility function of every agent is $u(x_0, x_2, z) = x_0^{0.5} + x_2^{0.5} - z$, where x_0 and x_2 are consumption of the good at dates 0 and 2 and z is consumption of the public bad at date 2. There are 95 poor agents, each endowed with 10 units of the good at date 0, and 5 rich agents, each endowed with 300 units of the good. There are two firms and three states of the world. The production function for firm j in state s is

$$g_s^j(x, z) = a_s^j x^{cj} z^{(1-cj)}, \text{ where } c_1 = 0.7, \ c_2 = 0.3, \ (a_1^1, a_2^1, a_3^1) = (5, 13, 30),$$
$$\text{and } (a_1^2, a_2^2, a_3^2) = 9, 13, 16).$$

16.   This section is based in part on Pranab Bardhan and John E. Roemer, 'Market Socialism: A Case for Rejuvenation', *Journal of Economic Perspectives* 6 (1992), pp. 101–16.

17.   Friederich A. Hayek, 'The Nature and History of the Problem', in Hayek, ed., *Collectivist Economic Planning*, London: Routledge 1935; 'Socialist Calculation: The Competitive "Solution"', *Economica* 7 (1940), pp. 125–49.

18.   Janos Kornai, *The Socialist System: The Political Economy of Communism*, Princeton, NJ: Princeton University Press 1992; 'Market Socialism Revisited', in P. Bardhan and J. Roemer, eds, *Market Socialism: The Current Debate*, New York: Oxford University Press 1993, pp. 42–68.

19.   Bardhan and Roemer, 'Market Socialism: A Case for Rejuvenation', 1992.

20.   Raj Sah and Martin Weitzman, 'A Proposal for Using Incentive Pre-Commitments in Public Enterprise Funding', *World Development* 19 (1991), pp. 595–603.

21.   Mathias Dewatripont and Eric Maskin, 'Centralization of Credit and Long-Term Investment', in Bardhan and Roemer, eds, *Market Socialism*, 1993, pp. 169–74.

22.   Michael Porter, *Capital Choices: Changing the Way America Invests in Industry*, Washington, DC: Council on Competitiveness 1992.

23.   See J. Corbett and Colin Mayer, 'Financial Reform in Eastern Europe: Progress with the Wrong Model', *Oxford Review of Economic Policy* 7 (1991), pp. 55–75. See also J. Franks and C. Mayer, 'Corporate Ownership and Corporate Control: A Study of France, Germany, and the UK', *Economic Policy* (1990), pp. 189–231.

24.   P. Bardhan, 'On Tackling the Soft Budget Constraint in Market Socialism', in Bardhan and Roemer, eds, *Market Socialism*, 1993, pp. 145–55.

25.   Samuel Bowles and Herbert Gintis, *Democracy and Capitalism*, New York: Basic Books 1986.

26.   For definitions of democracy, see P. Schmitter and T. L. Karl, 'What Democracy Is . . . and Is Not', *Journal of Democracy* 2 (1991), pp. 75–88. For general skepticism concerning the feasibility of democracy, see W. H. Riker, *Liberalism against Populism*, 2nd edn, Prospect Heights, IL: Waveland 1988.

27.   M. Hashimoto reports that, in Japan, the Honda training program for workers involves their studying manuals. When Honda set up its US plant, it discovered that workers were unable to learn by reading manuals. See Hashimoto, 'Employment-Based Training in Japanese Firms in Japan and in the United States: Experiences of Automobile Manufacturers' (working paper, Department of Economics, Ohio State University 1992).

28.   To put the argument in the language of section 5, we would say that, after a point, the *lack* of public education is a profit-increasing public bad.

29.   The four countries that contribute the greatest fraction of their GNP to official development assistance are Norway, Sweden, the Netherlands, and Denmark. Each of these contributes at least 0.94 per cent of its GNP. Among the 18 countries constituting the Development Assistance Committee of the Organization for Economic Cooperation and Development (OECD), the United States ranks last, contributing only 0.15 per cent of its GNP. See Organization for Economic Cooperation and Development, *Development Cooperation Efforts and Policies of Members of the Development Assistance Committee*, Paris: OECD 1990.

PART II

Commentaries, Criticisms, Extensions

The Role of Markets in the Socialist Project

2

Inequality and Alienation in the Socialist Capital Market

William H. Simon

The case for the practical importance of markets is far stronger than the case for private ownership of capital, and the case for private ownership *in general* is far stronger than the case for the particular ownership arrangements that currently prevail in Western capitalism. Thus, John Roemer's effort in 'A Future for Socialism' to revive the market-socialist tradition of speculation about how alternative property arrangements might square equality with efficiency is promising.

I have some doubts, however, about the specific institutional proposals Roemer makes, and I want to explore two of them here. The first concerns technical difficulties in trying to advance socialist egalitarian goals by equalizing equity ownership in a liquid, national capital market. The second concerns potential effects of the recommended market arrangements on political motivation and culture that even a socialist determined to avoid utopian views of human nature should confront.

Both lines question the viability of achieving socialist goals through the limitation of ownership rights in a conventional capital market without more directly democratizing economic processes. The doubts resonate with what might be called a romantic or petty bourgeois socialist perspective centered on worker and community-controlled enterprise. While Roemer, following Oscar Lange, operates on the Walrasian terrain of perfect competition, the romantic perspective has more affinity, as both normative and prescriptive propositions, with the Williamsonian perspective of shared monopoly and relational capital.

I hope it is apparent that these remarks arise from great sympathy with Roemer's aims and deep admiration for his brilliant contribution to reopening and advancing the debate over market socialism.

Inequality

In Roemer's capital market, equity can be purchased only with
coupons, not with cash. Every citizen receives an equal allotment of
coupons at some point in her life, and the coupons, or shares
purchased with them, escheat to the state on the citizen's death.
People with cash to invest have to do so by purchasing debt (unless
they start their own small businesses).

The goal is to constrain inequality in consumption opportunities
by precluding inheritance and to constrain inequality in corporate
ownership by limiting the use of cash to acquire shares, while maintaining a capital market that appraises corporate performance
through the coupon price of shares. A major virtue of equality in
corporate control is pressure for the reduction of 'public bads', such
as pollution, through the reallocation of economic incentives.

I fear that the goals of equalizing consumption and ownership will
prove vulnerable to opportunities for substitution that the capital
market will likely generate.

Consumption

In a conventional capital market, an investor's valuation of shares
is not affected by her consumption plans or her life expectancy. In
the coupon economy, the investor will be strongly influenced by the
latter and probably somewhat influenced by the former.

To take the clearest case, consider someone with a short life
expectancy. Her self-interest is to maximize her income during the
brief remainder of her life, and she does this by trading for stocks that
promise the largest dividend payout during that period.

Managers can cater to this clientele (which also includes younger
people who would rather not wait for their dividends) in a variety of
ways. One is simply to accelerate the pace of dividends by cutting back
on investment, deferring maintenance or selling off assets. Another is
to spin off projects with shorter payoffs into separate entities represented by separate securities. For example, in the 1980s, oil company
executives were urged to divide among entities with separate securities
but common management their 'cash cow' producing wells on the one
hand and their more long-term drilling and exploration efforts on the
other. A few undertook restructurings along such lines.[1] Under the
influence of the financier Carl Icahn, USX restructured so that its steel
business and its non-steel assets, which were thought to have a more
short-term payoff, were represented by distinct securities.[2] Managers

and investment bankers could package investments in myriad ways to satisfy almost any time preferences.

Such practices would be damaging to the aspirations of Roemer's program. First, the ability of the first generation of coupon recipients to capitalize shareholdings during its lifetime would create a major problem of intergenerational equity and jeopardize the long-term viability of the program. Secondly, the signalling function of coupon prices would be compromised by the fact that such prices will be functions, not just of expectations about profits, but of the varying time preferences of investors. Thirdly, the general effect would probably be to shorten undesirably the time horizon of investment planning.

It is hard to think of a rule governing income realization and dividend payments that would solve the problem. It would not be practical to distinguish the extent to which managerial decisions are motivated by illegitimate time preferences of investors. Moreover, proper investment and dividend decisions would require managers to make use of market-given discount rates that themselves would reflect to an indeterminate degree time preferences induced by the limitation of property rights.

In a recent amendment to the scheme in the book, Roemer proposes an ingenious response to the time horizon problem: require that citizens invest through mutual funds that in turn must have a representative age distribution of holders. This seems an improvement, but it still leaves problems.

First, even if this scheme proved administrable, the time horizons of the funds would still be considerably shorter than the horizons under conventional capitalism. This is because under Roemer's scheme no one will have a horizon greater than her life expectancy, whereas under capitalism, which permits bequests, many will have longer ones.

Secondly, the administrative requirements of the age-mix condition seem daunting. The market creates strong incentives for non-compliance or sham compliance. Funds dominated by older people looking for 'cash cows' would have incentives to make side payments to younger people to allow them to achieve their age quotas. Young people with shorter life expectancies might be assiduously recruited. One thinks of the difficulties of enforcing 'set aside' contracting programs for minorities and women in which questions constantly arise as to whether the benefited firms are 'really' minority or female.

Thirdly, even if enforcement were perfect, the age-mix condition might not mitigate short-term pressures very much. If, as seems likely, the bond market can offer young people plausible substitutes for long-term equities, then even young people with long horizons should be relatively indifferent as between short- and long-term payoffs in the mutual funds. If they get paid off earlier than their consumption plans demand, they can simply reinvest in the bond market. Thus, they would not provide much of a break on the short-term propensities of their elders.

It may seem unfair to press this objection, since the time horizon problem plagues any effort to limit inheritance, and any plausible socialism will have to attempt this somehow. But Roemer's program seems vulnerable to the criticisms that, first, because of the time horizon problem, the optimal rate of inheritance taxation is probably considerably less than 100 per cent, and secondly, it seems administratively more practical to integrate limits on the transmission of equity at death into a single inheritance tax on all forms of property.

Ownership

Roemer touches on two types of ownership problems. One is the 'agency costs' of managerial self-indulgence at the expense of capital suppliers. The other is the 'public bads' that arise because of the incentives that share ownership gives the rich regarding the exercise of their political power.

For the 'agency' problem, Roemer relies on a combination of share market signals and bank control. In the proposal presented in the book, the issuance of coupons does not generate actual funds for the firms, and in this situation, as Louis Putterman explains, it seems unlikely the share price could perform much of a role.[3] Managers would not care about the price, since a high price would not bring them any funds and dispersed shareholders would have little effective control. Banks would not care because, as creditors, their interests would often be different than those of shareholders. (Note that German and Japanese banks, which have good reputations as corporate monitors, hold substantial equity as well as debt.)

Roemer's recent amendment that provides for funding the coupons so that the share price plays a direct role in determining the firm's cost of capital, seems an improvement. Moreover, the introduction of mutual funds seems likely to improve the 'agency' problem by introducing potentially more effective monitors. Mutual funds have not been active monitors in the United States, but their monitoring activities have recently picked up, and some commentators are optimistic that, with legislative reform, they might prove more effective.[4]

Agency problems surely remain, but they do not seem more daunting than they are under existing American capitalism.

The main focus of Roemer's program is the problem of 'public bads' such as pollution. In Roemer's political economy, the rich exercise power most directly, not over enterprises, but over the political process. The disproportionate share ownership of the rich under capitalism is important, not because it gives them control over enterprises, but because it gives them an interest in enterprise profits that leads them to exercise political control to permit enterprises to impose a large level of public bads.

Because the wealth of the rich gives them disproportionate political power, they are able to achieve public tolerance for a high level of public bads. Under market socialism, the rich continue to enjoy disproportionate political power, but since they have no more shares than anyone else, their incentives are different. Their gains from corporate profits due to public bads are lower relative to their share of the costs of the bads. Thus the rich support a lower level of public bads under market socialism, and the consequence is greater efficiency.

The problem with this argument is in the premise that the interests of the rich will be dramatically different when most of their wealth is no longer in corporate shares.

Under market socialism, the rich cannot use their cash for shares, but presumably they can buy as much as they want of other types of interests. Why is the accumulation of these other interests by the rich not a threat comparable to the accumulation of equity? Roemer does not say explicitly, but presumably the answer lies in an assumption that the other interests will carry a fixed, unconditional return of the sort conventionally associated with debt. If the return were literally fixed and unconditional, it would leave the holder indifferent to the conduct or profitability of the firm.

In practice, however, this assumption is unrealistic in several respects. First, securities markets now offer an array of derivative instruments that can be packaged easily to replicate the financial characteristics of corporate shares. With a combination of purchases of call options and sales of put options, an investor can achieve the economic equivalent of shareholding without holding shares. Shutting down the derivative market will not be easy, both because it serves some useful hedging functions and because evasion of controls is relatively easy in this market. Since the holder has no direct relation with the corporation, his identity does not have to be recorded, and the market can easily move offshore.[5]

Secondly, despite the stereotype, some debt explicitly provides for conditional returns. An 'income bond' promises payment only if the firm has income, and it thus strongly resembles a profit interest.[6] Thirdly and most importantly, even a nominally unconditional debt interest is implicitly conditional on the solvency of the firm. Moreover, even if the payment on debt is nominally fixed, the value and price of the interest will fluctuate with the risks to the firm's solvency.

The debtholder's concern about solvency is not especially intense where debt is small relative to the firm's assets or where it is secured by claims on 'redeployable' assets that retain their value after the firm becomes insolvent. But unsecured creditors in firms with a lot of debt have strong concerns about solvency. These interests may differ from equityholders' interests; because debtholders' claims are senior, they may prefer more conservative policies than shareholders, who may capture most of the benefits of successful risk taking. But it is not clear that more conservative policies will generate less public bads. For example, adopting a new technology may be risky but have the potential of reducing negative externalities, say by polluting less, or creating positive ones, such as demonstrating the efficacy of the new techniques or increasing the skills of the workers who work with them.

More importantly, when the firm becomes leveraged to the point that characterized some of the more spectacular financings of the 1980s, the distinction between debt and equity holders becomes fairly academic. In such circumstances the debt claims on the corporation can only be served through a dramatic increase in corporate income that can only be achieved through risky policies. Since the market socialist regime will shift wealth from the equity market to the debt market, one would expect the consequence to be an increase in leverage. Even with derivatives prohibited, there is no reason to expect that the interests in firm conduct of the rich, as holders of risky debt in leveraged enterprises (plus some equity), will differ from their prior interests as holders of proportionately more equity.

Alienation

Roemer rejects attempts to found socialism on revolutionary character reformation designed to produce a more solidaristic 'socialist person'.[7] Part of the appeal of markets for him is that they are compatible with 'ordinary' self-interested motivation.

Now it seems entirely right that selfish behavior will not disappear spontaneously with the inauguration of socialism and cannot be extirpated through the coercive inculcation of virtue by the state. On the other hand, many socialists who recognize these points would want to insist that motivations are not given independently of economic institutions. People's aims will be shaped in part by their experiences in the institutional settings in which they live.

This point suggests that in designing institutions we should take account of, not only their instrumental effects in satisfying given goals, but their constitutive effects in encouraging desirable motivations. (The distinction here is not between motives considered virtuous and desirable by the social architect and those held by ordinary individuals, but between the motives ordinary individuals, in reflecting on how society should be designed, would consider it good for society to foster and those on which they are currently patterning their private conduct.)

Traditionally socialists have objected to the capitalist market, not just because of its unequal outcomes, but also because its processes inhibit self-realization. The classic critique of this kind, of course, is Marx's analysis of the 'fetishism of commodities'.[8] On one interpretation, the critique charges capitalism with inducing a kind of political blindness and impotence in its participants. The market produces an experience of social life as beyond human agency. Individuals see themselves as passive objects of an autonomous process. The way their own actions contribute to the production of the system and the ways they might collectively restructure it are systematically obscured.

The point is not simply that capitalist *ideology* has a misleading conception of the market, but that participation in the capitalist market generates a sense of passivity, isolation and self-absorption inimical to effective democratic citizenship. The (sometimes implicit) contrast is to participation in collective democratic decision making in which people address their fellow citizens in terms of norms of common good (as well as individual satisfactions) and make systemic political choices.

Socialists influenced by such views have been concerned to expand the scope of democratic collective decision making over social life both by democratizing enterprises internally and by narrowing the range of impersonal markets. To those opposed to pervasive centralized planning, the challenge has been to show how this can be done in a substantially decentralized economy. One traditional socialist response to this challenge has recently been resurrected in, for the most part, non-socialist rhetoric by some recent theorists of industrial policy. Its typical prescriptions include increased investment in the relatively non-mobile factors of production (people, infrastructure), attempts to break up mass markets through the diversification and specialization of goods, and an emphasis on competition through innovation rather than cost (especially wage) cutting.[9]

Such programs attempt to create local economies of small institutions linked by concrete relational networks structured so as to give them a measure of immunity from the corrosive volatility of the surrounding markets. The convergence of political and economic logic in this strategy is expressed in the basic maxim of Transaction Cost Economics that 'nonredeployable' investments are often best protected through 'governance structures' rather than contracts and markets.[10]

From this perspective, Roemer's system raises at least two major concerns: first, the coupon capital market seems likely to generate a lottery culture that would stunt citizen capacities for political participation; and secondly, on Roemer's analysis, the coupon regime creates powerful disincentives for political participation.

The Lottery Culture

The coupon regime turns the entire citizenry into players in the stock market. Finance theory teaches that most people should not be stock pickers. It is not in their interest to do so (since they assume, without compensation, risk they could avoid by buying into a diversified mutual fund), and they contribute nothing to the efficiency of the market by doing so.[11] Indeed millions of new lay stock traders would probably exacerbate the volatility of the market and its casino-like features.

At worst, the popular capital market would resemble current state-operated lotteries where manipulative publicity encourages the masses to make investments with negative present values by manipulating superstitious hopes of getting rich quickly and without work. Lottery markets represent in the most extreme form some of the psychological qualities that the 'fetishism of commodities' argument deplores: the sense of impotence and irrationality that comes with the feeling that one's fate is in the hands of a process beyond human control and the sense that one's fate is radically separated from one's fellows'.

There are two objections here. One is that by leaving so much of existing capital markets intact Roemer forgoes an opportunity to extend collective control over the investment process. Another is that the expansion of participation in what for many will be a psychologically corrosive process will diminish citizens' capacities for effective participation in other spheres of collective decision making.

A more mundane but still important problem is that many citizens will take more risk than is in their interests. Presumably a securities commission will prevent outright swindles, but it seems impractical to prevent middle- or low-income people from betting the store on high-risk projects, though such practices seem objectionable either on straightforward paternalist grounds or what might be called second-order paternalist grounds – the probability that society will feel compelled to bail out the improvident.

Of course, not everyone will want to pick stocks. Most will probably prefer to turn their coupons over to mutual funds, and Roemer's amended program requires them to do so. However, if given the chance, some mutual funds will create lottery conditions by trying to attract coupons through promises of fantastic returns, as recently occurred in Eastern Europe, with sometimes catastrophic consequences.[12]

No doubt others will behave responsibly, and some will simply index to the market. If everyone invested in responsible mutual funds, the system would work plausibly, but that raises the question of what value the coupons add. Ordinary citizens have no plausible role to play as stock pickers. It seems almost as unlikely that they can play any plausible role in monitoring the funds. (If the funds have sectoral or specialized investment plans, then picking funds has much of the difficulty of picking stocks; on the other hand, if they are diversified, there is no substantial basis for choosing among them.)

So why not forget about coupons and have government-owned funds with independent budgets and competition between them? (Some such system may be emerging now in China.) Such funds could be designed either to provide income to the government for public expenditures or to maintain individual accounts to fund consumption (for example, retirement) benefits to particular citizens.

Alternatively, what about funds entrusted to participatory institutions such as unions, industrial associations, occupational groups and local governments? Such funds could be hemmed in by ERISA-type regulation, especially to the extent they were intended to facilitate retirement saving. Of course, coupons might find their way into such funds, but it would seem preferable to have the payments made (by employers, the government) directly to them.[13]

Disincentives to Participation

The second set of concerns arises from one of the most striking and original suggestions of Roemer's analysis. Roemer's formal modeling of the welfare of rich and poor in the coupon and capitalist economies confirms that the poor are better off under the coupon system. But the comparison suggests a startling conclusion about the relation between economic welfare and political power under the two systems. While in the capitalist economy the welfare of the poor, as one would expect, increases fairly steadily in proportion to the political power of the poor; in the coupon economy, over a wide range of political possibility, the welfare of the poor *decreases* as they gain political power.[14]

Roemer explains the increase in welfare by the fact that the coupon economy remedies externalities resulting from a collective action problem: the inability of the poor collectively to decide not to sell their shares to the rich at the outset. But the strange relation of economic welfare and political power results from another collective action problem under the coupon economy. In the coupon economy, the poor, through individually rational decisions, borrow more than their collective interest dictates. This borrowing has the consequence of making them dependent on firm profits to pay off their loans and hence compels them politically to support higher levels of public bad. The rich, who in the aggregate have a comparatively lower stake in firm profits (because they are fewer and shares are equally distributed), thus become 'a force for reducing the public bad' and everyone benefits as the rich gain increasingly disproportionate power until they approach total control of the government ($\lambda = 0.68$).[15]

Surely this situation is intolerable to democratic aspirations. While both economies have the familiar problem that individual incentives for political participation are low, the capitalist one at least has the virtue of collective incentives for the poor; their collective welfare seems likely to increase through collective participation. But the coupon economy punishes participation by the poor and rewards them for giving up the political struggle to the rich.

On this particular modeling, the coupon economy thus has the opposite tendency from the one socialists who have previously advocated individual rights in capital have sought to create. They have seen property as a means of giving people a 'stake' in the economy – something to protect from bad political decisions and that benefit from good political decisions – that would motivate participation in politics.[16] But coupon rights seem likely to motivate passivity and privatism. Only a very narrow and uncompromising utilitarianism could reject a strong disincentive to political participation as a major cost.

Moreover, if we look at the system dynamically, the model suggests that in many variations, the welfare gains to the poor from instituting the coupon economy would not be stable. For example, we might imagine that the economy would be implemented in circumstances of popular mobilization in which a high degree of democracy is also achieved, so that the political influence of the rich is only slightly disproportionate. In these circumstances, the efforts of political organizations of the poor will be counter-productive; the organizations will become discredited, and the poor, passive and demobilized. Once the rich achieve great power they may be able to change the rules of the game and expropriate from the poor. The poor can try to remobilize but they will be less organized than the rich are now or than they themselves were earlier. If the poor can foresee this danger from the outset, they would be unwise to agree to the Roemer system.

Conclusion

I think Roemer is on the right track in trying to redefine property rights and preserve a role for markets in his reimagined socialism. However, a liquid, national capital market is not the most promising setting for institutionalizing socialist goals. For both practical and idealistic reasons, I would favor reforms that, rather than trying to universalize participation in conventional capital markets, seek to expand control over investment decisions by organizations – unions, trade associations, governments – that are structured to afford *political* participation.

Notes

1. Hayes, Thomas, 'The Oil Industry's Shake-Up', *New York Times*, December 7, 1985, at D1.

2. Hecks, Jonathan, 'USX to Issue Stock Linked to Steel Unit', *New York Times*, February 1, 1991, at D1.

3. Putterman, Louis, 'Comments on *A Future for Socialism*, paper presented at the conference on A Future for Socialism; see this volume, chapter 9, pp. 151–70.

4. Black, Bernard, 'Agents Watching Agents: The Promise of Institutional Investor Voice', *UCLA Law Review* 39 (1992), pp. 811–93.

5. Grundfest, Joseph, 'The Limited Future of Limited Liability: A Capital Markets Perspective', *Yale Law Journal* 102 (1992), pp. 387–425.

6. See Richard Brealey and Stewart Myers, *Principles of Corporate Finance*, 2nd edn, New York: McGraw-Hill 1984, p. 519.

7. John E. Roemer, *A Future for Socialism*, Cambridge, MA: Harvard 1994, pp. 38–39.

8. Karl Marx, *Capital*, vol. 1, London: Penguin 1976, pp. 163–76.

9. See Michael Piore and Charles Sabel, *The Second Industrial Divide: Possibilities*

for Prosperity, New York: Basic Books 1985 and Robert Reich, *The Next American Frontier*, New York: Penguin 1983.

10.   Oliver Williamson, *The Economic Institutions of Capitalism*, New York: Free Press 1985, pp. 72–83.

11.   See Brealey and Myers, *Principles of Corporate Finance*, pp. 80, 263, 140–58 and Andrei Schliefer and Lawrence Summers, 'The Noise Trader Approach to Finance', *Journal of Economic Perspectives* 4 (1990), pp. 19–33.

12.   Michael Specter, '10,000 Stampede As Russian Stock Collapses', *New York Times*, July 30, 1994, p. 1.

13.   William Simon, 'The Prospects of Pension Fund Socialism', *Berkeley Journal of Employment and Labor Law* 14 (1994), pp. 251–74.

14.   Roemer, *A Future for Socialism*, pp. 71–72.

15.   *Ibid.*, pp. 70, 72.

16.   William Simon, 'Social-Republican Property', *UCLA Law Review* 38 (1991), pp. 1335–1413.

3

Roemer's Market Socialism: a Feminist Critique

Nancy Folbre

John Roemer offers a new low-fat recipe for socialism, very different from one that clogged the economic arteries of the state socialist countries and contributed to their collapse. In nouvelle left economics, markets (everywhere in fashion) are a key ingredient – and I think they should be. I agree with Roemer's claim that market competition promotes the kind of dynamic efficiency crucial to economic health, and I welcome his emphasis on egalitarianism as a key element of the socialist vision.

But Roemer's confidence in markets is excessive, and his approach to egalitarianism is disturbingly incomplete. Ironically, the most obvious shortcomings of his approach reflect the legacy of the Marxian orthodoxy he otherwise rejects. Largely preoccupied with differences among groups defined by differential ownership of the means of production, Roemer underestimates other forms of collective identity and action such as those based on nation, race, gender, age and/or sexual orientation. His approach is class-centric.

Perhaps because he focusses on the 'productive' sector of the economy, he slights the problems of the contemporary welfare state. Treating it in a cursory fashion as simple 'redistribution of income', Roemer overlooks important problems and sidesteps current political debates over the appropriate organization of education, health care, social insurance and family life. In these respects, Roemer's priorities are eerily reminiscent of Lenin's: socialize the 'commanding heights' of the economy first, then address other problems of social inequality.

In contesting these priorities, I will argue that the market-socialism debate would be enriched by more attention to the feminist and anti-racist literature, but will also express my affection for a central aspect of the socialist feminist tradition: its critique of the selfish proclivities of 'rational economic man'. Roemer fails to specify any limits to markets, and his lack of concern with the type of values, preferences and behavior that markets may foster is an ugly aspect of his vision. It may also be an inefficient aspect, especially where the care and nurturance of people (also known as social reproduction or the production of human capital) is concerned.

Class-centrism

In *A Future for Socialism*, as in his previous work, Roemer focuses on class differences, defined in economic terms. Indeed, he generally treats asset ownership as the only structural (rather than social-psychological) factor differentiating social groups. Forms of discrimination based on aspects of social identity such as race or gender are attributed to exogenously given tastes and preferences, often reinforced by capitalist strategies of profit maximization.[1]

Roemer seems to believe that the traditional Marxian emphasis on class was once appropriate, but no longer quite up to date. Even today, in Roemer's view, most 'public bads', including environmental degradation and the Gulf War are exacerbated by the existence of a 'small, powerful class of people deriving gargantuan amounts of income from profits'.[2] This is true to some extent. But the existence of other small (or not so small) groups of people with distinct collective interests is also relevant. Environmental 'bads' have long been far worse in the Soviet Union than in the United States, largely because of lack of accountability of the technical/managerial class. The spatial distribution of air pollution and toxic wastes in both the Soviet Union and the United States shows that they have a disproportionate impact on people of color.

Class is one among many dimensions of social division. Contrary to Roemer's claims, capitalist countries have not indulged in demonstrably greater abuses of military force than state socialist regimes. Military aggression cannot be attributed simply to the concentration of wealth ownership. Roemer emphasizes that the Gulf War served the interests of US capitalists, and cites polls showing that most citizens were initially opposed to the war.[3] This is hardly evidence that they did not benefit from preservation of the current structure of political power in the Middle East, which deters oil-exporting nations from collectively increasing the price of oil. Further, the middle- and upper-class white population paid a much lower cost for that military sortie than did less affluent people of color, who were disproportionately represented among ground combat troops.

Of course, it is difficult to compare 'public bads', because there are so many of them, and they are bad in so many different ways. But it is not hard to think of many that are unrelated to profit maximization per se. For instance, the history of public income transfers in the US shows that a predominantly white majority has laid claim to the lion's share of entitlements, restricted public assistance to the poor and is currently engaged in an energetic effort to scapegoat welfare mothers. Similarly, the gross inequities that characterize education finance in the US (which Roemer seems to attribute simply to some 'lack of community') are the product of explicit collective strategies devised and implemented by predominantly white middle- and upper-class communities.

There is no prima facie reason to believe that the unequal distribution of profits generates more profound inequalities than the unequal distribution of government spending and of earnings. Relative to taxes, corporate profits represent a relatively small 'surplus'. In the US in 1991, the sum of federal, state and local tax receipts was more than five times greater than total corporate profits.[4] Similarly, we might ask how much money we would need to transfer from full-time male wage earners to bring their income into rough equality with those of full-time female wage earners. The answer, for the US in 1992, is about $53 per week per male employee or about $132 billion, over a third of corporate profits.[5] And this calculation is an underestimate, because it leaves part-time market work and household work out of the picture.

What does Roemer have to say about earnings inequalities? In his earlier work, he suggested that it might be analyzed in class-theoretic terms. *Free to Lose* treated human capital in the form of education, training and experience as an asset and correctly emphasized that this form of capital cannot easily be expropriated from its owners.[6] Indeed, Roemer noted that inequalities in human capital associated with the emergence of a professional managerial class lead to a type of exploitation characteristic of state socialist societies. This form of exploitation would likely persist, if not intensify, within the market socialist economy he proposes in his more recent work.

Apparently this no longer troubles him. He now explains that 'As long as a market for labor exists and people are differentially educated and talented, there will be wage differentials' and ignores the role that forms of discrimination and cultural valorization play in shaping wage differentials.[7] In fact, he stipulates that 'considerations of efficiency pretty much determine the distribution of wages among workers'.[8] Not surprisingly, the book contains no discussion of racial or sexual discrimination in the labor market, and no mention of affirmative action or pay equity.

Roemer downplays the significance of racism and sexism as social phenomena: 'I do not ignore the fact that people themselves have racist and sexist ideas, and so one cannot expect changes overnight with respect to these practices.'[9] How many nights, exactly, before one could expect changes? Roemer's language evokes the traditional Marxist notion that forms of inequality based on race and gender are merely 'superstructural'. He does not even deign to cite the literature that treats race and gender as forms of collective identity and action. Roemer's only concession to feminist theory is his careful utilization of female as well as male pronouns. If there is any reference in his manuscript to the non-Marxist literature on race, I cannot discern it.[10]

The class-centrism of Roemer's market socialism (which shines through most of his work) is accentuated by his emphasis on the substantive and strategic primacy of equalizing financial assets. He observes that differential education is a major source of earnings inequality, but would defer any efforts to equalize per-student educational expenditure until after his revolution, until his proposed reforms have created the social solidarity that could foster a genuine egalitarianism.[11] Redistribute wealth first (the material base), then build social solidarity (the superstructure). But where is the social solidarity that is required to redistribute wealth going to come from?

As many critics, such as Fred Block and Joel Rogers, pointedly emphasize, Roemer offers no political theory of how or why his proposals might be adopted in this or any other country. In my view, his narrow, wealth-based definition of egalitarianism would make it very difficult to build the kind of political coalition needed to implement market socialism. It is certainly unlikely to garner much support from women or minorities.[12] And Roemer's lack of attention to current political struggles leads him to a misplaced emphasis on the viability of redistributing financial assets as the first step from which other noble steps would follow.

No 'share the wealth' movements are evident in US politics today, but campaigns for school funding equalization, a virtual continuation of the civil rights movement, have long been under way in many states, including Texas and New Jersey.[13] A nationwide campaign around this issue could well enjoy more direct support than efforts to redistribute financial assets. Obviously, the two political strategies are not mutually exclusive. In fact, more egalitarian schooling may be a requirement for the success of financial asset redistribution. Without it, the less educated are likely to fare poorly as investors or pay exorbitant commissions to better-educated investment advisors.

There would be distinct political advantages to a strategy aimed at more egalitarian distribution of both human and financial capital. Steep increases in inheritance taxes, such as Roemer advocates, could be used to finance additional investments in education for children living in poverty. The legacies of class and racial/ethnic inequalities could be addressed simultaneously. My point here is that a broader definition of egalitarianism would not only serve Roemer's political ends, but could also provide a better means to those ends.

One more comment on the legacy of class-centrism: it fosters the economistic assumption that egalitarian distribution of wealth and income is more important than egalitarian distribution of work, responsibility and authority. Thus, measures to increase the income of workers, women, people of color and the poor are considered more important than measures to increase their access to education, training and interesting jobs. Are cash transfers really sufficient to compensate for crummy working conditions? There is no simple correspondence between market income and self-realization. Surely this is one of the most precious insights of Marx's critique of bourgeois social values. It is an insight that applies to indignities based on nation, race, gender, age and sexual orientation, as well as class. And none of these dimensions of inequality is necessarily any more 'attitudinal' or less 'economic' than the other.

The Welfare State

Perhaps because he appreciates the limited impact profit redistribution alone might have, Roemer clearly states his allegiance to the welfare state. But, true to form, he defines it in class-centric terms as something brought about by a highly disciplined labor movement and a relatively homogeneous work force and possibly an indirect result of the egalitarian example set by the Bolshevik revolution.[14] He views social democracy, like the welfare state it promotes, as a means of redistributing income in a more egalitarian fashion.

Consider an alternative perspective: the welfare state is not a byproduct of class-based struggles over the surplus, but the outcome of a complicated interaction between the family, the market and the state, shaped by collective interests based on nation, race, gender and age, as well as class. More than mere 'redistribution', social programs are afflicted by problems similar to those that beset both markets and central planning, including the exploitative strategies of social groups, perverse incentives and externalities.

The rhetoric of social democracy has always been based on the metaphor of the social family, and cross-national differences in social policy have been significantly influenced by racial/ethnic composition, demographic circumstance and perceptions of national interest. In general, the growth of labor markets based on individual wages has weakened the traditional patriarchal family and attenuated intra-family income flows, with some positive and some negative effects. On the one hand, women and children have gained new freedom from elder male authority. On the other hand, a set of complex social institutions designed to provide support for the care and nurturance of dependants has eroded. State social programs developed largely in response to this erosion have had a very uneven impact. In most cases, men have fared better than women, the elderly better than children, non-parents much better than parents, and whites much better than people of color. Income transfers in the advanced capitalist countries alleviate some forms of poverty and exacerbate others.[15]

The welfare state, far from 'egalitarian', is the site of distributional conflict. Further, its policies contribute to the development of political coalitions based on gender, race and age that undermine the potential for class-based solidarity. Thus, left political economists need to rethink the principles upon which public income transfers should be based, not only because this is crucial to a larger egalitarian vision, but also because it is necessary to the development of a political coalition capable of redistributing productive assets.

Reconsideration of the moral and political principles of the welfare state is a daunting task in and of itself. But it must also be accompanied by a careful and sustained analysis of the economic inefficiencies of social welfare programs. The most obvious of these fall into the category of agency problems, including the lack of incentives to maximize efficiency. One of the best progressive critiques of Aid to Families with Dependent Children (AFDC) emphasizes the tremendous administrative costs of the current system and argues that public transfers should be directly distributed to the needy through a guaranteed income.[16]

Most economists agree, in principle, that a negative income tax system would be far superior to the existing AFDC program, which suffers from obvious incentive problems. While there is, as Roemer notes, a large literature describing these problems, most of it is empirical in nature, avoiding even the least mention of economic justice. On the Left, the widespread notion that assistance to the poor could be financed entirely by taxing the idle rich has made it easy to avoid a more substantive issue: what kinds of restrictions and requirements should be placed on recipients of public assistance who are capable of productive work? Both socialist and liberal egalitarian principles mandate some quid pro quo, but both quid and quo are open to debate. I would argue that adult recipients of AFDC already perform some productive work – child rearing – in return for the assistance they receive (this does not imply that they should not be encouraged to find paying work as well). But left economists, other than feminists, have been remarkably reticent about the punitive 'workfare' measures recently imposed by several states and under consideration on the national level.

Roemer implies that market competition is the appropriate solution for agency problems. In my opinion, this is more likely to be the case in the realm of production than in the realm of social reproduction. It is hard to tell whether or not, or where, Roemer would draw the line. Take education. Many critics correctly point out that public (state) schools are administratively top-heavy and fail adequately to monitor or reward good teaching. Would Roemer advocate the type of increased competition among schools that a voucher system would provide? If so, he must concede that schools do not produce a homogeneous product whose quality can easily be measured. Should teachers' pay simply be determined by their students' scores on standardized tests? Also, school vouchers pose a serious agency problem: parents who do make a choice of school may not act in the best interests of students. What if a significant subset of children is penalized simply because their parents are too constrained, too poorly educated themselves or just too apathetic to make the best choice?

Health is another classic case: asymmetric information, high transactions costs and fearful risks make it difficult for consumers to make optimal choices. And of course, insurance itself creates third-party problems. Many health care experts argue that a single-payer system provides the best health care for the money. Does the logic of Roemer's market socialism militate instead towards 'managed competition'? And if so, how exactly would it be managed (presumably not in Clintonesque style).

Another crucial issue is the impact of social policy on family formation. While the decline of intra-family transfers helped motivate the development of welfare programs, these have had the reciprocal effect of weakening family ties. Socialists and feminists need to ask themselves exactly what kinds of family commitments should be encouraged. I would argue that the state should strictly enforce both parents' financial responsibilities for their children, and provide some financial compensation for unpaid family labor involved in the care of children, the sick and the elderly. However, I do not believe that it should subsidize non-market work in general (i.e., housework) or discriminate against gay and lesbian families. These are *economic* issues of considerable significance. Where do Roemer and other market socialists stand on them?

The incentive problems described above are exacerbated by a particular externality problem. Current fiscal and welfare state policies have socialized many of the economic benefits of children for tax-payers as a whole, who enjoy significant claims on their future earnings. Public contributions to the cost of raising children, however, have remained relatively small. Individuals who devote relatively little time, energy or labor to child rearing are essentially free-riding on parental labor. In the fiscal sense, at least, children are public goods.[17]

A socialist feminist strategy would promote more equal distribution of the costs of children, as well as more equal opportunity for children themselves. Improved child support enforcement would help, as would increased public subsidies for childcare. But however necessary, these are not sufficient. Parents should be compensated for their efforts through a greater tax exemption or credit for raising children. And families with children should be guaranteed the means to obtain a minimum income above the poverty line. How do Roemer and other market socialists propose to provide support for child rearing? Or do they not?

As should be apparent, by now, I do not think that the most serious ailments of the welfare state can be successfully treated by the prescription of more markets (though small homeopathic doses may be useful here and there). One reason for this is fairly obvious: the public provision of health, education and welfare is more complex than the provision of impersonal commodities, if only because the 'consumers' are often too young, too sick or too desperate to exercise sovereign choice. The welfare state, like the family, is primarily a site of social reproduction, and its primary product is welfare itself. If we refuse to treat people as commodities (as I think we should) we cannot use profit maximization as a palliative for the problems of welfare management. Whatever the role of markets elsewhere in the economy, some aspects of state planning simply need to be better planned.

Competition versus Caring

Human nature is at the heart of the question. Roemer, like other advocates of market socialism, rejects the notion that people either are, or should be expected to be, unselfish. If people always acted out of concern for others, the agency problems that he describes would hardly exist. 'I therefore remain agnostic,' he writes, 'on the question of the birth of the socialist person, and prefer to put my faith in the design of institutions that will engender good results with ordinary people.'[18] Me too.

But the juxtaposition between socialist persons and everyone else is not terribly helpful. Just how selfish are ordinary people? The design of social institutions affects what they want and how they act. What if institutions designed to harness the energy contained in the pursuit of self-interest ultimately discourage altruism and solidarity? In the old-fashioned vocabulary of dialectical materialism, people are partly the product of their historical circumstances. In more neoclassical terminology, ordinary people are not exogenously given.

As Amartya Sen pointed out long ago, most rational choice theories depend far too heavily on the assumption of perfect selfishness.[19] No society based entirely on individual self-interest (defined narrowly as the absence of love, altruism or otherwise positively dependent utilities) would be capable of the forms of cooperation crucial to social reproduction. Left-wing critics of market socialism, like Michael Albert and Robin Hahnel, do not prophecy the birth of socialist economic persons. They argue, rather, that a socialist society should foster and encourage unselfish behavior.[20]

One need not agree with their views to wince at Roemer's lack of concern for values and norms of cooperation. He explores the tensions between democracy and equality without even mentioning solidarity. The Frenchmen who stormed the Bastille in 1789 added 'brotherhood', at least, to their slogan. The problem is not that ordinary people are somewhat selfish, which is indisputable, but that they could become even more selfish than they already are.

Much of the work of social reproduction in both the family and the market can be described as 'caring labor'. It is undertaken, at least in part, out of concern for the happiness and well-being of others. Historically, women have had a greater propensity than men to specialize in caring labor, partly because their access to other types of labor has been severely restricted, partly because cultural norms define femininity in terms of altruism and caring.[21] With increases in women's participation in the labor market, the erosion of family commitments, and the cultural redefinition of gender, the social space for caring labor has been reduced. The traditionally masculine pursuit of individual self-interest has become a prescription for appropriate human behavior in every realm.

Karl Marx believed that an economy based on competition would eventually lead to economic anarchy. While he exaggerated the instability of capitalist market economies, he clearly foresaw the adverse impact of competitive individualism on family life, as did Karl Polanyi.[22] A wide body of literature suggests that caring, altruism and reciprocity are reinforced by social norms that can be considered long-run implicit contracts. These norms help overcome the free-rider problems that would otherwise make such exchanges risky and inefficient.[23]

Some norms, such as those that discourage robbery, cheating or extortion, are fostered by the successful institutionalization of exchange relations. But other norms, specifically norms of caring for other people, are discouraged by impersonal spot markets. In fact, the primary ideology of market exchange is based on the claim that the individual pursuit of self-interest benefits everyone. It seems entirely possible that legitimation and reiteration of this claim has a negative impact on caring behavior. For instance, empirical evidence suggests that studying neoclassical economics encourages students to act in more narrowly self-interested ways.[24]

In any short-run bargaining situation, a party that cares more about the other party (or cares more about the consequences to a third party, such as a child) is in the weakest position to advance their own economic interests. This matters little if their 'care' is unaffected by an unfair economic outcome, because they derive intrinsic pleasure from the other person's gains. But once burned, they may become less likely to care next time around. Nice guys (or gals) finish last. No good deed goes unpunished.

Market transactions may penalize care for another reason: it is extremely difficult to monitor. The theory of efficiency wages suggests that employers often benefit by paying more than a market-clearing wage. By doing so, they not only gain some leverage over their employees (by increasing the cost of job loss) but also gain intangibles such as loyalty and good will that improve job performance. By this reasoning, we might expect employers to pay an especially high wage premium for jobs that involve care of children, the sick or the elderly, because the quality of genuine care is so difficult to observe.

But these jobs tend to be very poorly paid. In her analysis of the relationship between the pay rates and types of skill required by detailed occupations, Paula England finds a net negative return to nurturance; by contrast, the exercise of authority has a very positive impact on occupational pay.[25] It seems that our economy places a low value on caring labor, perhaps because it is generally performed by workers with little bargaining power.

On the other hand, perhaps caring, unlike other dimensions of job performance, cannot be successfully elicited by greater pay. If you can get more by simply paying more for it, maybe it isn't caring labor at all. For instance, remunerating parents on the basis of how well their children 'perform' undermines the principles that elicited parental commitment. Put in more vulgar terms, a high-priced hooker may be skilled at faking her emotions, but the buyer still knows they are fake.

Performance-based pay may actually lower quality. There are precedents for this argument in the growing literature criticizing androcentric models of 'rational economic man'.[26] The most direct, though perhaps most macabre, analogy lies with Richard Titmuss's classic research on the donation of blood for transfusions.[27] In an era when the quality of blood was difficult to monitor, he found that countries that relied on voluntary donations of blood, like the United Kingdom, fared much better than those, like the US which paid donors. People who gave blood for money were more likely to lie about their medical history and less likely to offer uninfected blood.

In general, the cheapest way to screen workers or partners for caring may be to offer them a lower pecuniary reward (or, as Gershwin put it, 'I can't give you anything but love, baby'). The only reason someone would accept a job as a daycare worker that pays far less than the alternatives is that he or she truly enjoys caring for children. Profit-maximizing employers may actually have a productivity-related incentive to pay less for caring labor.

Here again, the consequences are less troubling in the short than in the long run, as preferences, norms or values are modified. For instance, daycare workers find that the intrinsic pleasures of children wear thin after a few months of poorly paid, highly stressful work, and their turnover rates are quite high. This probably has unfortunate, though difficult to measure, consequences for the quality of childcare. Changes in the organization of family life may also have a significant long-run impact. A woman who plans to marry, have children and receive a share of her husband's income rather than be paid the market value of her labor may be willing to supply caring labor to the market for a short period of time, because the cost to her is relatively small. But a woman who predicts that her long-run economic welfare will be largely determined by her own market earnings will be more reluctant to pay the caring labor penalty. Rational economic woman does not want to depend on or care for rational economic man.

Probably more important than such individual calculations are the changing social norms and values that accompany the transformation of work. The celebration of new opportunities for women is often accompanied by the stigmatization of traditional gender roles. When a choice to specialize in non-market labor, or in caring jobs that are 'stereotypically female', is interpreted as a sign of passivity or stupidity, individuals may reduce their own caring and encourage their sisters, daughters and friends to do the same. Increased rewards for individual performance, along with cultural depreciation of family and social commitments, threaten what might be termed a 'masculinization' of society.

A concern for caring as a distinctive and valuable aspect of women's values helps explain why socialist feminists, unlike liberal feminists, argue that women's liberation should be measured not only by women's access to men's jobs, but also by men's willingness to take on tasks traditionally performed by women. It also helps explain why any vision of market socialism must explicitly consider not only public support for family labor, but also the larger balance between market and non-market institutions.

Where is the 'social' in Roemer's socialism? He envisions a just and egalitarian society that rewards intelligence, initiative and effort. With a major redistribution of intangible, as well as tangible assets, markets could help realize this vision. But markets would do little to reward affection, solidarity or caring. And these traditionally feminine qualities – too often assumed to be natural, God-given or otherwise exogenous – are also important to the efficient functioning of the economy as a whole.

Conclusion

The general concept of market socialism is the offspring of two otherwise disparate traditions – Marxism and liberalism – that share a legacy of economism and androcentrism. Most market socialists, like Roemer, are more interested in the specific mechanisms of asset reorganization than in its implications for race, gender or social reproduction. Most who read or listened to this critique were more sympathetic to feminist concerns than Roemer, but equally unwilling to engage feminist theory. Their overwhelming response was: 'There is nothing in Roemer's model that actually precludes dealing with these concerns. Can't they just be added on?'

The answer is no. A feminist reading of Roemer does not generate a list of policy measures that could be appended to a program of asset redistribution, but a set of questions that remain not only unresolved, but largely unexplored. Will market socialism, or its attendant welfare state, do anything to weaken forms of privilege based on race and gender? How far should markets extend within the realm of social reproduction? Do markets encourage what we think of as 'masculine' as opposed to 'feminine' behavior?

These questions bear directly on the economic desirability and the political viability of the market-socialist vision. Since we do not yet know the answers, we should construe them as a serious and sympathetic challenge, rather than a hostile critique. In his concluding chapter, Roemer reiterates that socialism should be conceived as egalitarianism and build upon those aspects of capitalism that have had good effects. Yes; that is exactly why socialism should draw from the theory and practice of feminism.

Notes

1. See also John E. Roemer, 'Divide and Conquer: Microfoundations of a Marxian Theory of Wage Discrimination', *Bell Journal of Economics* 10 (1979), pp. 695–705.

2. John E. Roemer, *A Future for Socialism*, Cambridge, MA: Harvard University Press 1994 p. 57.

3. Roemer, *A Future for Socialism*, p. 111.

4. See *Statistical Abstract of the U.S., 1993*, Washington, DC: Government Printing Office, pp. 292, 446.

5. Ibid., p. 426.

6. John E. Roemer, *Free to Lose. An Introduction to Marxist Economic Philosophy*, Cambridge: Harvard University Press 1988.

7. Roemer, *A Future for Socialism*, p. 50.

8. Ibid, p. 120.

9. Roemer, *A Future for Socialism*, p. 112.

10. For a more detailed critique of class-centrism, and a review of the relevant feminist and anti-racist literature, see Nancy Folbre, *Who Pays for the Kids? Gender and the Structures of Constraint*, Routledge 1994.

11. Roemer, *A Future for Socialism*, p. 111.

12. A similar criticism applies to most models of market socialism. For instance, those based on worker ownership could actually intensify race and gender differences by reinforcing the advantages that white male workers already enjoy, by virtue of their employment in relatively stable, profitable firms.

13. Nancy Folbre, 'Showdown in Texas', *Dollars and Sense* (June 1993), pp. 6–8, and 'Remember the Alamo Heights', *Texas Observer* (November 13, 1993) 1, pp. 6–9.

14. Roemer, *A Future for Socialism*, p. 25.

15. Folbre, *Who Pays for the Kids?*, pp. 91–125.

16. Teresa Funiciello, *Tyranny of Kindness. Dismantling the Welfare System to End Poverty in America*, New York: Atlantic Monthly Press 1993.

17. Nancy Folbre, 'Children as Public Goods', *American Economic Review* 84:2 (May 1994), pp. 86–90.

18. Roemer, *A Future for Socialism*, p. 114.

19. Amartya Sen, 'Rational Fools: A Critique of the Behavioral Foundations of Economic Theory', *Philosophy and Public Affairs* 6:4 (Summer 1977), pp. 317–44.

20. Michael Albert and Robin Hahnel, *Looking Forward*, Boston: South End Press 1991.

21. Nancy Folbre and Heidi Hartmann, 'The Rhetoric of Self-interest: Selfishness, Altruism, and Gender in Economic Theory', in Arjo Klamer, Donald McCloskey and Robert Solow, eds, *Consequences of Economic Rhetoric*, Cambridge, MA: Cambridge University Press 1988 pp. 184–206; Nancy Folbre, 'Holding Hands at Midnight: The Paradox of Caring Labor', manuscript, Department of Economics, University of Massachusetts, Amherst, MA, 01003.

22. Karl Polanyi, *The Great Transformation*, Boston: Beacon Press 1944.

23. David Collard, *Altruism and Economy*, New York: Oxford University Press 1978; Geoffry Hodgson, *Economics and Institutions*, Philadelphia: University of Pennsylvania Press 1988.

24. Robert Frank, Thomas Gilovich and Dennis T. Regan, 'Does Studying Economics Inhibit Cooperation?', *The Journal of Economic Perspectives* 7:2 (Spring) 1993, pp. 159–72.

25. Paula England, *Comparable Worth: Theories and Evidence*, New York: Aldine 1992, p. 164.

26. Marianne Ferber and Julie Nelson, *Beyond Economic Man: Feminist Theory and Economics*, Chicago: University of Chicago Press 1993.

27. Richard Titmuss, *The Gift Relationship: From Human Blood to Social Policy*, London: George Allen and Unwin 1970.

4

Status Inequalities and Models of Market Socialism

Debra Satz

In the last several decades, the hopes and claims of socialists have been transformed.[1] The labor theory of value, the Marxian concept of exploitation, the belief in a single, unified agent of social trans-formation and the ideal of a completely conflict-free society no longer define the politics of reflective people who consider themselves socialists. Most importantly, contemporary socialists have recognized that no modern economy can dispense with markets. Socialists must thus confront questions about where, why and how society is to rely on markets; they must examine the complex relationships between markets, equality and human motivation.

Liberalism, too, has undergone significant reformulation since the 1970s. Egalitarians have challenged those strands of liberalism which permitted the arbitrary factors of inherited wealth, social position and the 'genetic lottery' of talents to determine the life chances of individuals. The assumption that individuals have ownership rights in their talents and abilities (and that therefore welfare state redistribu-tion as well as socialism are unjust) has been subjected to a compelling attack.[2] Liberals and socialists are no longer rigidly divided along a priori lines of principle as to the question of what forms of property – capitalist or socialist – best realize human flourishing. Thinkers from both schools have converged on the thought that it is equality which people should want, and that we ought to be committed to whatever forms of property, politics and political economy best realize that ideal.

To be sure, there is considerable disagreement about the type of equality which socialists and liberals think people should want. Should we want equality of opportunity, equality of income, equality of welfare, equality of opportunity for welfare or equality of resources? However, whatever metrics of equality contemporary theorists have adopted, their focus has generally been on distributing some benefit

among individuals, and not on the refiguration of the (given) relationships within which those individuals stand.[3] For example, although
John Roemer mentions three dimensions of equality of opportunity
which socialists want – self-realization and welfare, political influence
and social status[4] – *A Future for Socialism* concentrates on designing
a feasible mechanism for advancing only the first of these (via redistribution of profits), and ignores or downplays the other dimensions of
equality which explicitly call our attention to the unequal power of
individuals and the hierarchical relationships between them. Roemer's
model of market socialism challenges neither gender inequality, racial
and ethnic marginalization, nor elite control of economic decision
making.

There is undoubtedly an important rationale for focusing on
redistributing those goods and opportunities which causally effect the
degree of material equality between individuals. Material inequalities
(for example, inequalities in income and wealth) support and sustain
inequalities in political influence and social status. Money talks, and
its language translates into corruption, unequal political influence
and unfair access to scarce opportunities. Furthermore, material
inequalities play a role in maintaining relationships based on unequal
status: people who hold material advantages can coerce those who are
economically vulnerable. For example, poor women with dependent
children are less likely than others to leave abusive relationships
or oppressive work situations. As vulnerable women receive greater
material security, they become more likely to leave purely instrumental
and degrading relationships; they become less likely to make what
Michael Walzer terms a 'desperate exchange'.[5]

But there are forms of inequality, best characterized in non-material
terms, which also have a profound effect on human well-being and
quality of life. For this reason, I believe that the narrow focus on
distributing some metric of material benefits,[6] common among many
contemporary egalitarians, is a mistake. The socialist and liberal
traditions offer us another vision of what equality is. I will call this
conception *status equality* although it is not simply concerned with the
juridical relationships within which people stand.[7] People who bear
formally equal political status to each other can also stand, at the same
time, in 'non-political' relationships of unequal status.

Relationships of unequal status are characterized by lack of
reciprocity, hierarchy and a lack of accountability. There is a distributional component to status inequalities: they are relationships of
unequal power. An agent A has power over an agent B where A can
command B to act in A's interests through imposing or threatening

to impose sanctions, but B cannot reciprocally command A. In relationships of unequal status, people cannot speak up or exercise control over their circumstances because they are dependent upon others who can fire them, demote them, tyrannize them, harass them or abandon them at will.

Relationships of unequal status can also involve attitudes or norms which marginalize people or degrade them and which shape their self-conceptions in ways which serve the interests of others. Gender inequalities, in particular, have historically functioned, at least in part, through (male) attitudes and norms which have shaped women's conceptions of what women should want. The emphasis on degradation, discounting of interests and marginalization is crucial to my analysis of why (and which) status inequalities are wrong. Some inequalities – those that produce the Michael Jordans and Linus Paulings of this world – are not based on either the exclusion and discounting of others' interests or the exercise of unaccountable and asymmetric power. Even where such inequalities lead to differentials in status, for example, in honor and regard, they are not here considered objectionable.

I believe, and will argue, that redressing those status inequalities based on hierarchy, discounting of interests, and asymmetric and unaccountable power requires more than simply giving people more money (or resources or opportunities for welfare. . .). Their relationships must be reshaped to provide them with opportunities for recognition, reciprocal influence and dignity.

This paper has three parts. In the first part, I develop the idea of status equality, drawing on strands in socialist and liberal thought. I elaborate several virtues of status equality and defend it as an ideal. In the second part, I examine John Roemer's explicit arguments for rejecting worker-management versions of market socialism in favor of what he terms 'managerial' market socialism. I challenge those arguments first on their own terms. Despite my criticisms, I hope that my sympathy with Roemer's often brilliant attempt to develop a feasible model of market socialism will be apparent. Secondly, I argue, more externally, that Roemer's version of socialism is an incomplete and unnecessarily narrow moral ideal. By ignoring status inequalities, Roemer weakens the moral appeal of his market socialism. In the third part of this paper, I explore the relationship between material inequality and status inequality. I am particularly interested in exploring this relationship as it bears on the case of gender inequality. I argue that material equality is not sufficient for the achievement of gender equality; the latter requires independent political and cultural measures, centering around a redistribution of power between men and women.

1 The Ideal of Status Equality

A great deal of recent egalitarian theory de-emphasizes what I am calling status inequality. Workplace, firm and family relationships do not stand at the center of the kind of equality which many egalitarians aim to advance. Rather than focusing on mechanisms of domination, unaccountable power, marginalization and the attitudes which sustain them, egalitarians have instead concentrated their debate on the material benefits (however these are understood) which they believe should be distributed to people equally.

Roemer's own recent work parallels this trend, in focusing almost exclusively on the redistribution of income and wealth.[8] Discussion of gender and race relations, hierarchy, alienation and asymmetric power are noticibly absent from his discussion. This is surprising, since the quality of social relationships has been a central concern of socialist theory. But it is also surprising given that most people actually care a great deal about the nature of their relationships and not simply about how the benefits those relationships produce get distributed. For example, the objection most people have to slavery or indentured servitude is not captured by focusing solely on material inequalities (e.g. on the fact that slaves are almost always poor).[9] Rather, it is because slaves are given a degraded and unequal status, their fundamental interests discounted, their opinions and values treated as insignificant, and because they are treated as 'dishonored' people,[10] that most of us think slavery is an abominable and 'evil' institution.

The human species has shown itself to be deeply creative in finding ways to deny equal status to people. Beyond the extremes of torture, mutilation, arbitrary imprisonment and genocide, we do not have to look far to find contemporary examples of marginalization, scapegoating, denigration, subordination and domination.

Social movements have been inspired as much by the need to win recognition and inclusion, as by the need to rectify unfair economic outcomes. Consider the examples of the Chartist movement in Britain, the civil rights movement, movements in favor of the rights of ethnic minorities, the women's movement. In addition to the facts of material inequality there are facts of exclusion and subordination, facts which people care about and act upon. Traditionally, some socialists and liberals have been moved by these latter facts to make status equality one of their central objectives.

Marx's own view of equality helps to illustrate the distinction I am drawing between status inequality and economic inequality and to place a socialist pedigree (if one is needed) on the idea of status inequality. In his writings, Marx is not only a critic of formal juridical conceptions of equality, but also of distributive conceptions of justice which seek to provide people with equal reward for equal amounts of labor.[11] Marx's criticisms have led theorists like Allen Wood to argue that Marx was 'no friend to the idea that "equality" is something good in itself'[12] and even to claim that Marx was an immoralist. But I think Wood's view is mistaken. Marx's criticisms are directed against precisely those conceptions of equality which leave the unequal status relationships between people untouched. There is a powerful passage in *Capital*, volume 1, which makes this point:

> The sphere that we are deserting, within whose boundaries the sale and purchase of labour-power goes on, is in fact a very Eden of the innate rights of man. There alone rule Freedom, Equality, Property, and Bentham. Freedom, because both buyer and seller of a commodity, say of labour power, are constrained only by their own free will ... Equality, because each enters into relation with the other, as with a simple owner of commodities, and they exchange equivalent for equivalent. Property, because each disposes only of what is his own. And Bentham, because each looks only to himself ...
>
> On leaving this sphere of simple circulation or of exchange of commodities, which furnishes the 'Free-trader Vulgaris' with his views and ideas, and with the standard by which he judges a society based on capital and wages, we think we can perceive a change in the physiognomy of our dramatis personae. He, who before was the money owner, now strides in front as capitalist; the possessor of labour power follows as his labourer. The one with an air of importance, smirking, intent on business; the other, timid and holding back, like one who is bringing his own hide to market and had nothing to expect but – a hiding.[13]

In this sardonic passage, Marx objects to the capitalist workplace not because of its outcomes in terms of economic inequality, but because it subjects the worker to the power and domination of the capitalist owner. This power is asymmetric[14] – the capitalist 'smirks', the worker is 'timid and holding back'. Beneath the formal equality of the market, this passage reveals the hierarchical and despotic relationship of capitalist to worker.

Status inequality, and not inequality in material outcome, was central to Marx's criticism of capitalism. While he criticized (inconsistently) the distributional outcomes which advantaged the owners of capital,[15] he focussed his criticism on two types of unequal and degrading status relationships which he thought characterized the capitalist system. *Capitalist production relationships* necessarily subordinate the interests of workers to the interests of capitalists. In a capitalist system, if capitalists do not generate profit, workers' interests cannot be met and workers lose their jobs and livelihoods. Moreover, workers have no control over the production process and no say in the investments of their firms, the mechanism by which profit is generated. These decisions are made by others who are not accountable to them. Marx believed that workers in capitalist firms were treated, by the very logic of the capitalist system, as 'appendages to machines'.

Marx also believed that *capitalist market relations* involved people in relationships of unequal status because they placed (or at least appeared to place) human interests under the control of things. When confronted with the complexity of the capitalist market, people become passive; they cannot see the market's outcomes as the result of their independent, atomized decisions. In the capitalist market, things, commodities, become endowed with the power to dictate social and economic life: people are subordinated to things.

The idea that some group (or even inanimate things) should not be able to exercise asymmetric and unaccountable power over others is not only part of the socialist tradition, but of the liberal tradition as well. For example, John Stuart Mill questioned the morality of a system of relationships which gave husbands unaccountable power over their wives as well as employers unaccountable power over their workers. Such relationships, he argued, were not compatible with equal dignity and respect.[16] The 'equality' term of the celebrated triad of 1789 – liberty, fraternity, equality – similarly referred not simply to material equality but also to status equality.

A concern for status equality is thus central to both the socialist and liberal traditions. It is also a central part of our culture, part of the way that people evaluate their lives and their environment. People make judgments about the quality of their relationships which are independent of how well those relationships distribute material goods. They make judgments about whether or not those relationships degrade, marginalize or discount their needs and interests.

We should criticize those who look only to the economic consequences of institutions, rather than to their internal relations and to the treatment of the individuals involved in them. Many contemporary egalitarian theorists (including most welfare economists) still fail to note that people often have preferences for relationships and institutions which are *direct*, that is, that people prefer certain institutions and relationships not simply for their independent, external consequences, but because they are fulfilling, reciprocal, and sources of self-realization and self-respect. To focus *only* on an institution's economic consequences is to elevate the importance of material goods over persons; equality's moral bite and appeal is lost when we lose sight of what we want equality *for*.

I do not believe that people should (or will) find attractive a model of socialism which disconnects the distribution of goods from the quality and equality of their social relationships. Models of socialism should focus not only on the distribution of material goods and opportunities, but also on the relationships between people and between people and institutions. Socialists should oppose relationships based on exclusion, marginalization, dependency, and unaccountable and asymmetric power. In addition, relationships based on status equality realize important moral goods which socialists should want: reciprocity, self-respect, autonomy and accountability. Such goods are part of the ideal of a democratic politics in which people deliberate and make choices as free and equal citizens. Why, then, should these relationships be confined to the political process alone when so much asymmetric power, marginalization and degradation occurs in society's other fundamental institutions and social practices?

2 Status Equality and John Roemer's Model of Managerial Market Socialism

The 'central innovation' of John Roemer's model of market socialism is to simulate the powerful incentive and informational mechanisms of markets in the context of restrictions on the ownership and transferability of shares of stock. In Roemer's system, the price of labor, capital and consumer goods is determined by competitive markets, as in a capitalist system. But shares (or equity) in firms and enterprises can be purchased only with coupons and not with cash. As every adult will receive the same quantity of coupons and cannot transfer them to others, the effect will be to equalize the distribution of profits. This equalization is postulated to have several positive social effects: the diminishment of public bads such as pollution and war; the equalization of the opportunities for political influence; and the raising of the level of well-being of the worst off members of society.

This socialist stock market leaves a great deal of existing inequalities intact, since it does not address either disparities in wage earnings or the unequal division of labor within the family. Roemer proposes supplementing his model with social democratic welfare state distribution,[17] a 'massively improved' education system aimed at raising the life chances of the poor,[18] a system of estate taxes,[19] and the need for a constitution which limits the accumulation of private property in productive assets.[20] But even if Roemer's capital market and the additional welfare state measures reduce material inequality, they fail to directly redress the systematic status inequalities which constitute capitalist production relations.

Roemer rejects versions of market socialism that feature a greater democratization of workplace relations and worker management, and which yield to people more deliberative control over the economy. In Roemer's model, managers run firms in the interest of maximizing profit. In order to ensure that managers efficiently meet their goals, a consortium of firms and banks, modeled after the Japanese *keiretsu*, monitors their behavior. Groups of firms are organized around a small number of main banks who are responsible for monitoring them and disciplining the behavior of their managers through the control of debt-financing.

From the perspective of status equality, this proposal has several main defects. First, it concentrates a large amount of power in the hands of banks. As Roemer himself asks, 'Who . . . would monitor the monitors?'[21] Concentrations of power enhance the possibilities of, and incentives for, corruption and the manipulation of information. Secondly, the proposal provides no mechanism for workers' own monitoring of managers who harass, demean and arbitrarily threaten them. Thirdly, it provides no mechanism of input for workers who want their workplaces to pursue other goals besides that of maximizing profit, such as environmental preservation, gender and racial justice, occupational safety, or the reform of the work process.[22] Finally, the asymmetric power of managers, bankers, and workers helps to sustain a culture in which powerful and powerless regard each other with growing fear and contempt.[23]

Why does Roemer reject workplace democratization? *A Future for Socialism* gives two main reasons.

1. Managerial market socialism is preferable to worker management socialism in that it proposes fewer departures from the status quo. As Roemer puts it, 'an organism with one mutation is more likely to survive than one in which two mutations occur simultaneously'.[24] A proposal which endorses fewer changes is likely to be more stable (and more acceptable) than a less modest proposal.

2. Labor-managed firms may be inefficient. Workers, for example, cannot be expected to lay themselves off by closing down an obsolete plant which they own. More critically, their adversity to risk may lead them to view innovation with suspicion; they may therefore adopt policies which lead to lower levels of productivity.

How serious are these criticisms? The first argument, I believe, stems from an inappropriate analogy between consciously formulated social changes and the random mutations which occur in biology. It is true, as Roemer states, that organisms with a small number of mutations are more likely to survive than those with many mutations. But that is because in the biological case, mutations are largely random and generally harmful to the organism. In the case of sociological 'organisms' such as Roemer's managerial market socialism, we are not dealing with randomly introduced changes but changes designed to bring about some beneficial effect. In such cases, the achievement of that effect will often require altering other parts of the social structure as well.

Consider the following example. The adoption of no-fault divorce laws was designed to introduce formal equality into divorce. California, along with several other states, directed that marital property be divided equally upon divorce and that financial support following divorce be designed only for a transition period. Yet Lenore Weitzman's study[25] concluded that these few and simple reforms have made women worse off, by failing to take into account the long-term economic disadvantages which accrue to women who do not work outside the home during marriage, and by failing to anticipate that, despite the legal preference for joint custody, most women continue to perform the major parenting role. Here, 'one change is better than two' does not work as moral arithmetic. Reforming divorce laws requires a myriad of measures which address the unequal social and economic relationships between men and women.

Roemer's second argument – that worker-managed firms tend to be too conservative toward risk-taking and therefore will tend to underinvest – is sensitive to the background environments in which worker-managed firms are assumed to operate. These background assumptions are crucial because both empirical and theoretical research shows that the behavior of worker-managed firms is highly sensitive to external financing arrangements as well as to internal criteria for firm membership. The worker-managed cooperatives in Mondragon, for example, are forced to compete with other firms for loans.[26] These loans are scrutinized by other cooperatives (each of which has shares in the others) which help to determine the conditions under which their assets are used. Such 'outside' financing constraints can help mitigate the tendencies of worker-managed firms to take a conservative attitude toward risk and hence toward innovation. But the 'outside' control exercised by worker-creditors is quite different from the type of hierarchical, managerial control that characterizes Roemer's model. In Mondragon, workers engage in mutual monitoring (a move which may increase their efficiency[27]), participate in the running of their cooperative, and receive shares in the profits that their cooperative produces. They, and not bank boards and corporate elites far from the scene of production, elect their managers and can dismiss managers who abuse, degrade and exploit them, as well as managers who are technically incompetent.

Empirically, the claim that hierarchical firms will necessarily outperform labor-managed firms has yet to be seriously tested. In capitalist economies, workers who wish to run their own firms face serious obstacles. Most importantly, workers are asset poor. They are therefore unable to secure bank loans on terms comparable to wealthy capitalist owners and more likely to be conservative toward risk since their assets are not diversified. But even if the empirical claim should be substantiated and labor-managed firms turned out to be somewhat less productive than capitalist ones, why should that fact be decisive against labor-management? There are other values besides maximal productive efficiency. Indeed, capitalist firms already allow non-market values to shape workplace organization. Even in poor countries, where pressure on raising the standards of labor productivity is greatest, commonsense morality and decency should condemn certain types of labor organization. Indentured servitude, the violation of workers' basic interests in health and safety, sexual and racial discrimination, harassment, and forms of work which diminish human capacities and lifespans are rightly rejected and condemned, even where such practices would increase productive efficiency. Why should we think that productive efficiency, even when we can tack on to it redistributive material equality, is the *sole* virtue of an economic arrangement?[28]

Apart from the values of mutuality, democratic accountability and greater autonomy, worker-management also provides room for the values of occupational safety, environmental conservation and sexual and racial equality to play a role in the organization of the production process. At a time when women and minorities still disproportionately occupy the least well paid and least prestigious jobs, worker-management is attractive to socialists insofar as it allows for democratic debate on the restructuring of work tasks, and allows for the possibility of restructuring leave time to redress the gender inequalities which result from women's unequal work in the home.[29]

Furthermore, worker-management may help to minimize the opportunities for managerial abuse. We have seen that Roemer's managerial model of market socialism raises the worry: who guards the guardians? This is a significant concern in a system in which financing and management selection rests in the hands of the banks and experts, and in which workers and citizens participate in economic decision making largely as atomized and self-interested owners of coupons.

Perhaps most significantly, Roemer's model of managerial socialism runs the risk of heightening the pathologies of individual choice which emerge in large impersonal markets where each individual's contribution to the collective good is indirect and numerically insignificant. In particular, what prevents individuals from directing their coupons to investments which promise high-risk, high-yield returns even when such investments are dubious from the point of view of social production?[30] Why should we believe that atomized and dispersed coupon holders will achieve an optimal outcome on environmental issues? What, in short, prevents individuals in the socialist stock market from behaving in the familiar short-term, selfish ways which already generate collective action problems and exacerbate public bads?

One answer to these problems is to try to increase what biologists refer to as the 'degree of community' or relatedness among individuals. Biologists and game theorists[31] have found that when the degree of community of a group is enhanced, the group's ability to cooperate and to reach collectively beneficial outcomes also increases. The degree of community is affected by (1) the extent of shared beliefs and preferences among individuals; (2) the expectation that individuals will continue to interact with one another in the future (that membership in the group is more or less fixed and that interactions are repeated); (3) the respective rewards for cooperation and defection; and (4) the extent to which individuals engage in face-to-face direct relations with one another.

The equalization of wealth, by making the population more homogeneous, is one way in which Roemer's proposal does increase the degree of community. But he relies heavily on markets to do this whereas each of the above factors is affected by the operation of markets. By fostering short-lived and indirect relations between strangers, characterized by the possibility of exit, markets can change the costs and benefits associated with cooperation. The ability of individuals to secure goods independently of others erodes incentives to participate in efforts to improve a common life. (Consider the collapse of public education in the United States.) Atomized decisions motivated by narrow and short-term interests can give market outcomes a volatility which will disrupt the provision of many social and political goods.

Of course, not all forms of 'cooperative' behavior are good, for example, cartelization. And 'exit' is one important way of exercising freedom. But in order to encourage individuals to have a sense of the common good, markets need to be embedded in a larger social order which encourages norms of reciprocity among equals, sharing and participation. Creating this larger order requires, I believe, the reorganization of production relationships, making managers democratically accountable to their workers, and encouraging mutual monitoring and the decentralization of certain economic decisions.[32] Reforms of gender and race relations, and changes in our treatment of children and those with disabilities, are also part of creating a more humane and egalitarian society. How can we expect people who are harassed, rendered passive, discounted, and subordinated to processes and people that they cannot control to develop a sense of the common good?

3 The Relationship between Status Equality and Material Equality

Material equality can affect status equality in several ways. Status equality is conditioned, although not determined, by material equality. As I have noted, where there is greater economic equality, it is easier for people to 'exit' from oppressive and degraded relationships. Equalization of material resources also gives to people a greater opportunity to represent their interests and to bargain effectively, thus allowing them to attempt to transform oppressive and degraded relationships. It makes it less likely that some particular person or persons will have the power to control processes of public deliberation (where such processes exist). A high degree of material equality is, arguably, a precondition for a democratic society.

Material equality is also a way of acknowledging the status equality of persons.[33] For example, consider Rawls's difference principle, which justifies inequalities in income and wealth only insofar as they improve the position of the least advantaged. This principle forces us to *justify* material inequalities to the least advantaged person, because it assumes her initial interest in an equal share in society's wealth. The baseline for Rawls's difference principle (against which inequalities are to be justified) is absolute equality in the distribution of primary goods because this is assumed to follow from the equal worth of persons and from an acknowledgement of their fundamental (and equal) interests.

Conversely, it is plausible to assume that status equality will render material equality more likely. The incorporation of people into social institutions on terms of equal respect allows for the interests of each to be equally counted. Where people's interests are equally counted, we can expect that relationships based on personal subordination will be less stable.[34] Moreover, status equality can change people's sense of what their fundamental interests are and what they are entitled to. For example, the growing acknowledgment of the injustice of status inequality based on gender has spawned movements for comparable worth and pay equity.

There is an additional potential effect of status equality on material equality which directly bears on Roemer's version of market socialism. In his book, Roemer focuses on changing the unequal distribution of profits; his model does not attempt to reduce wage differentials. He writes, 'Indeed, the key to the market-socialist proposals outlined in this essay is the fundamental asymmetry between wages and profits as categories of national income: while considerations of efficiency pretty much determine the distribution of wages among workers, they do not determine the distribution of profits.'[35] Roemer does not provide evidence for this assertion, but neoclassical economics has many arguments designed to show that wages are determined by the efficiency of the marginal worker. Such theoretical explanations of wage differentials ignore the role of politics, culture and norms in shaping wages. In the real world, compensation is determined not only by efficiency but also by unionization levels, racism and sexism, incomplete information, monopolistic power and unequal political influence. The vast differentials in the wages of American and Japanese CEOs, or American and British physicians, cannot be explained without taking into consideration the effects of both institutions and values.[36] If this is right, then there is a degree of flexibility in the determination of wages. Giving workers more control over their managers and executives might thus lead to a compression of wage differentials. Status equality might lead workers and managers to adopt norms which rule out large inequalities in material income.[37]

Status equality and material equality may thus mutually and

beneficially support each other. Both, I believe, are moral imperatives. But it would be a mistake to conflate these two kinds of equality, or to think that one kind of equality reduces to the other kind. While distributing certain material goods more equally will improve the bargaining position of the poorest, it will not by itself end either domination or marginalization. I have argued elsewhere that the cases of commercial surrogacy[38] and prostitution[39] provide us with powerful examples where improving the economic equality of women might actually worsen the gender (status) inequality of women. In allowing women to 'capitalize' on their reproductive and sexual 'assets', the economic position of women may be improved: prostitution and commercial surrogacy open up new market opportunities for women. At the same time, both practices have the potential to reinforce sexist assumptions about women and to place women's sexual and reproductive capacities under the control of others. Prostitution and surrogacy, like pornography, influence people's preferences and perceptions; in particular, these practices shape men's perceptions of women and women's perceptions of themselves. Negative perceptions of women's worth can reinforce features of the caste-like system which now defines relationships between the two genders. For example, they can reinforce views about women as essentially providers of sex and childcare.

If the problem with practices like pornography, prostitution and commercial surrogacy is that they reinforce *unequal relationships* between men and women, then giving women more money to engage in these practices does not redress the problem. Instead, encouraging such practices can potentially undermine equality between men and women, by fostering relations of domination, marginalization and status hierarchy,[40] and attitudes of superiority and contempt.

How might gender equality be achieved? Surely, pay equity is one component of gender equality, establishing the equal worth of men and women workers. A further component would include positive measures to establish and protect a women's right to control her sexual and reproductive capacities and not to give over control of these capacities to others, for example, through access to abortion, contraception and sex education and establishing a minimum age of consent. Additional measures might include the public provision of childcare, and the availability of parental leave regardless of gender.

From the perspective of status equality, there is no justification for drawing a sharp distinction between the principles which govern 'public' political relations between people and those which govern their 'private' relations in schools, workplaces and families. Both the realm of the economy and that of the family have crucial constitutive effects on people and powerfully shape their life chances, their conceptions of themselves and of their interests, their quality of life, their sense of worth, and their ability to participate actively in shaping their own lives and circumstances.[41] It is an important theme in some strands of American republicanism, such as Jeffersonianism, as well as some strands of socialist thought, that dependent people make poor citizens.[42] The contemporary workplace, the economy and the family all involve people in relationships of dependence and subordination, in which they are often beholden to others who, in turn, are unaccountable to them. Models of socialism need to be assessed not only in terms of their motivational realism and their potential for achieving greater economic equality, but also for the kinds of relationships they sponsor.

4 Conclusion

In this paper, I have sought to establish two principal points. First, I have argued that Roemer's model of managerial market socialism provides insufficient scope for certain important forms of redistribution. By focussing narrowly on the distribution of material income (and, indeed, only on the distribution of material income derived from profits), Roemer's model ignores the necessity of redressing the unequal relationships which characterize many of the most important social institutions in our society. I believe that models of market socialism which explicitly address these unequal relationships as well as inequalities in material income, should be preferred to the model offered in *A Future for Socialism*. This conclusion, I have argued, is supported by the powerful influence of status inequality on people's sense of self-respect, on their autonomy, and on their ability to freely participate in deliberations about the public good. (It may be supported by efficiency considerations as well, although I do not pretend to have established that conclusion in this paper.)

Secondly, I have argued that Roemer's model needs to pay more explicit attention to the non-market institutions and values which are required to stabilize the socialist stock market and guide it to beneficial outcomes. The guardians need to be guarded: there must be institutions of accountability and public control over the behavior of banks, managers and technical experts.[43] We cannot rely on the behavior of atomized and self-interested coupon holders to realize the common good: there are too many externalities and too many incentives to manipulate information or to seek a free ride. Even from within Roemer's own model, status equality has a role to play.

Despite these criticisms, I want to acknowledge that Roemer's book revitalizes an important debate and does so with both analytical rigor and imagination. His work highlights the importance of reconciling a more egalitarian distribution of income with dynamic market efficiency. *A Future for Socialism* also rightly emphasizes the need to avoid utopian assumptions about human nature and motivation. My aim here has been to bring into sharper relief a kind of equality, absent from many contemporary egalitarian proposals and, in particular, neglected in Roemer's model, which I think is important to the socialist ideal. Socialism has never been simply about redistributing income; a large part of socialist aspiration has centered around the need to design institutions and relationships which foster independence, self-respect and dignity, and which give people a greater degree of control over their lives and circumstances. That is one reason why conceptions of the goal of socialism have been so intertwined with those of the process of its achievement, and why so many socialists have rejected managerial or elite conceptions of political organizing.[44]

My view of status equality as central to socialism's ambitions raises a number of broad questions which I think should rank high on the agenda of anyone concerned with achieving greater distributive justice. Among these questions are the following.

1. How do we institutionalize forms of firm-based worker management in an age of extreme labor mobility, the disintegration of the traditional 'proletariat', and heterogeneity of interests?[45]

2. What kind of work and family relations best support the development of the deliberative capacities needed to support democratic institutions?

3. What limits does liberty set to the restructuring of social and economic relationships?

I cannot address these questions here. But I believe that a concern with the central status inequalities between people should guide our efforts to reform society and to theorize alternative models of markets and politics. We need never to lose sight of what we want equality for.

Notes

1. This paper is a revised version of comments prepared for the conference on 'A Future for Socialism'. While revising this paper, I have benefited from reading a fine essay by Elizabeth Anderson, 'Equality and Market Socialism' (forthcoming in Justin Schwartz, ed., *Socialism and the Market*, New York: Guilford Press) which converges with the critical perspective on managerial socialism I take here. Anderson counterposes a concept she calls relational equality to distributional equality. By contrast, the concept of status equality which I defend here is a distributional one. (I discuss my views of the relationship between status inequality and material inequality in the third part of this paper.) I have also benefited from discussion of the issues with John Ferejohn, Elisabeth Wood and the participants in the original conference.

2. Cf. G.A. Cohen, 'Marxism and Contemporary Political Philosophy, or: Why Nozick Exercises Some Marxists More Than He Does Any Egalitarian Liberal', *Canadian Journal of Philosophy*, Supplementary Volume 16 (1990), pp. 363–67.

3. See also Anderson, *Equality and Market Socialism*, on this point.

4. John E. Roemer, *A Future for Socialism*, Cambridge, MA: Harvard University Press 1994, p. 11.

5. Michael Walzer, *Spheres of Justice*, New York, Basic Books 1983, p. 102.

6. Where this phrase is taken to include the opportunity for material benefits.

7. Although J. Rawls is clearly concerned with more than material equality – i.e. the first principle of justice in *A Theory of Justice*, Cambridge, MA: Harvard University Press, distributes liberties between people – I think that he fails to explore adequately the implications of his view for the status relationships of individuals outside their formal juridical relationships. Thus, he says little about the structure of the family and the workplace. And although he frequently refers to the 'social bases of self respect' as a primary good to be distributed in accordance with the difference principle (indeed, the most important primary good), he does not consider the implications of its distribution for the actual social relationships between people. The 'social bases of respect' appears most centrally and explicitly in the third part of *A Theory of Justice* in the section on 'Ends' and has a lesser role in the second part of the book on 'Institutions'.

8. See also my review of Roemer's book *Free to Lose* (Cambridge, MA: Harvard University Press 1988) in *Economics and Philosophy*, vol. 6, no. 2, October 1990, pp. 315–22.

9. Nor have the groups denied equal status always been materially poor: the Jews of medieval Europe were often wealthy, but were still denied equal treatment and respect in their society's basic institutions.

10. See Orlando Patterson, *Slavery and Social Death*, Cambridge, MA: Harvard University Press 1982.

11. Cf. 'The Critique of the Gotha Program', in R. Tucker, ed., *The Marx–Engels Reader*, 2nd edn, New York: Norton 1978, pp. 530 ff.

12. A. Wood, 'Marx on Right and Justice', *Philosophy and Public Affairs* 8 (1979) p. 281.

13. Karl Marx, quoted in ed. R. Tucker, *The Marx–Engels Reader*, 2nd edn, New York: Norton 1978, p. 343.

14. Cf. Louis Putterman, 'On Some Recent Explanations on Why Capital Hires Labor', *Economic Inquiry* 22 (April 1984), pp. 171–87.

15. Recall that in *Capital* Volume 1 Marx writes that the existence of surplus value 'is a piece of good luck for the buyer, but by no means an injustice towards the seller'.

16. See, for example, John Stuart Mill, *Principles of Political Economy*, Harmondsworth: Penguin 1970, especially book IV, ch. VII.

17. Roemer, p. 119.

18. Ibid., p. 110.

19. Ibid., p. 119.

20. Ibid., p. 110.

21. Ibid., p. 76.

22. See also Anderson.

23. For a funny and heartbreaking account of the culture of the hierarchical workplace, see Ben Hamper, *Rivethead: Tales From the Assembly Line*, New York, NY: Warner Books 1991.

24. Roemer, p. 122.

25. Lenore Weitzman, *The Divorce Revolution: The Unexpected Social and Economic Consequences for Women and Children in America*, New York: Free Press 1985.

26. Cf. Ana Gutierrez Johnson and William Foote Whyte, 'The Mondragon System of Worker Production Cooperatives', *Industrial and Labor Relations Review*, 1977.

27. Cf. Sam Bowles and Herb Gintis, 'A Political and Economic Case for the Democratic Enterprise', *Economics and Philosophy*, vol. 9, no. 1 (April 1993), pp. 75–100.

28. This is not to deny the need for, and value of, dynamic efficiency. Roemer is right to argue that the material equality that socialists want is not 'levelling-down' but equality at a high level of provision. I am not convinced, however, that worker-managed firms will be unable to successfully pursue profit goals, nor do I believe that these are the only goals that they should pursue.

29. I say 'possibility' here, fully aware that some workers oppose the sexual and racial desegregation of their workplaces.

30. As Bill Simon notes, in his contribution to this volume (ch. 2), managers would have incentives to package their firms' investment returns to manipulate (and probably to shorten) the time preferences of the investors, a move which could inflate the value of coupons for the next generation.

31. Cf. Michael Taylor and Sarah Singleton, 'The Communal Resource: Transaction Costs and the Solution', (unpubl. MS, May 1992); Elinor Ostrom, *Governing the Commons: The Evolution of Institutions for Collective Action*, Cambridge, MA: Cambridge University Press 1990; Sam Bowles, 'Mandeville's Mistake: The Myth of the Self-Regulating Market' (unpubl. MS).

32. Exactly *which* economic decisions should be handled by the workers of an individual firm is an important and difficult question which I do not address here.

33. While I am very sympathetic to the analysis of 'relational equality' that Elizabeth Anderson presents in her paper, 'Equality and Market Socialism', I disagree with her that the liberal concern with distributive equality is a form of commodity fetishism. Distributive equality in income and wealth can be a form of equal respect, in addition to serving as the precondition for a political democracy.

34. Cf. Peter Railton, 'Moral Realism', *Philosophical Review* 95 (1986), pp. 183–207 for an elaboration of this point. Railton does not acknowledge, however, the collective action problems which can emerge even where individuals have the power and opportunity to bring about some desired and beneficial end.

35. Roemer, p. 120.

36. See Derek Bok, *The Cost of Talent*, New York: Free Press 1993.

37. It is also possible that worker-management will increase efficiency, since workers may be more likely to work where they believe that the authority exercised over them is legitimate, and also where mutual monitoring, and not hierarchical and centralized supervision of tasks, prevails.

38. Debra Satz, 'Markets in Women's Reproductive Labor', *Philosophy and Public Affairs*, Spring 1992, pp. 107–31.

39. Debra Satz, 'Markets in Women's Sexual Labor', unpubl. MS.

40. I make this claim only with reference to prostitution and commercial surrogacy in contemporary American society under prevailing social conditions. It is not a claim about these practices per se. See Satz, 1992. op. cit.

41. Cf. Susan Okin, *Justice, Gender and the Family*, New York: Basic Books 1989, for an illuminating discussion of the ways in which inequalities between men and women in the home shape, and are shaped by, broader social inequalities.

42. Cf. Hal Draper, *The Two Souls of Socialism*, New York: Independent Socialist Clubs of America 1966, for a vision of socialism which emphasizes the need to change the relationships between people as well as the distribution of things between them.

43. The *keiretsu* variation of Roemer's model allows for a greater degree of accountability than the pure market model.

44. Eugene Debs once remarked, 'Don't vote for me because you think that I will lead you to the promised land. Because if I could lead you there, someone else could lead you out.'

45. See the Joshua Cohen and Joel Rogers contribution in this volume (chapter 6) for scepticism about workplace democracy in an age of labor mobility.

Coupon Socialism, Democracy and Politics

5

My Utopia or Yours?

Joshua Cohen and Joel Rogers

Like all of John Roemer's work, *A Future for Socialism*[1] casts analytical light on an intellectually deep, practically urgent problem: in this case, the problem of reconciling equality and efficiency. Roemer's proposed solution to this problem – his managerial model of market socialism – is characteristically ingenious. His argument for it is exemplary in uniting technical precision, imagination and a long view of the possibilities for social justice.

Roemer's proposal rests on three premises: (1) economic, social and political equality are fundamental values; (2) dynamic efficiency – important if equality is to mean levelling up, not down – requires markets; (3) because people are not indifferent to how they fare individually, and will not become so merely through education or a change in property rights, incentive schemes are needed to establish congruence between individual motivations and egalitarian outcomes. To promote equality in this world of markets and incentive problems, Roemer would establish a new property right, providing each citizen with claims on firm profits by endowing each with coupons that can only be used to purchase shares in firms (either directly or through mutual funds). Because the endowments are equal and the coupons cannot be cashed in, income would be more equally distributed in the coupon economy than its capitalist counterpart. To ensure dynamic efficiency, Roemer would have firms compete in markets. To solve principal–agent problems, those firms would be controlled by managers and monitored by banks.

We agree with Roemer about the importance of equality, markets and incentive problems, and share the intellectual project that follows from this agreement: to develop models of political-economic regimes, alternative to contemporary capitalism, that have sufficient *institutional* richness to show how equality might be achieved despite market and incentive constraints. Accepting a need to economize on the scarce motives of solidarity and public-spiritedness – that shared commitments to equality will not suffice for the stability of an egalitarian social regime – means accepting the need to say something about the organizational glue that will hold the regime together.

A variety of egalitarian models or strategies might satisfy these different conditions. Roemer mentions several, including our own model/strategy of 'associative democracy' (pp. 51–53). What distinguishes the associative conception from Roemer's is that it does not premise a fundamental change in property rights, though it would welcome such a change. Instead, it seeks to further egalitarian aims chiefly by improving the terms and kinds of *popular organization* on which egalitarian democratic regimes customarily rely for social and political support. Taking note of the fact that the 'right' (democratic, equality-enhancing) kinds of popular organization do not arise naturally under modern capitalism,[2] and thus that egalitarian regimes 'naturally' face an organizational deficit at their base, the associative view recommends curing that deficit through the deliberate use of public powers – using subsidy and other means to encourage the development of the missing organizational bases of support.[3]

The concerns that have led us to this recommendation also summarize our differences with Roemer's managerial model. These stem in part from differences in normative emphasis, in part from skepticism about the political feasibility of the managerial model. In what follows, we explore these differences and then speculate briefly on what taking our side in them might presently imply for socialist practice.

Differences with Roemer

Norms and politics

When Roemer surveys the demise of state socialism and asks what is left of the socialist project, his answer is 'equality'. Our answer is 'democracy'. Certain differences in institutional recommendation follow from this difference in normative emphasis.

With respect in particular to the organization of the economy, we are as concerned with democratic *control* of the economy as with the likely consequence of that control – the material equality that has long provided Roemer's principal focus. Property has two aspects – control and benefit – and the socialist critique of private property embraces both. The best in the socialist tradition was always about, and in our view the best continuation should centrally be about, collective control of economic resources – about 'economic democracy' broadly understood as popular control of the kind and conditions of economic activity – as well as equal sharing in the material benefits of that activity. Indeed, far from recommending a retreat from this democratic aspect of the traditional socialist project, present circumstances recommend special insistence on it, with 'democratic control of the economy' understood as one instance of the radical democracy we take to lie at the core of socialist ideals.[4]

Having drawn attention to this normative difference with Roemer, we do not wish to exaggerate it. Roemer mentions the importance of political equality – 'equal opportunity for political influence' (p. 11) – as one dimension of socialist concern, and his model of market socialism has parties competing for office in part on the basis of different proposals about investment. Reciprocally, we are attracted to the associative view in part because we think that the changes in organization will produce changes in bargaining power, and that those changes are needed to bring greater equality in the distribution of resources.[5] Still, a difference of emphasis remains. Our associative conception is focused as much on the organization of power as on the distribution of resources. Managerial market socialism is democratic, but it does not take the democratization of economic power as a principal concern.

Our second area of disagreement with Roemer concerns the feasibility of managerial socialism as a *political* project. Roemer would grant that what we are discussing here – and whether it is called 'socialism' or 'egalitarianism' hardly matters for this point – must be thought of as a political project, not just an intellectual one.[6] Taking that seriously, however, requires more than describing institutional models that achieve equality consistent with protecting markets and addressing incentive problems. It means also saying something about the likely *agents* of institutional reform (who would carry it out) and the continuing social bases of *stability* in reform arrangements (how they would be supported once in place). In addressing these concerns, moreover, political projects assume the burden of starting from somewhere – some determinate place in the social world. However remote their goal, they need to offer a strategy for advancing toward that goal from that place, taking measure of the barriers as well as opportunities it poses for reform. As the world changes, they correlatively need to assume the burden of rethinking their strategy in light of those changes.

Roemer ignores most of these problems and concerns. Most strikingly, perhaps, he ignores this last requirement to take notice of changes in that place from which his political project must start. Roemer's managerial model could perfectly well have been offered at the beginning of the century and defended in much the same terms (equality, dynamic efficiency, incentives, etc.) that Roemer now defends it. To be sure, *A Future for Socialism* is informed by one major change, the collapse of the Soviet 'experiment'.[7] But it is much less concerned with changes in contemporary capitalism – in the structure of labor markets, working class composition, firm operation, relations among firms and between them and the state, relations among national economies to one another and between them and the international economy – that provide the more relevant context for projects of egalitarian reform. Roemer observes that 'modern capitalism provides us with many fertile possibilities for designing the next wave of socialist experiments' (p. 125). It is all the more surprising then that he offers no account of how social and organizational developments within capitalism bear on the appropriate institutional expression of the egalitarian project; in particular on the issues of agency and stability that mark political projects off from their intellectual analogues.

Roemer's silence on these matters amounts to admission that the managerial model is not a *political* project at all, since without attention to this world he cannot offer an account of how to get from it to his goal. And that is a serious problem, if it aims to be more than an intellectual exercise.

Lost in the real world

To sharpen this criticism, consider a few features of the contemporary world. Familiar enough, we think they bear decisively on just which sorts of strategies – within the range of alternatives concerned with equality, dynamic efficiency, and incentives – are most promising *as* political projects.

1. *Social heterogeneity.* Social democracy is the only egalitarian politics successfully practiced under democratic conditions in a modern economy. But the 'natural' or 'organic' social base of social democracy – an organized working class – has largely disappeared. Made under conditions of mass production, that class is now highly fragmented under the decline of those conditions and the world of the family wage that accompanied them. Several factors have served to disrupt existing working-class organizations and deepen the heterogeneity of interests within the working class itself: transformations in

the organization of production (decentralization within firms and more joint production across them, along with new technology and greater returns to differentially supplied human capital in its use); changes in the composition of the work force (in particular, increased female labor force participation); and shifts in the terms of competition (more exacting, owing to new entrants, more rapid technology diffusion, internationalization). Even construed as limited to class concerns, then, mass egalitarian politics finds itself without a unified agent.

2. *Diversity of interests.* At the same time, a variety of interests not best organized from the standpoint of formal class positions – interests in gender or racial justice, the environment, or other 'non-class' concerns – are expressed today with a robustness and intensity exceeding those of class. Moreover, these interests are seen as irreducible to class, and are jointly pursued at least in part by those with antagonistic class positions. So any mass egalitarian politics limited to class concerns would likely be doomed. At the same time, no new and politically efficacious solidarity has emerged out of this heterogeneity of interests.

3. *Limits of the state.* If working-class organizations provided the social foundation for democratic egalitarianism, the state was its immediate agent. But the state is a less resourceful ally than it once was. Increased internationalization of product and capital markets has qualified a centerpiece of traditional egalitarian economic policy – Keynesian demand management – by qualifying the degree to which demand will be met by domestic firms. The same factors have enlarged domestic capital's possibilities of exit from progressive national tax regimes. Changes in the sorts of problems the state is asked to address have also highlighted longstanding incapacities of state institutions.[8] With a greater recognized range of social interests and less self-regulation by disintegrating communities, the state is asked to regulate more broadly and extensively than in the past. But government often lacks the local knowledge needed to determine appropriate standards or the most appropriate means for satisfying those standards in diverse circumstances; its monitoring and enforcement capacity, especially in areas requiring compliance across numerous and dispersed sites, is inadequate. So too is its ability to administer solutions, ever more in demand, that require coordination across multiple policy domains and communities of interest.

Why this is a problem for Roemer

Roemer needs to worry about these familiar facts of the present world for the same reason any egalitarian reformer with a political project needs to worry about them: because they obscure the agents of reform, and the stability of reform arrangements.

Consider stability. Any political alternative needs a social base to support it, against opposition, in the everyday politics and practical administration of a social order. Given general possibilities of defection from general social norms and the enlargement of those possibilities by the existence of markets, egalitarian democratic alternatives are particularly in need of some significant measure of social integration and solidarity. The basic reason why is that no social design is 'strategy proof'. No matter how carefully designed the scheme of social cooperation, no matter how ingenious its incentives to behavior that produces egalitarian outcomes, individuals motivated only by self-interest will find a way to muck it up. And once they do, even those earlier prepared to be bound by solidaristic norms will depart from them; to be solidaristic is, after all, not to be a sucker.

Roemer thus needs an account of stability more robust than that provided by calculations of individual material advantage within his property rights regime. 'Those who benefit will provide the base' is not an answer to the question of social support. Even if all those with convergent interests improbably agreed to initial cooperation,[9] subsequent defections might be rewarded and begin to spiral. A social base is not simply a collection of beneficiaries. Something needs to be said about their motivations. To *maintain* equality, Roemer needs something like an egalitarian political culture, nurturing a 'civic consciousness' in its participants congruent with egalitarian ends.[10]

Such consciousness depends in turn on social organization; it cannot live exclusively off the fact that individuals enjoy the status of equal citizenship. Assuming democratic conditions and rights of association, *organized groups* will emerge that provide potentially competing bases of political identity, with dispersed 'veto powers' to block alternatives that do not conform to their particular ends. So, a political culture friendly to equality requires support in those groups themselves. Such organizations must be sufficiently rooted in the particularity of individual experience to be regarded by members as compelling expressions of their identity and instruments of their interests. At the same time, their behavior needs to be congruent with a general interest in equality, else the constitutionally equalizing property regime fall prey to the same group rent-seeking and particularism that now plague all pluralist democracies.[11] Minimally, the stability of managerial socialism requires the cooperation of such organizations in its mass politics and daily administration: in the debates within formal political arenas about alternatives investment strategies and in the public monitoring of the banks in turn entrusted with the monitoring of firms.

One way or another, working along this chain of stability requirements, Roemer will thus come face to face with the present disarray of solidaristic institutions and the ways that present economic organization advances that disarray. He will need, in short, to confront the facts about heterogeneity, diversity and the limited capacity of present governing institutions. The fact that, in the present proposal, he has nothing to say about these matters is fair grounds for worry about its feasibility as a stable model.[12]

Even before indulging worries about managerial socialism's stability, however, Roemer needs to say something about the *agents* who might put that model in place. Again, the reasons are straightforward enough. Any reform as radical as his coupon scheme will be fiercely resisted by the holders of wealth. Its beneficiaries will need to struggle for it, and the result of that struggle will depend importantly on how well they are organized. Such organization is almost entirely lacking at present, remote, given the present state of division, and unlikely to get closer by building a political movement around coupon socialism. It is almost inconceivably absent from some project for coordination more immediate and concrete than his distant 'future'. Whatever the content of that more immediate project, however, advance on it will not only risk a redefinition of goals away from his model – perhaps toward once familiar proposals to 'attenuate class struggle through social-democratic concessions' (p. 129) – but also again raises the problems of group faction and coordination that he now mistakenly feels safe to ignore. Once again, he will be forced to address the demands of a political project and the special problems of actually organizing egalitarian politics under present circumstances, which show a decomposition of solidarity proceeding not only within existing groups but between them.

In making these points, we do not mean simply to be restating the obvious – that politics is hard, egalitarian politics harder still, and that someone's moving from here to there requires a sense of *who* and *here* as well as *there*. We also think that acceptance of what we have said provides a basis for real doubt about the desirability of Roemer's project *as against alternatives*.

Take, for example, our own proposal of an associative egalitarian strategy.[13] Roemer concedes that its endpoint – again limiting ourselves to the material equality dimension that principally concerns him – may be indistinguishable from his own. But notice of the organizational politics he will need raises two questions. First, in facing those politics is he better off with or without a deliberate politics of association of the kind we recommend, with regularized possibilities for the support of the social base he needs? Leaving prudent doubts about the possibility of our own proposal aside, to ask that question is to answer it. He is better with an associative strategy available to help him – a strategy for rebuilding now-decaying solidarities.

Secondly, if implementing his proposal requires the same sort of social base we aim to construct, and if the result of its construction is to achieve a reasonably egalitarian result, why bother implementing his proposal at all? Institution building has costs. If a successful effort to build the institutions Roemer recommends (new property rights, monitoring banks, all the rest) requires the organizational base we recommend, and if that organizational base is sufficient for the common aim of equality, the cost of building those new institutions is sheer waste for the egalitarian project. Instead of reconciling equality and efficiency, Roemer's model would provide another case study in their divergence.

Roemer's partial answer to this question is that his strategy is preferred in those circumstances where the associative strategy has least initial base. This turns out to be countries lacking a recent history of liberal association, viz. developing capitalist countries of both the 'authoritarian' and 'democratic' variety, and especially the nations of Eastern Europe and the former Soviet Union. In such settings, where the underdevelopment of capitalist democracy minimizes the 'opportunity costs of adopting market socialism' (p. 126), Roemer speculates that his scheme might be mandated, electorally or not, by what would effectively amount to a coup. Elsewhere, the temptations of 'social-democratic concessions' stopping short of the real reform he has in mind will likely still the model's advance.[14]

But even if we agreed with Roemer's handicapping of the managerial model's prospects in different systems,[15] this is not much of an answer, given the difficulties associated with *maintaining* any egalitarian project without widespread and democratically organized popular support. Among the lessons of the Soviet 'experiment', surely this is every bit as prominent as the vagaries of centralized planning. And once the need for democratic oganization is recognized – whatever the historical setting and traditions of association – Roemer is back in the difficult territory marked above in our discussion of regime stability.

What Do We Have in Mind?

Thus far, we have only criticized Roemer. Have we got something better? To get to an answer, let's first see what 'better' entails. A political project worthy of support must be organized around a set of political commitments attractive enough to encourage its adherents to stick with it, especially during the reversals of fortune that inevitably befall any project of radical reform. It must accompany those commitments with a vision of a stable institutional order that would realize them more fully than they now are. It must address the issue of agency – who might plausibly be moved to carry the project from here to there. And its account of stability and agency must of course be guided by an understanding of the circumstances to which it is addressed.

Suppose we take these points about political projects seriously, and that we accept the stylized facts, about heterogeneity, diversity, and the limits of the state, as important elements of the circumstances that political projects need to consider. Suppose, too, that we add in a commitment to the idea of democratic control, as an additional element of an egalitarian project. What, then, might an attractive political project look like?

Economic democracy?

One possible answer is 'economic democracy', a suggestion that seems to follow naturally from taking the *control* aspect of socialism more seriously than Roemer does. As commonly interpreted, however, economic democracy runs into problems as an answer, for it shares many of the difficulties Roemer encounters from not looking hard enough at present capitalism.

Of course, the content of the idea of economic democracy is a matter of longstanding dispute in the socialist tradition. By turns it has been interpreted to require: national planning as an alternative to market coordination; parliaments of industry to supplement territorial with functional representation and coordinate particular sectors; or worker cooperatives or self-management at the level of individual firms. Today, national planning and parliaments of industry are objects of limited enthusiasm; the idea of firm-based worker cooperatives and self-management, however, continues to enjoy support.

Even that support, we believe, needs now to be qualified. We are all for democracy at the workplace, and certainly believe that associational rights within the workplace should be strengthened to that end. But we are much less confident than traditional workplace democracy advocates that the firm provides an appropriate unit of organizational analysis in the construction of a democratic society.

Our reasons go back to the stylized facts offered above. The collapse of the old mass production system has been associated with a rise in decentralized firms with more permeable boundaries and less stable internal labor markets, growing workforce heterogeneity and work 'casualization', greater dependence of individual welfare on the ability to move successfully across several firms in a working lifetime, and, at least in many areas of manufacturing – and perhaps more generally in an increasingly service-driven economy – a dominance of regional labor market effects over particular industry effects in wages, working conditions, benefits, and lifetime earnings. All this makes the individual firm less compelling as locus for the aggregation of interests and for the formation of solidarities that contribute to democracy. Interest heterogeneity also suggests a need for varied mechanisms to address different dimensions of concern (for example, wages, environment, health and safety). While the degree to which the real economy approximates a 'virtual' one, with Moebius-like boundaries between carnivalesque firms and plastic identities of workers within them, is commonly exaggerated, we take it now to be beyond question that an exclusively firm-based system of economic democracy no longer fits the actual economy. In addition to institutions within firms, we need institutions of popular economic control articulated on a supra-firm basis.

What then?

But if a simple revival of traditional understandings of economic democracy does not define a plausible political project, a modern effort to assert democratic control over the economy, and to unleash the productivity gains potentially associated with such control, may well be.

The need for control is evident from the record of present failure: inequality, unemployment, environmental degradation, relentless stress on working families. And if it could succeed, certainly, a project of democratic control would enjoy very broad support. But precisely what is popularly in doubt is whether such control is *practical*; whether it can be administered in ways that are efficient, and not fatal to the engine of economic welfare.

Egalitarian concerns benefited during the Keynesian age from rough congruence between politically organized demands (in trade unions, for example, a promise of stable employment, job ladders, and higher wages) and the requirements for advancing broader social welfare. High and rising wage floors helped to assure effective demand for goods produced within national economies. Capitalists within those economies thus had reasons to invest. Their investment increased productivity. Steady productivity growth lowered the real costs of consumption and other goods. And for those needs not satisfied by the organized market economy, or those individuals not succeeding in the labor market, high-employment capitalism provided the tax base for a decent welfare state.

Today, however, Keynesianism is again compromised by international product and capital flows, high-wage/high-employment capitalism is receding, and the welfare state is fiscally compromised both by increased need and the decreased willingness of remaining 'winners' to subsidize their brethren. Most immediately, increased competition and firm variety have reduced the ability of trade unions to mandate wage norms. In this world, popular organizations appear not as guarantors of social welfare, but as obstacles to the efficient, flexible, rapid, productive redeployment of social resources.

At least, they do to the extent that such organizations focus only on distributional concerns and not on improving, within an egalitarian frame, the productivity of the economy itself. Again, in the recent past the productivity benefits of redistribution, via the higher wages, greater investment, higher productivity cycle just described, were key to establishing popular confidence in and support for egalitarian institutions. And the requirement that such institutions be useful in this most profane of senses remains operative today, a de facto precondition of a truly mass egalitarian politics.

How to further that profane project? Perhaps, building off the attractions of greater democratic control over the terms and conditions of economic activity, by organizing that control as a source of productivity advance. Certainly evident within advanced capitalisms, and increasingly apparent in developing ones, is the need for a variety of collective goods that are important for economic performance, that firms will not provide on their own, and that the state cannot be relied on to provide. These include such goods as effective systems of training, technology diffusion, regional labor market administration, and the consolidated delivery of now discrete welfare services. They include as well the more fugitive goods of 'trust' and 'civic consciousness' that themselves rely for their provision on some degree of equality of opportunity and welfare, democratic rights and clarity on the mutuality of obligations in a new social contract.

The only organizations capable of assuring the provision of such goods, albeit always working with firms and the state, are popular organizations rooted in the economy and society itself. They alone have both the political clout to declare and enforce the terms of the new social contract and the local knowledge and capacity to assist firms in meeting its terms.

Consider, then, a rejuvenated egalitarian-democratic program, focussed on the democratic control of the economy that is one aspect of the democratic ideal, and focussed within that both on controlling the terms of economic association and on increasing social productivity with support from – and in response to demands by – democratic institutions. The supports we have already glossed; they consist in the collective goods that a disorganized capitalism is unable as well as unwilling to provide but upon which the most productive capitalisms depend. What of the demands? Assistance to firms might naturally be coupled with insistence that wage, employment, and other welfare norms be accordingly raised and more generally enforced. In an age of unstable product markets and insecure jobs, those norms might include full employment (in part as a productivity whip), and a direction of labor market and welfare services toward providing career (vs job) security and lifetime (vs cross-sectional) equalities in reward. To reduce market dependence without bankrupting the state, they would likely include steeply progressive taxation of social benefits, which should come to be regarded (very much in a Roemerian spirit, we might add) as simply another source of income.

'Nice work if you can get it', it might be observed; and fairly enough. Our point is that getting this nice work requires some deliberate attention to building the organizations responsible for carrying it forward; it requires an associative strategy.

To take one step backward, that associations are needed to play this role is almost self-evident. They are needed to serve as instruments of democratic control and because they have competencies that naturally complement the limited capacities of the state noted earlier. In a world of heterogeneity and diversity, of course, just the right kind of organizations commonly do not exist. But their predecessors, as evident in trade union efforts to assert control over training programs, or community organizations to monitor compliance with environmental regulation, are struggling to be born into maturity. With some deliberate encouragement, that maturity might be achieved.

To take one step forward, such encouragement is what associative democracy is about. The associative strategy recommends using public powers to encourage the development of secondary associations congruent with egalitarian-democratic ends. Thus, where manifest inequalities in political representation now exist, we recommend promoting the organized representation of presently excluded interests. Where associations have greater competence than public authorities for achieving democratic ends, or where their participation could improve the effectiveness of government programs, we recommend encouraging a more direct and formal governance role for groups. And where group particularism undermines democratic deliberation or popular sovereignty, we recommend organizational changes that encourage the organized to be more other-regarding in their actions.

Suppose, then, that such acts of creation, encouragement and subsidy were directed first to those organizations directly assisting in the democratic reconstruction of the economy. This would help to provide some rationale, structure and immediate attraction to a concerted program of public supports of secondary association. For example, trade unions and employer associations that took on responsibility for the joint development of training curricula, might be encouraged by public grants contingent on their assumption of such responsibilities. For the associations, this would mean a gain in resources for doing what their members wanted them to do anyway: in the case of workers, to assure transportability of credentials across unstable employment contracts; in the case of firms, to assure a more qualified labor market pool and lower search costs in finding skilled labor. A second example would be support for regional labor market institutions that underwrote wage norms across metropolitan economies. This might be done through 'sectoral' bargaining, in which newly organized workers were automatically accreted to labor pools with defined wage and benefit standards, or it might be done, more simply, by applying construction union 'pre-hire' norms throughout the labor market. By either route, the result would appeal to workers in its assurance of some generality in wage conditions; it would also appeal to reasonable-wage firms because it would remove ruinous competition from fly-by-night 'sweating' firms. A final example would be the empowerment of community organizations to serve as 'early warning' sentinels for industrial dislocation or monitors for enforcement of public norms on toxic emissions, non-discriminatory hiring, or other matters of use to all because their contact with local contexts gives them monitoring capacities superior to state inspectorates.

In such a world, popular capacities for economic administration, achieved through organizations extending beyond individual firms, would grow in tandem with the elaboration of social norms on economic activity. The state, and politics generally, would devote itself to securing the social-institutional bases of democratic administration.

Full employment, a high social wage, and appropriate popular organizations – interacting as mutually enforcing points on a triangle of supports for a highly productive and highly egalitarian capitalism – would be an appealing package indeed. But now imagine what would be obvious to all in this world: that the coordination of those organizations was key to social welfare. As the economy came gradually under increased popular control, the material bases of democratic solidarity – commitment to the democracy that was the gist of such control – would become more visible. A strengthening of democratic solidarity out of the present heterogeneity of interests would then be thinkable. The mutual respect of equals that lies at the heart of the democratic ideal would be recognized as a functional contributor to well-being, not just an attractive norm.

In this economy, democratic organization would really determine, in part by taking responsibility for it, the organization of the production system; the content of a growing share of employment would be determined by social deliberations about the values the society wishes reflected in the organization of production; democratic control over the economy and with it the rest of social life (not just the equality in distribution that such control would premise as one ingredient) would again be the self-conscious aim of radical democracy.

How does such a project fare by the criteria of successful political projects sketched above? The focus on democratic control should strengthen the moral attractions of the project beyond those that attach to a project focussed principally on distribution. The immediate attention to issues of broad concern – reconstructing the economy – should help to address the agency question. The constructive artifice of associations will help to ensure stability by building the social foundations for a more egalitarian form of democracy. Finally, the fact that just such a project is already suggested in all manner of popular struggles, large and small, suggests that it is more immediately organizable than Roemer's, even as it is almost equally remote in its mature realization.

But if Roemer needs to take politics more seriously, do we need to get more serious about property rights? Won't the associative strategy face debilitating opposition if it does not transform property rights? Perhaps the success of associative democracy (its stability as an egalitarian scheme) will depend finally on market socialism. Perhaps we ought to think of these schemes as mutually supportive rather than as competitors.

One thing seems clear: radical democratic reconstruction would be immensely aided by a fairer distribution of property rights of the kind that Roemer describes. Might such a distribution be *necessary* to the stability of our egalitarian future? Nobody knows the answer to this question, but these appear to be the relevant considerations. We know that: (1) enormous gains can be made in equality without fundamental disturbance of capitalist property rights; this, among others, is the lesson of social democracy; (2) no massive reorganization of property rights, under democratic conditions, is possible without the social supports we have emphasized here; supports that are presently lacking and cannot reasonably be expected to arise without deliberate encouragement. Putting (1) and (2) together, it appears that the associative strategy is necessary background to property rights reform, and, if pursued more adventurously than social democracy, may be a sufficient condition for equality. Assuming it is sufficient, that is the end of the argument. Assuming it is not, then our discussion of stability suggests that: (3) any regime based on reorganized property rights would *require* continuing support from group organizations, again not arising naturally; moreover, (4) the precise content and character of market socialist arrangements (for example, how managerial they ought to be) is best discussed in light of explicit assumptions about the associative environment from which they emerge. Thus, we agree that associative democracy may require market socialism, but we are confident that market socialism needs something like associative democracy and that assessments of alternative versions of market socialism must take this social background into account.

We understand and expect that this telegraphic exposition convinces no one that the associative project is any more feasible than Roemer's. Our burden here, however, is not to make a compelling case about feasibility, but to indicate how the *kinds* of considerations we have entered as grounds for skepticism about Roemer's project might be incorporated in an alternative strategy. Our point is not that the managerial model is a bad one – it certainly is not – but that it is unnecessarily inattentive to the requirements of politics. However unformed our own speculations, they should at least persuade that it is possible to seek to meet such requirements; to discipline institutional speculation by reference to the demands of political projects. This is the discipline we miss in Roemer's speculations.

Notes

1. John E. Roemer, *A Future for Socialism*, Cambridge, MA: Harvard University Press 1994. References to Roemer's book will be included parenthetically within the text.

2. Not that they arise naturally under an alternative to capitalism. Instead we mention capitalism to indicate the context for our discussion.

3. For details, see our 'Secondary Associations and Democratic Governance', *Politics and Society* 20 (December 1992): pp. 393–472; 'Associations and Democracy', *Social Philosophy and Policy* 10 (Summer 1993), pp. 282–312; 'Associative Democracy', in K. Pranab, J. Bardhan and John E. Roemer, eds, *Market Socialism*, New York: Oxford University Press 1993 pp. 236–52; 'Solidarity, Democracy, Association', in Wolfgang Streeck, ed., *Staat und Verbände*, Sonderheft der *Politischen Vierteljahresschrift*, Wiesbaden: Westdeutscher Verlag 1994.

4. In thinking this, of course, we are not alone. Compare what Jürgen Habermas and Adam Michnik recently had to say in response to the question 'what is left of socialism?':

> Habermas: Radical democracy.
> Michnik: I quite agree with that.

Jürgen Habermas and Adam Michnik, 'Overcoming the Past', *New Left Review* 203 (January–February 1994), pp. 3–16, at 11.

5. Of course, changes in bargaining power can rise to the level of the liquidation of competitive markets and the innovation they encourage – the familiar nightmare of rent-seeking, soft budget constraints and the rest. But as we indicate in the sources cited in note 3, increased popular organization can also enhance economic efficiency. The problem (discussion of which lies beyond the scope of this article) is to show how to capture the gains and avoid the nightmares. Suffice it to say here that associations with the power to cause troubles for dynamic efficiency do not originate with associative democracy. Instead the associative view departs from the premise that such associations are part of the terrain in a modern democracy, and seeks to address the troubles that they can cause.

6. Roemer offers only the barest of suggestions on how his managerial model might be taken up as a political project, but clearly recognizes the need to think of it as such. '[F]or any end state of a social process to be feasible, a path must exist from here to there, and so at least a rough sketch of possible routes, if not a precise map, may reasonably be asked of someone attempting to describe the final destination' (p. 126).

7. While the point may not bear emphasis, in general and throughout we are less preoccupied with the collapse of the Soviet Union, and less regretful of it, than Roemer appears to be. Specifically, we are less inclined to look to the Soviet 'experiment' for instruction on the importance of markets or the recalcitrance of human motivations to sweeping revision; and (with our own long view of the possibilities for human justice) we unambivalently welcome the collapse of that dungeon.

8. To be more precise, these incapacities are not just 'longstanding', but more or less definitive of modern state governance.

9. For a classic argument why such initial cooperation should be thought an improbable outcome of shared individual interests, see Mancur Olson, *The Logic of Collective Action*, Cambridge, MA: Harvard University Press 1965; for a recent extension and qualification of it, see Gerald Marwell and Pamela Oliver, *The Critical*

Mass in Collective Action: A Micro-Social Theory Cambridge: Cambridge University Press 1993.

10. If this seems inconsistent with our earlier agreement on the need to economize on scarce motives, we note that economizing is not the same as abstaining.

11. Roemer observes that we 'view "factionalism" as a possible problem in [our associative democracy] proposal, that society would become partitioned into groups each concerned only with its own parochial interest' (pp. 52). While he goes on to say that faction 'may be a generic problem of all democracies', he apparently takes our attention to the problem to amount to an 'admission against interest' – good evidence of the weakness of our proposal. If we have Roemer right in this, he is mistaken. We take the problem of 'faction', broadly understood to denote pathologies of both inequality and particularism in secondary organization, *now* to be pervasive in existing liberal democracies. Our proposal is offered to relieve it.

12. Our concern about Roemer's inattention to the critical role that supportive group politics play in the stability of his model may suggest an equally powerful concern about our own proposal for associative democracy, viz. that its stability will turn on changed property rights assignments to which we are inattentive. We respond to this objection at pp. 118–20.

13. We believe the same points could be made for other proposals, but feel no burden to carry them here.

14. Once he makes this distinction, however, Roemer immediately fudges it with the suggestion that partial programs of egalitarian denationalization might provide a natural cross-walk between the demands of his model and the politics of emerging mass democracies. We agree, but then resist too sharp a distinction between the 'social wage' now provided by social democratic welfare states and the reform he has in mind.

15. Recent experience in Eastern Europe and the former Soviet Union is not promising on this score.

6

Market Socialism as a Culture of Cooperation

Mieke Meurs

Introduction

'[I] look forward to a state of society ... different from that which now exists, in which the effort of all is to outwit, supplant, and snatch from each other; where interest is systematically opposed to duty; ... and where the whole motley fabric is kept together by fear and blood. [I] look forward to a better state of society, where ... restless and anxious competition shall give place to mutual co-operation ... '

William Thompson to Anna Wheeler, 1825[1]

Socialism requires more than an allocative mechanism. It requires a culture, specifically a culture of cooperation and generalized reciprocity among diverse individuals and groups. More importantly, this culture is not something which can be added, perhaps optionally, once a feasible allocative mechanism has been defined and implemented. Recent game theoretic and institutionalist literature emphasizes that institutions (allocational and other) are themselves important determinants in the emergence of cooperative or individualist cultures. In turn, these cultures of cooperation or atomization will have a strong impact on the functioning of most allocative mechanisms, and therefore on economic performance.[2]

John Roemer's model offers an allocative mechanism which he suggests could serve as a basis for feasible socialism. The model is a significant advance over earlier market socialist models in that the author takes seriously the problem of motivating managers in the absence of concentrated ownership.

Much less attention is directed to the problem of guiding and monitoring the state, however. Roemer notes the importance of democratic elections which can serve to hold planners accountable for their actions. But no mechanisms are suggested to ensure that elections effectively promote accountability; nor does Roemer address how the state will aggregate conflicting interests into an efficient program of guiding markets and correcting their failures.

Without adequate attention to these issues, the market socialist model is likely to be plagued by rent seeking and other allocational distortions. These, in turn, will prevent the model from achieving the desired equality in opportunities for self-realization and reduction in public bads.

Recent literature suggests that institutional forms, particularly those based on regular, participatory interaction among relative equals, may promote *cultures of cooperation*. These cultures, in turn, may facilitate the resolution of conflicting interests and reduce collective action problems in monitoring the state. Cultures of cooperation have also been shown to mitigate other forms of market failure unrelated to state intervention.

The allocational institutions which Roemer has proposed to promote efficiency in the economy are likely to undermine the development of such cultures, however. The economic mechanisms, as designed, are more likely to create a culture of atomization than one of cooperation. This culture of atomization is likely to generate behavior inimical to the development of institutions which can effectively aggregate citizen interests and promote efficient monitoring of the state.

Rent seeking and atomization are, of course, also characteristics of capitalism, and their persistence might not reduce economic performance of Roemer's model below levels achieved by capitalism. I will argue, however, that in addition to perpetuating inequality of opportunity and excessive production of public bads, these characteristics reduce the performance of Roemer's model below that of another feasible alternative: one which actively develops the beneficial cultures of cooperation.

While recent research suggests that cultures of cooperation can contribute to economic performance, the evidence also indicates that the development of such cultures may itself be highly problematic. Their development will depend greatly on previously existing socio-historical conditions. The complexity of developing monitoring institutions compatible with market socialist goals undermines Roemer's claim that the market socialist model offers more general feasibility than social democracy. In addition, it implies that expectations of the market socialist model's applicability to the transforming, former centrally planned economies (CPEs) are misplaced.

The Market Socialist State

In his treatment of the state, Roemer adds little to earlier models of market socialism. Although Roemer mentions the possibility that rent seekers may bias state policy, state behavior remains seriously under-theorized. Planners are meant to smooth market failures and implement social welfare policy. At least two kinds of monitoring problems may arise in this process: the state may fail to implement the democratically chosen maximand or to do so efficiently; or the state may fail to disaggregate the maximand in a manner which promotes both economic efficiency and equality of opportunity. Nothing is said, however, about what kind of institutions might address these problems.

Historical experience suggests that planners may, in fact, use their power to promote their own interests, making monitoring essential. Moreover, theoretical work on the problem of monitoring firm managers indicates that periodic elections are unlikely to provide a satisfactory mechanism for monitoring. In the absence of large individual shareholders, collective action is needed for effective monitoring of firm management.

At the level of the state, large 'share holders' are precluded in democratic systems based on the principle of one person one vote. Collective action is thus necessary to assure effective monitoring of the state. Unfortunately, the individual returns to monitoring the state (change in profit income/population) are likely to be small compared with the organizing costs any one individual will bear, since non-participating individuals cannot be excluded from benefits of improved state performance. Free-rider problems among the atomized electorate will result in an underprovision of monitoring, unless countervailing mechanisms exist.

A second set of problems arise from the fact that the relationship between citizens and planners is much more complex than between managers and shareholders. Rather than implementing a unique maximand, such as maximizing returns, planners will be expected to protect a wide variety of citizen interests about which the citizens will disagree.

Disagreements stem from differences in preferences, but also from the continued possibility of concentrating the benefits (or costs) of planners' decisions, while costs (or benefits) are dispersed. Concentration by class will be eliminated, but other forms of concentration will persist, including concentration in relatively well-defined subsets of the population, such as those based on ethnicity, gender, and place of employment or residence. Preferential interest rates in a particular industry, for example, will provide income benefits concentrated on workers and managers in the industry, whereas the reduction in investment that this implies for each of the other industries will be small. Thus while inadequate incentives are generated for monitoring in general, incentives will exist for certain social groups to seek rents due to concentration of benefits among well-defined groups.

In addition to affecting income distribution and capital allocation, this rent seeking may perpetuate the production of public bads. Roemer's model shows how the concentration of profits results in an increase in the level of public bads over the levels chosen when profits are diffused, but a concentration of wage income may have a symmetric effect. When the wage benefits of a public bad are concentrated and the costs are diffuse, incentives are created for successful rent seeking to reduce regulation and increase the production of public bads.

The monitoring institutions proposed by Roemer are insufficient to address these problems. Democratic elections are subject to free riding, while organized minorities are more likely successfully to influence planners. Agency problems between citizens and the state, like those between workers and employers, and between shareholders and managers, are, of course, endemic to capitalist market economies as well. The centralization of investment decisions in the hands of planners is likely to *increase* incentives for rent seeking, but reductions in income inequality will *decrease* the concentration of resources available for such activities. On balance, the change may not be significant.

If the market socialist model is to achieve the desired equalization of opportunity and reduction in public bads, and not risk replacing one set of capital market failures with another, additional attention to institutional design is necessary. Institutions are needed to promote collective action in monitoring the state, while at the same time reducing the likelihood of particularistic rent seeking.

Cultures of Cooperation

Recent literature, highlighting the relationship between agency and structure, emphasizes the impact of institutional form in successfully overcoming these problems. Formal game theoretic models indicate that institutions affect outcomes in multiple ways: by changing agents' perceptions of their own interests, their expections of others' behavior, their expectations of the likelihood of meeting other agents again (and therefore the likelihood of effective retaliation against uncooperative action), and by promoting empathy.

Robert Bates, for example, shows if others' preferences are not known with certainty, certain institutions can permit signaling and other soft behavior which allow players to 'rationally gamble on cooperation'.[3] Paul Seabright[4] argues that repeated interaction may form habits of cooperation, because of the increased potential for effective retaliation in the case of repeated interaction, and because of the impact of successful cooperation on expectations of others' behavior.

These findings indicate that certain institutional structures may promote cultures of cooperation which could contribute significantly to overcoming principal-agent problems between citizens and the state. The cooperative culture may reduce free riding in general monitoring, and also increase the likelihood of compromise when conflicts of interest exist regarding investments and other economic policy.

Recent empirical work supports these findings. In his research on institutional evolution in contemporary Italy, for example, Robert Putnam[5] finds a strong relationship between institutional structures, perceived conflicts of interest, and the way in which interested parties respond to these conflicts. Specific changes in institutional structure (to be discussed below) successfully reduced ideological polarization. Parties were less likely to perceive conflicts as zero-sum, and accommodation was facilitated. Institutional structures also influenced the prevalence of rent seeking, and the efficacy of government in implementing the chosen policies.

Elinor Ostrom's survey[6] of institutions of collective resource management also reveals that institutional design can have a strong impact on the level of conflict between agents. In her many cases, institutional structure consistently affected agents' perceptions of their interests and their willingness to participate in monitoring of agreed upon rules and distributions.

John R. Freeman,[7] building on a large body of research on the political-economic impact of democratic, corporatist institutions, compares the functioning of corporatist (cooperative) and pluralist (competitive) political structures in Western Europe. He finds that the presence of cooperative versus competitive institutional forms has a strong impact on the potential for compromise among distinct social groups and the generation of greater policy stability. The empirical work of both Putnam and Freeman[8] also confirms that reduced conflict is correlated with increased economic efficiency (measured by economic growth rates) and commitment to equity.

These studies indicate that beneficial cultures of cooperation are created by institutions which promote ongoing interaction and are horizontal ('bringing together agents of *equivalent* status and power' and thereby increasing the potential for effective retaliation).[9] In Ostrom's study, institutions which successfully overcame coordination problems were those in which individuals interacted closely (reducing anonymity), were relatively equal, shared a past and expected to share a future (allowing reputations to be formed and making them matter). Successful institutions were also participatory: individuals affected by rules could participate in modifying those rules.[10]

Putnam's study also finds that repeated interaction is important, creating a 'virtuous circle'[11] of increasingly dependable cooperation. In addition, the study highlights the importance of horizontalness in promoting cooperation. Effective cooperation increases the rationality of a future 'gamble on cooperation' which, in turn, permits the generation of a web of generalized reciprocity, reconciling self-interest and solidarity.

'Denseness', or frequency of occurrence of institutions of 'social exchange' also promotes cooperation. By increasing the likelihood that individuals will be organized along more than one axis of interest, denseness exposes individuals to a greater range of perspectives and priorities, increasing knowledge of others' preferences and thus of potential common ground. Moreover, denseness broadens the webs of both enforcement and reciprocity. To perform their role in attenuating political-economic conflicts and promoting effective monitoring of the state, organizations need not be explicitly economic or political. In the Italian case, increased activity in organizations as diverse as sports clubs, professional associations and trade unions was strongly correlated with increased cooperation in the political sphere.[12]

Vertical networks show less potential to promote the trust and cooperation needed to effectively and efficiently monitor the state. In vertical relations, subordinates may not be able to credibly threaten sanctions against those higher up. In addition, they may cause subordinates to withhold information 'as a hedge against exploitation'.[13] Ostrom's cases similarly illustrate the way in which horizontal structures encourage use of locally available information and increase the effectiveness of monitoring and enforcement.[14]

Horizontal structures may provide some additional contributions to economic efficiency, beyond those involved in the reduction of rent

seeking and improved monitoring of the state. Putnam[15] finds that
complex systems of markets evolve and perform more effectively in
the context of trust and social bonding, as these reduce opportunism.
Freeman finds that the climate of policy stability created by
cooperative policy making lengthens time horizons, permitting better
investment planning and further reducing incentives for rent seeking.[16]

Market Socialism as a Culture of Cooperation

Unfortunately, the economic mechanisms proposed in Roemer's model
appear more likely to promote a culture of atomization than the needed
culture of cooperation. Under the structures for monitoring management, firm management will need to bargain vertically with banks and
planners in order to protect firm interests. Firm workers, likewise, will
bargain vertically with firm management, in order to elicit management
support in bargaining with banks. Management is likely to have an
ongoing relationship with banks; but workers, between decisive
moments in which they mobilize to defend a particular interest, are
encouraged to leave management to profit-maximizing managers.

In the monitoring of planners, too, periodic, vertical organization
is proposed. The relationship between individual voters and planners
involves a great inequality of power. In addition, the electoral mechanism on its own invites only very periodic interaction between the
two parties. In the interim, voters have no role to play. Voters in
capitalist countries with similar electoral structures and few supporting
institutions have become apathetic.

One might argue that in Roemer's model voters will have a lot at
stake, increasing the payoffs to active monitoring; but voters in
Eastern Europe have even more at stake, as the national economic
wealth is being divided and the rules of future accumulation are
being written. In the absence of supporting horizontal institutional
structures, their high stakes have not kept them involved: voter
participation dropped to well below 50 per cent in the second round
of elections. Sweden, with its highly developed, dense networks of
social exchange, has historically done much better at promoting
effective voter participation.

Finally, the heavy reliance on competitive markets as an allocative
mechanism in Roemer's model contributes further to atomization and
thereby to a proliferation of cooperation failures.[17] While increased
income equality may foster some increases in feelings of shared
condition, the dominant form of interactions will continue to tend

toward anonymity and occasionality and rely on self-interest for motivation. These are precisely contrary to the type of social relations needed to foster cooperative outcomes.

Market socialists could address principal-agent problems more effectively by promoting dense sets of horizontal institutions. Our understanding of the relationship between institutional form and the creation of cultures of cooperation is still in its early stages. Nonetheless, a few easily implementable possibilities suggest themselves.

Roemer notes that worker-managed firms could also be used to monitor managers, but suggests that worker management could be optionally added, once the new, market socialist allocational mechanisms are in place. Rather than being an optional, separable aspect of successful market socialism allocation, however, I believe worker management to be part of a set of cooperation-inducing institutions necessary to elicit adequate monitoring of planners.

Worker-managed firms, instead of reinforcing the atomizing, capitalist traditions of vertical relations, would create a relative equality of power between workers and managers. At the same time, the participatory management structures would build in ongoing interaction. Both changes could be expected to increase the efficiency of solutions to coordination problems at this level, while at the same time contributing to the development of dense horizontal networks.

Worker-managed firms could create the same problem of firm-based factionalism that Roemer's model creates. In this case, alliances would be horizontally, as opposed to vertically, organized, but rent seeking might still be encouraged. Cohen and Rogers[18] have suggested some institutional designs to reduce factionalist outcomes. Additional denseness will also serve to mitigate this problem.

Institutions for discussing national macroeconomic policy, perhaps based on the democratic corporatist model could also contribute to the development of cultures of cooperation and to a reduction in firm-based factionalism. With the emergence of worker-managed firms, bargaining between workers and banks or workers and planners would replace the traditional corporatist bargaining between workers and employers. The tasks of national bargaining would remain much the same, however: to generate agreement on levels of wage growth and investment.

Open, public bargaining increases pressures for solidaristic wage policy. Horizontal national structures for bargaining national macroeconomic policy also increase the likelihood of high, stable levels of employment. Both factors would do much to build trust and solidarity and reduce wage benefits to rent seeking.

The national bargaining structures would also provide a forum for generating compromise on a program of market interventions. In place of the heavy emphasis on profit maximizing, bargaining organizations could elaborate a more complex set of goals, including programs to overcome market failures, smooth market adjustments and select desired growth rates.

Such interventions will, of course, introduce 'distortions' into the competitive market equilibrium, but democratic states (and all but the most terrifying undemocratic states) always face pressures to intervene in the face of market failures, uneven development and market adjustments. The point here is not to replace markets as the most widely used allocative mechanism, but to create a set of institutions which will allow people to define the limitations on markets in a way which reduces rent seeking, wasteful conflicts and other public bads. Unfortunately, it may not always be possible quickly to create these necessary institutions. Social scientists know even less about the way people create institutions than they do about the way people respond to varying institutional forms. The government may, if properly motivated, intervene to promote the creation of certain types of institutions.[19] Putnam's study suggests, however, that the success of such intervention will depend greatly on the historical context and existing social structures. Other West European experiences suggest similar conclusions.[20]

The importance of institutional design to the performance of the market socialist model, combined with our limited ability to implement our designs, suggests that market socialism may have few practical advantages over social democracy. It is certainly true, as Roemer argues, that social democracy has flourished only under very specific historical conditions and is subject to erosion in response to voter dissatisfaction. There appears little reason to believe that the successful implementation of market socialism (one which satisfactorily resolves problems of monitoring the state) requires any less particular social-historical conditions. If both models have the potential to equalize income and opportunity, then adequate reasons for preferring one to the other remain to be developed.

Market Socialism for Transforming CPEs?

In view of the above discussion, Eastern Europe would seem a poor prospect for developing market socialism along the lines Roemer proposes. Clearly, certain aspects of the current situation make the region a good candidate for the proposed system. The problem of altering property rights would be minimal, since many East European countries are currently experimenting with a system of share distribution quite similar to Roemer's 'clamshell economy'. In addition, the prospects for economic growth under a capitalist market economy appear dim in many countries, opening the way for serious discussion of an alternative.

Other characteristics of former centrally planned societies are less well suited to the implementation of market socialism, however. In particular, the behaviors necessary to ensure adequate monitoring are weakly developed. While the absence of such behaviors will also have a negative impact on the development of a capitalist market economy, the concentration of investment decisions and extensive power of banks in the market socialist model is likely to exacerbate the danger of inadequate monitoring.

Over the decades between World War II and 1989, social relations in Eastern Europe were consciously and massively restructured along vertical lines. The highly centralized Communist Party strove to control everything from industrial production to religious behavior to sexual practices among married couples. Horizontal organizations without a vertical component were essentially illegal, and horizontal relationships of all kinds were subject to information leakage to vertical organizations (through spying; witness the East German experience).

A number of authors have documented the impact of this change on interpersonal relations among the members of East European populations.[21] The resulting attitudes have been characterized as those of extreme individualism (an interesting outcome for a collectivist society), widespread distrust, and apathy and cynicism regarding political participation. In short, this is a culture, despite a number of apparently feudal aspects, of extreme atomization.

At the same time, people have little experience with meritocratic evaluation. The 'corporate culture of competitive bidding in the market' necessary to motivate the bankers and managers in Roemer's model[22] is absent, as are the feelings of efficacy which contribute to a population's willingness to monitor state officials. (In recent elections, with the very rules of the new economic game at stake, East Europeans turned out at rates well below 50 per cent.) In any case, information is thin and markets weakly developed, making effective evaluation extremely difficult, even where motivated monitors exist.

In this context, the prospects for successful resolution of principal-agent problems are not good. These problems will also plague efforts to organize capitalist production, of course, but the concentration of power implied in the monitoring role of large powerful banks and the investment-guiding role of planners in the market socialist model creates prime targets for rent seekers.

Conclusions

The lack of mechanisms for monitoring the state reduces the ability of Roemer's market socialist model to increase equality of opportunity and reduce public bads. Recent literature suggests that cultures of cooperation could contribute to the generation of effective monitoring. Unfortunately, the institutions Roemer proposes for promoting economic efficiency are more likely to reinforce cultures of atomization than to create the beneficial cultures of cooperation.

While our understanding of the relationship between institutional structure and agent behavior is far from complete, certain well-known types of institutional structures promote the ongoing, horizontal relations which contribute to cooperation. Among these, the development of worker-managed firms and national bargaining over economic policy (on the corporatist model) hold particular promise for promoting cooperation and efficiency.

It is less clear, however, that the desired institutions can be generated at will. Studies reviewed here indicate that sociohistorical context plays a significant role in the formation of institutional structure, and attempts to manipulate institutions in line with externally imposed criteria have met with limited success. These considerations shed doubt on market socialism's claim to be a more generally applicable alternative than social democracy and a viable systemic alternative to the struggling countries of Eastern Europe.

Notes

1. Barbara Taylor, *Eve and the New Jerusalem*, London: Virago Press 1983.
2. Perhaps this will appear tautological. The relationship between institutions and culture clearly involves a great deal of (dialectical? overdetermined?) interaction, but my claim here is not to assert a particular causality. Instead, I wish to emphasize the central role cultures of cooperation can play in economic performance.
3. Robert Bates, 'Contra Contractarianism: Some Reflections on the New Institutionalism', *Politics and Society* 16 (1988), pp. 387–401.
4. Paul Seabright, 'Is Cooperation Habit Forming?', in P. Dasgupta and K.-G. Maler, eds., *The Environment and Emerging Development Issues*, Oxford: Clarendon Press, in press. See also, H. Sabourian, 'Repeated Games: A Survey', in F. Hahn, ed., *The Economics of Missing Markets, Information and Games*, Oxford: Clarendon Press 1990, pp. 62–105.

5. Robert Putnam, *Making Democracy Work: Civic Traditions in Modern Italy*, Princeton: Princeton University Press 1993.

6. Elinor Ostrom, *Governing the Commons: The Evolution of Institutions for Collective Action*, Cambridge: Cambridge University Press 1990.

7. John R. Freeman, *Democracy and Markets: The Politics of Mixed Economies*, Ithaca: Cornell University Press 1989.

8. Putnam, *Making Democracy Work* and Freeman, *Democracy and Markets*.

9. Putnam, *Making Democracy Work*, pp. 172–73. Mancur Olson (*The Logic of Collective Action*, Cambridge, MA: Harvard University Press 1965) is well known for arguing that collective action problems (of the sort involved in monitoring the state) are best overcome through vertical relations. Since actors are incapable of organizing themselves, monitoring and other collective action depend on the leadership of a few, powerful actors. In any case, since members of the population will organize only to protect their particularistic interests, these are seen as dangerous lobbyists for special treatment (Olson, *The Rise and Decline of Nations: Economic Growth, Stagflation and Social Rigidities*, New Haven: Yale University Press 1982). Once the relationship between structure and agency is introduced, however, the argument breaks down.

10. Ostrom, pp. 88–90.

11. Putnam p. 170.

12. Ibid., ch. 4.

13. Ibid., p. 174.

14. Ostrom, p. 186.

15. See Putnam, *Making Democracy Work*.

16. See Freeman, *Democracy and Markets*. Some descriptions of corporatism emphasize its 'vertical' aspects, due to its pyramidal structure. If the corporatist institutions are relatively democratic, however, at each level they will promote horizontal relations. Most importantly, at the national level, bargaining structures afford parties relative equality.

17. Michael Taylor, *The Possibility of Cooperation*, New York: Cambridge University Press 1987, p. 150 and Douglass North, *Structure and Change in Economic History*, New York: Norton 1981, p. 182, make similar arguments.

18. Joshua Cohen, and Joel Rogers, 'Associative Democracy', in Pranab Bardhan and John E. Roemer, eds, *Market Socialism: The Current Debate*, New York: Oxford University Press 1993, pp. 236–49.

19. For example, by directly funding institutional development, as suggested by Cohen and Rogers, *Market Socialism*.

20. For an elaboration of these points, see Freeman, *Democracy and Markets*, and Putnam, *Making Democracy Work*.

21. Istvan Rev, 'The Advantages of Being Atomized', *Dissent* (1987), pp. 335–50 and Elemer Hankiss, *East European Alternatives*, Oxford: Clarendon Press 1990.

22. Pranab Bardhan, and John E. Roemer, 'Market Socialism: A Case for Rejuvenation', *Journal of Economic Perspectives* 6, no. 3 (1992), p. 106.

7

Political Power, Democracy and Coupon Socialism

Erik Olin Wright

In this essay I will examine the relationship between coupon socialism, as elaborated in John Roemer's *A Future for Socialism*, and democracy.[1] Roemer affirms, and I concur, that the goals of socialists are not simply a certain kind of economic egalitarianism, but have also been concerned with the nature of the state and political power. He specifies this political goal as 'equality of opportunity for political influence'.[2] More conventionally, socialists frame this goal in terms of radically extending and deepening democratic governance, where 'radical democracy' includes the idea of political equality, but also envisions new forms of political participation, communication and consensus formation. Socialists have generally argued that, although capitalist societies may have democratic forms of government, capitalism in various ways thwarts the full development of true democratic practices. Socialism, then, is viewed as democracy-enhancing for two basic reasons: first, it eliminates certain key mechanisms that undermine democracy; secondly, if socialism is to be effectively implemented and sustained, it requires a significant extension and deepening of democracy. The question I want to address here is: in what ways might coupon socialism facilitate the democratic governance beyond the limits possible in capitalism? In what ways would it neutralize the distinctively capitalist barriers to democracy? And in what ways would its own institutional requirements encourage a process of extending and deepening democratic governance?

In section 1, I will briefly clarify the meaning of the democratic goal of socialists. I will argue that the goal is more than simply equal political influence, but also involves the extension of democratic authority over the economy. In section 2, I will discuss some core concepts in the neo-Marxist theory of power and the state which will help frame the specific analysis of coupon socialism and democracy. Section 3 will explore the ways in which coupon socialism might be democracy-enhancing with respect to a variety of dimensions of political power.

1 Why Do Socialists Want Enhanced Democracy?

There are two dimensions on which we can judge the democraticness of democracy: (1) the extent to which political power is equally distributed in a population; (2) the range of decisions which are subjected to the democratic decision-making process. The shallowness of capitalist democracy lies not simply in the ways in which money and wealth shape political decision making, but in the ways the protections of private property rights remove certain kinds of choices from the democratic arena.

Roemer strongly affirms the commitment of socialists to the first of these dimensions of democracy, but has an ambivalent attitude towards the second. He argues that

> popular or political control over investment . . . is important, but for only two reasons: in a market economy, the markets required to allocate investment efficiently do not exist, and investment has a number of external effects . . . that are not well managed with markets. . . . To state the contrapositive, if there were a full set of futures markets, if externalities associated with investment were small, and if people's preferences were formed under conditions of equal opportunity, I would have little objection to determination of investment by the market, that is, by citizens in the economy determining the rate of investment as a consequence of individual responses to prices.[3]

This argument implies that there is no intrinsic reason why the allocation of the economic surplus or even more broadly the 'running of the economy' should be under collective control, except for those situations in which democratic control is more efficient than markets (because of the absence of certain futures markets) or those situations in which various kinds of negative externalities of market allocations require democratic control for their solution. Basically Roemer believes that, all things being equal, it would be a good thing if atomized markets allocated everything; democracy should thus intrude only where this does not work. Democratic control potentially can solve problems of market failures.

An alternative perspective, defended by many contemporary democratic socialists, agrees that markets are important and should be allowed because they help to solve various problems in the democratic control of economic processes, but that democratic control of the economy is itself a positive value. If there were no incentive and information problems, then the best way of organizing much of economic life would be through a deliberative, democratic framework for deciding on investments. However, we know that this leads to lots of problems, and at least some of these can be solved by introducing markets. Markets potentially can solve problems of democratic failures.

It should be stressed that there is a large zone of pragmatic overlap between these two perspectives on the articulation of markets and democracy in the underlying goals of socialists. After all, market failures of various sorts are pervasive and open up a quite considerable space for democratic intervention in economic processes. On what grounds, therefore, can we defend the extension of democratic control in economic practices beyond those mandated by market failures?

One line of argument stresses the ways in which the preferences, and even the operative values, of actors are endogenous to the process by which decisions are made. This is not just a question of the formation of preferences under 'conditions of equal opportunity', but under conditions of democratic deliberation versus atomized private choices. Dialogue and deliberation can change people's minds. Isolated decision making in market transactions, therefore, can lead to suboptimal outcomes because people are not engaged in the settings in which they can be convinced to make other kinds of choices.

The issue of the endogeneity of preferences, however, goes beyond simply the problem of information and persuasion. Being in a deliberative context brings to the foreground issues of other people's well-being and various values beyond one's own self-interest. This is not just a question of hearing arguments and being exposed to new points of view; it is a question of being part of a collective project which triggers different moral codes and priorities. This is also not a question of fundamental transformations of human beings into different kinds of moral agents. Roemer is correct in insisting that we design institutions that accept people as they really are today rather than how they might become under some alternative cultural system. The point is that, even today, the preferences people act on in practice are shaped by the interactions and communications within which they make decisions. People are very complicated as moral agents and simultaneously hold values of generosity and selfishness, the welfare of their loved ones and the welfare of people in the wider community, individual success and collective harmony. Different contexts will call forth or reinforce different sets of these values. Atomized, private consumption choices in the market will strengthen different kinds of preference orderings than will involvement in more collective processes of decision making in a democratic community.[4]

The issue of the endogeneity of preferences to the process of decision making is related to another common argument for the desirability of democratic over atomized decision-making processes in allocating the social surplus. Atomized market allocations may make it harder to overcome certain kinds of prisoner's dilemmas. The choice of investments in public versus private transportation would be a classic example: each individual serially making autonomous choices results in everyone choosing private transportation, with the result that commuting takes longer than it would have taken if everyone had chosen public transportation. One can, of course, call the traffic congestion resulting from market allocations of transportation investments an example of a 'negative externality', and I assume that this is how Roemer would treat the problem (although perhaps the problem is a missing futures market in uncongested travel). But there is another issue here: the atomized decision-making process undermines the development of assurance game (or conditional altruist) preference orderings which would render the public transportation free riding problem easier to solve. It is not just that with fixed preferences democracy may solve market failures, but that democracy elicits different configurations of the preferences themselves.

The basic underlying principle here is that to the extent possible people should be able democratically to decide issues which shape the fates of their communities. Of course, there are many complications that have to be dealt with to give precision to this idea. Principles of democratic collectivity need to be balanced against issues of individual autonomy and individual rights. The meaning of 'community' needs to be precisely defined. I will not deal with these problems here. The point I do want to emphasize is that this kind of view gives a positive value to the process of democratic deliberation and public dialogue and sees it as desirable in principle for the collectivity to have as much control as possible over the social surplus.

The central question of this essay, then, is whether coupon socialism is a step in the right direction. As a way of organizing property rights, does it enhance the capacity of democratic politics to shape the fate of communities?

2 A Neo-Marxist Conception of Power and the State

To frame the discussion, it will be helpful briefly to review the central claims of the contemporary neo-Marxist critique of capitalist democracy. A useful place to begin is with a sketch of how some contemporary theorists understand the concept of political *power*. If democracy is fundamentally about organizing political power in such a way that people have 'equal opportunity for political influence' then it would do us well to know what we mean by power before we talk about the extent to which it is democratically organized. (What follows is a fairly didactic exposition of neo-Marxist views of political power and social class. Readers familiar with these concepts and arguments might skip to section 3.)

Robert Alford and Roger Friedland, building on the analysis of Steven Lukes and others, have elaborated a tripartite typology of 'levels of power' that will be useful in examining these issues.[5]

1. *Situational* power refers to power relations of direct command and obedience between actors, as in Weber's celebrated definition of power as the ability of one actor to get another to do something even in the face of resistance. This is the characteristic form of power analyzed in various behavioral studies of power. Typically, when we talk about people *having* power, it is this kind of instrumental, situational power to which we are referring.

2. *Institutional* power refers to the characteristics of different institutional settings which shape the decision-making agenda in ways which serve the interests of particular groups.[6] This is also referred to as 'negative power', or the 'second face of power' – power which excludes certain alternatives from a decision-making agenda, but not, as in situational power, which actually commands a specific behavior. Institutional power is above all power that is inscribed in institutional rules, regulations and protocols which make it hard to place certain concerns on the table, but easy to include others.

3. *Systemic* power is perhaps the most difficult (and contentious) conceptually. It refers to the power to realize one's interests by virtue of the overall structure of a social system, rather than by virtue of instrumentally commanding the behavior of others or of rules which shape the agendas of specific organizations. Systemic power, in Luke's analysis, is power that shapes *what people want*. If the first face of power is the ability to command people in spite of what they want, and the second face of power is the ability to define what wants get on the public table of political deliberation, the third face of power

concerns the very formation of the wants themselves. To the extent that the formation of wants is closely tied to the nature of the social system within which people live it is linked to 'systemic' power in the Alford–Friedland sense.

Alford and Friedland discuss this typology of power using a loose game theory metaphor:[7] systemic power is power embedded in the fundamental nature of the *game itself*; institutional power is power embodied in the specific *rules of the game*; situational power is power deployed in specific *moves within a given set of rules*. When actors use specific resources strategically to accomplish their goals, they are exercising situational power. The procedural rules which govern how they use those resources reflects institutional power. The nature of the social system which determines the range of possible rules and achievable goals reflects systemic power. There is thus a kind of cybernetic relationship among these levels of power: the system level imposes limits on the institutional level which imposes limits on actors' strategies at the situational level. Conflicts at the situational level, in turn, can modify the rules at the institutional level which, cumulatively can lead to the transformation of the system itself.

Alford and Friedland also relate this typology to common political terms for the degree of polarization in political conflicts: *liberal* versus *conservative* politics constitute conflicts restricted to the situational level, conflicts over moves in the game within a fixed set of rules; *reformist* versus *reactionary* politics are political conflicts at the institutional level of power over attempts to transform the rules within which situational conflicts occur; and *revolutionary* versus *counter-revolutionary* politics are conflicts located at the systemic level of power over which game to play. This does not imply that a change in the 'game itself' cannot be accomplished by gradual, incremental changes in the rules of the game. It is possible that reformist struggles cumulatively could have revolutionary consequences; this is the vision of certain strands of reformist socialism. But it does imply that the stakes are different when the nature of the game is at issue rather than simply rules within a game.[8]

The central thesis of neo-Marxist theories of the state is that at each of these levels of the analysis of power, capitalism undermines democracy by giving advantages to the capitalist class and its interests. The argument for situational power is the most straightforward. Class structures, among other things, distribute resources which are useful in political struggles. In particular, in capitalist societies capitalists have two crucial resources available to them to be deployed

politically: enormous financial resources and personal connections
to people in positions of governmental authority. Capitalists are in
a position to use their wealth directly to shape the direction of state
policies through a wide variety of concrete mechanisms: financing
politicians, political parties and policy think tanks; financially controlling the main organs of the mass media; offering lucrative jobs
to high level political officials after they leave state employment;
extensive lobbying.[9] When combined with the dense pattern of
personal networks which give capitalists easy access to the sites of
immediate political power, such use of financial resources gives the
bourgeoisie vastly disproportionate direct leverage over politics.

The analysis of the class biases in the institutional level of power
grew out of the recognition that capital*ists* are not always present as
the predominant political actors in the formation of state policies,
either overtly or behind the scenes. The argument is basically this: the
state should be viewed not simply as a state *in* capitalist society, but
rather as a *capitalist* state.[10] This implies that there are certain institutional properties of the very form of the state that can be treated as
having a specific class character. The idea here is not simply that there
are certain *policies* of the state which embody the interests of a specific class, but rather that the very structure of the apparatuses
through which those policies are made embodies those class interests.[11]

Claims about the class character of the institutional level of power
involve what is sometimes called non-decision-making power or
negative power. The basic argument was crisply laid out in an early
essay by Claus Offe.[12] Offe argued that the class character of the state
was inscribed in a series of negative filter mechanisms which imparted
a systematic class bias to state actions. 'Class bias', in this context,
means that the property in question tends to filter out state actions
which would be inimical to the interests of the dominant class. The
form of the state, in effect, systematically determines what does *not*
happen rather than simply what does.[13]

Three examples will help to clarify the idea that state apparatuses
can have a distinctively capitalist bias built into them. First, and
perhaps the most important property of the capitalist state, as
emphasized by Offe and Ronge[14] and Therborn[15], is the institutional
rules by which the capitalist state acquires financial resources: through
taxation and borrowing from the privately produced surplus rather
than through the state's direct appropriation of the surplus generated
by its own productive activity. By restricting the state's access to funds
in this way the state is rendered dependent upon capitalist production,

and this in turn acts as a mechanism which filters out state policies which would seriously undermine the profitability of private accumulation.[16] Second, the legal rules that 'protect' private property by prohibiting the state from appropriating private property without 'fair' compensation, typically interpreted as market-rate compensation, blocks the capitalist state from acquiring productive resources for democratic purposes. In the contemporary debates in South Africa over land redistribution, for example, the rules of fair compensation act as an enormous constraint on various land reform policies the post-Apartheid government might wish to pursue. Third, as Poulantzas[17] forcefully argued, the electoral rules of capitalist representative democracies, in which people cast votes as individual citizens within territorial units of representation rather than as members of functioning groups, has the effect of transforming people from members of a class into atomized individuals (the 'juridical citizen'). This atomization, in turn, serves to filter out state policies that would only be viable if people were systematically organized into durable collectivities or associations. To the extent that this filter can be viewed as stabilizing capitalism and thus serving the basic interests of the capitalist class, then exclusive reliance on purely territorial, individualized voting can be viewed as having a class character.[18]

The idea that power at the systemic level also embodies a distinctive class bias has been forcefully argued by Adam Przeworski,[19] building on the work of Antonio Gramsci. Przeworski writes:

> Capitalism is a form of social organization in which the entire society is dependent upon actions of capitalists . . . First, capitalism is a system in which production is oriented towards the satisfaction of the needs of others, toward exchange, which implies that in this system the immediate producers cannot survive on their own. Second, capitalism is a system in which part of the total societal product is withheld from immediate producers in the form of profit which accrues to owners of the means of production . . . If capitalists do not appropriate a profit, if they do not exploit, production falls, consumption decreases and no other group can satisfy its material interests. Current realization of material interests of capitalists is a necessary condition for the future realization of material interests of any group under capitalism . . . Capitalists are thus in a unique position in the capitalist system: they represent future universal interests while interests of all other groups appear as particularistic and hence inimical to future developments.[20]

So long as capitalism is intact as a social order, all actors in the system have an interest in capitalists making a profit. What this means is that, unless a group has the capacity to overthrow the system completely, then, at least in terms of material interests, even groups opposed to capitalism have an interest in sustaining capitalist accumulation and profitability.

This systemic level of power does not depend upon capitalists consciously using the dependency of the state on the rate of profit as a political weapon. The issue here is not the threat of a coordinated capital *strike* – the conscious decision by capitalists to disinvest and move their capital abroad in order to thwart a particular political project. Here the argument is that in the mundane, everyday practices of capitalists, acting atomistically in pursuit of profits, they affirm a set of interdependencies with other actors in which their interests will assume a privileged position in the society at large: everyone will want capitalism to thrive. This dependency, then, constrains the possibilities of democratic governance, for policies which seriously impinge on private profits and accumulation are seen as undesirable.

The arguments at the systemic level are in many ways the trickiest to defend rigorously, for some of what looks like a constraint rooted in the private ownership of profits may simply be a constraint rooted in the conditions for production of a social surplus which would exist under any regime of property rights. That is, democratic choices over the acceptable level of pollution must be attentive to the effects of the resource allocations required to accomplish such a level on the future availability of investments (surplus). Zero pollution would probably be 'too costly' in terms of opportunity costs, and would thus constitute a 'constraint', under any set of property relations. The claim about the systemic bias of capitalist property relations, then, is a claim that such constraints on the democratic allocation of resources are narrower by virtue of the private ownership of the surplus than they would otherwise be.

3 Coupon Socialism and the Three Levels of Power

Let us now turn to the question of how coupon socialism might affect each of these levels of power.

At the situational level of power, coupon socialism would seem clearly to weaken the constraints on democratic governance. Roemer's own discussions of democratic power mainly revolve around the situational level. Indeed, the rhetoric of Roemer's initial affirmation of the socialists' political goal – equality of opportunity for political *influence* – suggests a rather instrumental conception of power. Later, where he discusses his models of 'public bads', the emphasis is again on the level of the public bad that would be demanded by actors with differing capacities to influence state policy.

The reasons why coupon socialism enhances democratic situational power are easy to see. By eliminating concentrations of wealth, coupon socialism contributes to a relative equalization of the resources available to individuals to deploy politically. Even though the actual profit dividend each person receives is not enormous (under Roemer's calculations), fewer people will have gargantuan levels of discretionary income available to use for political purposes.[21] Furthermore, the threat of capital strikes and other forms of politically motivated disinvestment is also removed in coupon socialism.[22]

What about institutional power? It is less clear how this level of power will be directly affected by coupon socialism. One can imagine a variety of ways of organizing the institutions of political power which would be compatible with coupon socialism and which would, to varying degrees, be democracy enhancing. One attractive possibility would be the kind of associative democracy proposed by Joshua Cohen and Joel Rogers.[23] The core idea of Cohen and Rogers' proposal is that functionally defined associations of various sorts play an active role in democratic governance, both as vehicles for interest representation and deliberation and as players in the administration of various kinds of public policies. For example, works councils within factories could, on the one hand, be formally recognized associations where various kinds of policy were discussed and from which representatives would participate in various kinds of policy-making bodies, and, on the other hand, be delegated real responsibilities for the monitoring and enforcing of certain policy provisions, such as health and safety regulations. Democracy would be deepened through such associational practices by increasing the forms of citizen participation, enriching the arenas for consensus formation and enhancing the accountability of administrative bodies.

The question, then, is whether, *relative to capitalism*, coupon socialism would make it easier to institutionalize the associative democratic rules of the game. There are several reasons why we might think this would be the case. First, one of the groups whose interests would potentially be most threatened by associative democracy is the class of capitalists. While Cohen and Rogers seem to argue that associative democracy could exist in a capitalist society, strengthening the ways in which popular forces can have a serious voice politically is unlikely to be welcomed by capitalists. Eliminating the class of capitalist wealth holders, therefore, removes a powerful interest opposed to associative democracy.

Second, if the banks in coupon socialism are themselves public bodies which are democratically controlled, as Roemer suggests would be the case, then some kind of associative mechanism is a natural way of organizing the governance structure of banks with respect to their constituencies. The banks in Roemer's model of coupon socialism are meant to fulfill crucial monitoring functions of firms and are also the places where certain kinds of priorities of investment alternatives are decided. One of the strengths of associative democracy is its potential for accomplishing decentralized forms of monitoring and interest representation. Some form of associative democracy in which representatives of firms, unions and community groups sat on the boards of directors of banks would seem to be a natural way of accomplishing these functions.

Third, as envisioned by Roemer, the basic way that more centralized democratic planning of the market would occur in coupon socialism would be through strategic use of interest rate surcharges and subsidies to encourage investment in specific sectors. Since this planning mechanism is linked to the practices of the banks, it would seem that the possibility of coordinating and fine-tuning such policies might be enhanced under institutions of associative democratic governance involving associations of banks and other functional constituencies.

For these arguments to be convincing, of course, details of the institutional design of associative democratic coupon socialism would have to be elaborated. All that I have suggested here is that there is a certain organizational affinity between the idea of associational democracy and the institutions of coupon socialism.

The problem of systemic power gets to the heart of the relation of forms of property relations and political power. Certainly in the Marxist tradition, this is where the real power of the capitalist class lies. The key issue here is the extent to which the day-to-day investment and disinvestment decisions in coupon socialism, compared to capitalism, constrain the policy options of democratic political institutions.

The answer to this question undoubtedly depends upon the institutional details of the way coupon socialism would actually work. Thus, for example, in one place Roemer seems to offer some institutional suggestions which would potentially severely compromise the democratic potential of coupon socialism: 'Foreign investors would not have coupons, of course, but would invest real capital in return for some share of profits'.[24] Roemer expresses some concern about this only because 'citizens might use foreign firms as their agents to invest their capital in domestic firms'. He concludes that, 'This would have to be outlawed.' Depending upon the scale and scope of such direct foreign investment, however, a much more important issue than citizens circumventing the egalitarian norms of coupon ownership might be the recreation of systemic vulnerability of the democratic state to the private investment choices of capitalists. Democratic capacity is enhanced in coupon socialism because deliberative democratic bodies have to worry less about capital flight and disinvestment than under private enterprise capitalism. Direct foreign investment undermines this.

The pivotal institution for the problem of systemic power in coupon socialism seems to be the banks, for the banks make the basic decisions about the allocation of the economic surplus in the form of loans to firms and it is the banks that have primary responsibility for monitoring the performance of firms. Roemer is at pains to argue that the banks need to be relatively autonomous from government control. He fears that if they were too closely controlled by the government their loans would be allocated primarily on the basis of political criteria and thus they would cease to be instruments of profit-maximizing, market efficiency. On the other hand, since the banks are not themselves private firms, if they are not themselves closely monitored there is always the risk that they will have no particular incentive to monitor the firms effectively.

Roemer acknowledges that he has not worked out a solution to this problem, but he believes that a combination of democratically elected boards of directors and a proper incentive structure to managerial careers in the banking industry would solve the problem. If we assume that this problem is solved, then it would seem that coupon socialism with democratically controlled public banks would greatly relax the systemic constraints on democratic state power.

One way of thinking about this is to look at the capacity for sustainable tax rates as an index of the political capacity of the democratic state. A high, sustainable tax rate means that the state can control a significant part of the social surplus without it leading to a declining tax base. This is not to argue that a maximally unconstrained democratic state would necessarily opt for the highest sustainable level of taxation. For a wide range of reasons, a democratic state might choose lower than maximally sustainable taxes. Nevertheless, the scope of democracy is enhanced if the democratic state has the capacity to raise taxes to higher sustainable levels.

It seems likely that the democratic state in a coupon socialism would have considerably enhanced capacities for taxation since it would not face the threat of disinvestment and capital flight in the face of rising tax rates. The main constraint on tax rates would come from the effect of taxes on labor effort, and accordingly on the level of earnings that constitute the income tax base. While it is, of course, difficult to estimate what is the elasticity of labor supply (or effort) to taxation, it would certainly be less sensitive to taxation than 'capital effort' since most people are neither able nor willing to emigrate to avoid high taxes, whereas capitalists have no difficulty in moving investments to lower tax areas to reduce taxation. In fact, if we assume that people have target standard of livings which they try to achieve, then there would be reason to believe that, up to a point, increasing income taxes might even lead to an increase, rather than a decrease, in labor effort. The empirical experience of the increase in household labor supply since the early 1970s (mainly in the form of increased labor force participation of women) to compensate for declining real wages lends support to this argument.

If these arguments are correct, then the level of sustainable taxation in coupon socialism will be considerably higher than in capitalism. This, in turn, means that the democratic state in coupon socialism operates under weaker constraints in its deliberations over appropriate policies and priorities, and thus would have enhanced democratic capacity.

Coupon socialism is defended by John Roemer as a feasible first step away from capitalism, a first step that accomplishes at least some of what socialists want, particularly in terms of goals of economic egalitarianism. While the details of how this system of property rights would be articulated to a matrix of democratic institutions still needs to be elaborated, it would seem that coupon socialism might be a first step towards significantly deepening and extending democratic politics. Instrumental power would be less subject to manipulation by the wealthy; institutional arrangements for associational democracy would become more feasible and perhaps even encouraged; and the systemic constraints on democracy would be weakened.

Notes

1. John E. Roemer, *A Future for Socialism*, Cambridge, MA: Harvard University Press 1994.
2. Ibid., p. 11.
3. Ibid., pp. 20–21.
4. Perhaps one can call 'self-centered' preferences a 'negative externality' of market allocations. The desirability of expanding the scope of democratic decision making, then, could be subsumed under the general rubric of solving market failures. Such an extension of the idea of negative externality, however, is somewhat misleading, since this is a negative externality of the essential *process* of market allocating rather than of the outcome of the allocations itself.

5. Robert Alford and Roger Friedland, *The Powers of Theory*, Cambridge: Cambridge University Press 1985. Steven Lukes, *Power: a Radical View*, London: Macmillan 1974.

6. Alford and Friedland prefer the term 'structural power' for this second 'level'. All three levels of power, however, are 'structural' in the sense of being systematically structured by and through social practices. The distinctive characteristic of this second level of power is the way it is embodied in features of institutional design, and thus it seems more appropriate to call it simply institutional power.

7. The nature of conflicts within a sport can be thought of in terms of these three levels. Given that you are playing basketball, and given that basketball has a specific set of rules, then different players will have more or less 'power' in the moves of the game – more or less capacity to accomplish their goals (making baskets). Suppose the rule for goal tending was removed. This would enhance the power of very tall players. Given those rules, various strategies would develop to affect this 'balance of power', but it would be tough for many players to ever make a basket. The result is that conflict is likely to be displaced onto the rule-making body to reform the rules. However, so long as the game remained 'basketball', the basic desires of the players would remain oriented towards making baskets.

8. This set of metaphors also suggests that a crucial criterion for evaluating rule changes is the extent to which they alter the 'nature' of the game. Thus, widening the net in soccer is a different kind of rule change from allowing players to pick up the ball and run with it.

9. The focus on these kinds of mechanisms which link the state to the bourgeoisie are by no means limited to scholars who explicitly see their work as Marxist. For example, G. William Domhoff in his many books on the 'power elite' – including *The Powers that Be*, New York: Random House 1979, *Who Rules America Now?*, Engelwood Cliffs: Prentice Hall 1983, and *The Power Elite and the State*, Hawthorne, NY: Aldine de Gruyter 1990 – specifically situates his work in opposition to 'Marxism' (or, at least, to the main currents of neo-Marxism prevalent since the early 1970s) and yet places the networks and resources of capitalists at the center stage of his analysis of the 'power elite'.

10. This linguistic turn of phrase – 'the state in capitalist society' vs 'the capitalist state' – was, to my knowledge, first formulated by Nicos Poulantzas in 'The Problem of the Capitalist State', *New Left Review* 58 (1969), pp. 67–78, his well-known critique of Ralph Miliband's book, *The State in Capitalist Society*, New York: Basic Books 1969. The thesis itself, however, has a long Marxist pedigree, going back to Marx's own work, particularly his analysis of the class character of the state in his discussions of the Paris Commune. This theme was then forcefully taken up by Lenin in 'The State and Revolution', where he argued that because the very form of the state in capitalism was stamped with a bourgeois character, it could not simply be captured, it had to be smashed. For a general discussion of the problem of capturing vs smashing the state, see Wright, *Class, Crisis and the State*, London: Verso 1978, ch. 5.

11. Policies as such could embody particular class interests because actors external to the state with specific class interests were able to impose those policies on the state. That is, if capitalists were always actively present politically and always predominant in conflicts involving *situational* power, then, even if the state itself was a completely class-neutral apparatus, state policies could be uniformly pro-capitalist. The claim that the form of the state itself embodies certain class principles was meant to provide a way of explaining why state policies are broadly consistent with the interests of the bourgeoisie, even when they are not present as the ubiquitous, active initiators of state policies.

12. Claus Offe, 'Structural Problems of the Capitalist State: Class rule and the political system. On the selectiveness of political institutions', in Von Beyme, ed., *German Political Studies* vol. I, London: Sage 1974, pp. 31–57.

13. Offe emphasizes the extremely difficult methodological issues involved in empirically demonstrating such 'negative selections'. The basic issue is being able to

distinguish between things which simply have not *yet* happened from things which have been systematically excluded as 'non-events' and therefore *cannot* happen.

14. Claus Offe and Volker Ronge, 'Theses on the Theory of the State', *New German Critique* 6 (Fall, 1975).

15. Goran Therborn, *What Does the Ruling Class Do When it Rules?*, London: Verso 1978.

16. Logically, one could have a capitalist system of production in which the state directly owns a significant number of enterprises and uses the profits from these businesses to finance its general budget, thus not needing to tax private capital and wages at all. The fact that with very few exceptions, such as the ownership of Statoil (the North Sea Oil Company in Norway) by the Norwegian State, or perhaps (if they are genuine capitalist states) the oil sheikdoms in the Persian Gulf, capitalist states do not acquire significant revenues this way is not a feature of capitalism as such but of the way states have institutionally developed within capitalism.

17. Nicos Poulantzas, *Political Power and Social Classes*, London: NLB 1973.

18. There is some ambiguity in many discussions of the class character of the state over the status of the claim that a particular formal property of the state, in this case atomized territorial representation, has a particular class character. Some writers (Therborn, for example) seem to suggest that the element in question inherently has a given class character. Others, for example, Chantal Mouffe, 'Hegemony and Ideology in Gramsci', in *Gramsci & Marxist Theory*, Mouffe, ed., London: Routledge & Kegan Paul 1979 or Norberto Bobbio, 'Are there Alternatives to Representative Democracy?', *Telos* 35 (1978) pp. 17–30 suggest that the class character comes from the gestalt in which a given element is embedded. Territorial representation thus has a capitalist character because it is not articulated to various forms of more functional representation and direct democracy rather than because intrinsically territorial representation as such reproduces capitalism.

19. *Capitalism and Social Democracy*, Cambridge: Cambridge University Press 1985.

20. Ibid., pp. 138–9.

21. Since coupon socialism itself does nothing to reduce inequalities in employment earnings, there will still be people with very high incomes that can be used in politics, but there will not be any Ross Perrots.

22. In one place Roemer suggests that coupon socialism is compatible with direct foreign investment in the equity of firms. In such a model, the coupon system only applies to 'domestic' ownership, but foreigners can function as normal capitalists. If a significant amount of capital was invested in this way, then the threat of politically motivated disinvestment by private capitalists would once again become a source of antidemocratic situational power.

23. Joshua Cohen and Joel Rogers, 'Secondary Associations and Democratic Governance', *Politics & Society* 20:4 (December 1992), pp. 393–472 and *Associations and Democracy*, London: Verso 1995.

24. Ibid., p. 82.

Assessments of the Economics of Coupon Socialism

8

Coupons, Agency and Social Betterment

Louis Putterman

There are many things I like about John Roemer's essay. I share his view that those who would like to craft a better world should work with human beings as we know them – taking account of a tendency to pursue individual material interest – not people assumed transformed by revolution. I agree, too, that the collapse of Soviet-type socialism did not prove existing capitalism to be the end-stage of history or the best feasible social system. And I agree that greater equality of opportunity is central to what a better world would be about. Most of all, I applaud the fact that Roemer ventures to say with some specificity what kind of better world he thinks is feasible. I find it encouraging that challenging times have spurred an analyst of his stature to move in this direction and take the risks that such an enterprise entails. The critical thoughts that I would offer are in the spirit of contributions to that enterprise, not a rejection.

I see the essay as having four main components. First, it argues for defining socialism as a kind of egalitarianism, rather than as a doctrine favoring state management of the economy or state ownership of the means of production. Second, it argues that one way of achieving greater equality, the equalizing of profit income, is more immediately feasible than is the alternative of equalizing incomes from labor. Third, it suggests specific ways in which an equal distribution of profits would increase welfare. Finally, it sketches out a fairly specific blueprint of an economic system in which profits are distributed relatively equally.

The comments which follow are organized into four sections dealing in turn with each of the four components. A fifth section gives comments on some less central aspects of Roemer's essay, and the main points are summarized in the conclusion. Most importantly, these involve identifying some efficiency and financial incentive problems in the coupon proposal, and questioning both the view that

139

profit incomes are more easily redistributed than are those of labor, and the proposal's focus on redistributing profits rather than wealth.

1 Socialism as Egalitarianism

Roemer asks what socialists want and concludes that they want equality of opportunity for welfare, self-actualization, political influence and social status. Important socialists have also wanted to abolish or sharply curtail the roles of the market and of private property, but Roemer suggests that these were means, rather than ends in their own right, and that subsequent experience allows us to see them to have been poorly chosen means.

If the test of whether an idea is socialist is its consistency with the writings of Marx, then Roemer's emphasis on egalitarianism could be judged socialist, in my view, but more on the basis of subtext than of text. That is because, as far as I am aware, Marx the scientist never explicitly embraces the egalitarian ideal. Insisting on the scientific nature of his analysis, he claims to tell us how and why capitalism will end, not why it *ought* to end. When he writes of exploitation, he claims to do so on objective, rather than moralistic, grounds. In the end, however, he can provide no sensible explanation for why things do, as opposed to *ought to*, exchange at values proportionate to their labor contents.[1] Moreover, he eventually admits that they do not exchange at such values under actual capitalism. I think one is fully justified in concluding, and I take this to be the essential message of much of Roemer's work to date, that Marx's labor values are after all a normative metric, rather than a positive one. While Roemer initially reached this position through analytical rejection of the alternatives, one would also get there by going with the tone of *Capital*, that is, noting where the sarcasm and outrage get heavy, rather than with the formal scientific protestations. Not surprisingly, perhaps, the scientific Marx ends up a victim of the same quest for scientific validation that has impoverished so much of neoclassical economics. He would protest at our selection of his moral outrage instead of his positive analysis, but he left us with little alternative, since any attempt to support the analysis at a strictly positive level is doomed to fail.[2]

Discarding Marx's rejection of the market is also something of a blow to Marxist orthodoxy. While one might argue that 'to each according to his work' was a bit less negotiable for Marx's conception of socialism than was central planning, I suspect that Marx expected 'the anarchy of the market' as well as the inequality based on property ownership to be replaced.[3] Dropping Marx's antipathy toward markets as having been based on an unrealistic assessment of the planning problem as a straightforward administrative matter, and perhaps also on an undervaluation of the despotism to which centralized coordination might be prone, is a move with which I am fully in sympathy.

Although Roemer's essay shows a willingness to jettison much Marxist orthodoxy, it also shows a tendency to hold on to Marxian elements that may have little more to recommend them than that they are not yet discarded. The main not-yet-discarded Marxian proposition here is that profits but not labor income can be redistributed. This proposition may be well-rooted in Marx, but I would argue that it is poorly grounded in demonstrable support. Given the trend in progressive Marxist thinking towards abandoning old Marxist tenets little by little, clinging to what has not yet been discarded is disturbing, since one cannot help but wonder whether it is only a matter of time before these shreds, too, will be dropped.

To be sure, the essay takes another step from orthodoxy in arguing against 'to each according to his work' as a distributive ideal; socialists would not have the disabled starve. But even this position has some support in Marx's statement that a socialist society will spend more than a capitalist one on such things as health services, and that it will make available 'funds for those unable to work, etc.'. Moreover, the practical relevance of this principle is limited by an assumed need to distribute *mostly* according to work. It is noteworthy that in 'The Critique of the Gotha Program', the 'funds for those unable to work, etc.' are not said to exceed those distributed under capitalism; the amounts in question under the two alternative systems are implicitly treated as comparable when Marx explains the category as 'in short, . . . what is included under so-called official poor relief today'.[4] The limited scope of the essay's redistributive proposal suggests similar modesty in this respect.

Of course, there is no way to decide whether a set of ideas is 'socialist' or not without first delineating the boundaries of socialism. As one attracted by a communitarian brand of socialism, I have in my own mind tended to define the term as 'the belief that society and its individual members are linked by mutual obligations and responsibilities', which contrasts with at least a caricatured liberalism under which the individual and society owe one another nothing. But without agreed rules on what qualifies competing approaches to be called socialist, the definitional question can never be resolved. If the boundaries of what is socialist are to be drawn only around Marx and his followers, then as someone for whom Marx is neither a moral nor a scientific authority, I find the exercise to be of only academic interest.

Whereas the question 'what do socialists want?' is in my view either unanswerable or not terribly important, Roemer's essay can also be viewed as a response to the broader and more fundamental question 'what are the requirements of a good society?' Looking at Roemer's response to the latter question, his inclusion of equality of opportunity will probably engender little debate, except with respect to details. My only reservation, here, is that the equality that the essay focusses on turns out to be principally material, and that other desirables, such as liberty and fraternity (or whatever is its non-sexist counterpart), receive little or no attention. While I am encouraged to see the author devote more than a few lines to the topic of workplace relations, his ultimate decision to tackle the distribution problem first and perhaps exclusively is disappointing.

2 What is to be Equalized?

In the 'Critique of the Gotha Program', Marx says that equal earnings for equal labor can be achieved earlier than can 'to each according to his needs'. The reason people will still have to endure different living standards when their households have different amounts and qualities of labor to offer and different numbers of dependants to support is that workers will emerge from a capitalist epoch believing in the 'bourgeois' right to own what their hands have wrought.[5] But if the fruits of their labor cannot be redistributed, how then can that portion of those fruits which they choose not to consume, that is, their savings, be subject to redistribution? The problem would not arise in the world of *Capital*, where workers earn only enough to live, and all saving and investment is done by capitalists. But in our more complicated world in which labor incomes vary over a wide range and a good deal of society's investment funds come from workers' savings, it cannot be avoided.

Moreover, things are more complicated still when popular perceptions allow 'the fruits of labor' to include entrepreneurial earnings and perhaps even the returns on smart investment. With people viewing property gained by a wide variety of avenues as legitimate, a mandate to redistribute 'capital' is lacking.[6] In Marx's terms, the populace would seem to be not merely 'still stamped with the birth marks of the old society from whose womb it emerges',[7] but not yet ready to leave the capitalist womb at all.

In the end, the proposal in Roemer's essay essentially avoids the problem of redistribution, but it can do so only at great cost in terms of achieved inequality (and, the last section will argue, a possibly appreciable cost in efficiency). The mechanism involved is the re-distribution, not of existing assets, but of rights to future streams of returns. Each citizen is given an equal allocation of coupons with which to purchase rights to shares of firms' profits, but when the model is applied to an actual capitalist country such as the United States, the existing distribution of wealth is assumed to remain untouched.[8] Wealth holders can earn returns on their funds not only by lending them to financial intermediaries, which will pay them interest, but also by starting small business ventures, which are not subject to a public ownership requirement. The proposal's conceptual modesty is clear here, since income from both sources would be counted as profits by Marx, and as 'unearned income' by the US tax code. Whether its results would be large or small in quantitative terms is unclear, however.

The initial estimate of the adult dividend in 1981, $459.92, is about 30 per cent more than the average weekly earnings of production and non-supervisory workers in that year, thus raising worker incomes by some 2 or 3 per cent.[9] Capitalized at a 7 per cent interest rate, it is equivalent to an asset worth $6,570.29. While only about 18.6 per cent of US *average* wealth of $35,231 in that year, the hypothetical asset was worth over eighteen times the average wealth of persons in the bottom quintile of households, who held only 0.2 per cent of total wealth, or an average of $352.[10] Assuming it came entirely from upper quintile wealth, the additional asset would have raised the bottom quintile's wealth share from 0.2 to 3.9 per cent, a major increase, although one leaving that quintile's share still far from an egalitarian 20 per cent. Using the alternative estimate of Table A3 and the same 7 per cent interest rate, the 1981 dividend of $1,206.68 has an asset value of $17,238, which raises the bottom quintile's wealth share to an impressive 10 per cent. The questions that I will raise below about the effect of the proposal's change in property rights upon the share of capital returns going to creditors, as opposed to equity owners, place dividend estimates of such magnitudes in doubt, however.

Depending on which hypothetical computations one uses, then, the combining of 'distribution according to work' and non-redistribution of wealth may or may not render the essay's shift towards 'socialist' equality timid. With respect to the choice of leveling mechanism, however, it should be noted that Western industrial societies have already shown a significant willingness to redistribute labor earnings through progressive income taxes, and property, too, has been attacked by wealth, gift, and estate taxes. While there is thus a small chance that the essay's proposal could strike a receptive chord with some populist post-socialist regime,[11] it is hard for me to believe that a Western citizenry that became further predisposed towards equality would be more likely to implement its radical institutional experiment than to bolster the redistributive tendencies in existing tax codes. The incentive and other consequences of accomplishing redistribution by these methods are, after all, better understood.

Another way of looking at the problem is to consider Roemer's claim that 'there is a fundamental asymmetry between wages and profits', in that the distribution of the first but not that of the second category is primarily determined by considerations of efficiency. I do not agree with this claim when I think in terms of *any existing distribution of wealth*. Just like that of wages, the distribution of profits *for a given distribution of ownership of assets* tends to be one which induces financial resources to flow into highest-return activities, a requirement of efficiency.[12] The strongest argument for the claim that the existing distribution of profits is less necessary to efficiency than is that of wages, I believe, would be an argument that wealth, unlike skills, can be fairly easily redistributed, and with minimal efficiency effects. But whether wealth can in fact be easily redistributed is, as just discussed, a non-trivial political question, while the efficiency consequences of such a distribution are also unclear.[13] In any case, I note again that the Roemer proposal does not call for a redistribution of wealth. His argument that unequal profit distribution is not necessitated by efficiency must therefore rest on other grounds. By separating the variable from the predictable part of capital returns and redistributing rights to the former alone, his proposal attempts to redistribute profit without redistributing wealth.[14] But the claim that this will be without efficiency effects is not immune to challenge, as I will show below.

In sum, partly because of the complexity of the existing distribution of property and income, partly because of the tenacity of 'bourgeois' values, and partly for reasons to be discussed later, the Marxist supposition that the easy part of redistribution is the redistribution of profits appears to lack any strong basis. The most promising way of supporting it is by appeal to the distinction between alienable financial and inalienable human assets, but Roemer's proposal is not one of asset redistribution. It appears politically no more difficult to redistribute current incomes than wealth, and redistributing profits without re-distributing wealth requires an institutional revolution of unknown efficiency consequence that seems still less politically realistic than expanding conventional redistributive programs, at least in 'mature' economies. I would add here that redistributing endowments by improving access to education is not only a potentially more saleable approach, but also one that provides a bonus relative to other forms of redistribution by way of its favorable effects upon self-esteem, personal fulfillment, and social relations, and that is less easy to reverse by reason of its inalienability. It is for these reasons that I find starting with a not-yet-rejected nugget of Marxian doctrine and building a strategy to better the human condition upon it to be the weakest stone in the foundation of Roemer's proposal.

3 How Equalizing Profits will Raise Welfare

One way to judge how well-being would be affected by a more equal distribution of profits would be to use a social welfare function. Roemer stops short of proposing a single measure by which to judge his proposal, but one possibility would be to look at the Benthamite function that simply adds up the utilities of all individuals, which he reports for his simulation. While using such a measure has its pitfalls, I welcome the way in which it downplays Pareto efficiency and gives legitimacy to interpersonal tradeoffs, as the transfer of income from wealthier to poorer citizens raises social welfare, assuming declining marginal utility of income and a common utility scale.[15] Because the impact of redistributing profits on the distribution of income under Roemer's proposal is small, however, other arguments about the effect of the proposal on welfare become important. An argument emphasized by Roemer is that with the benefits from generating negative externalities distributed more similarly to the costs, which is to say more equally, the ensuing choice of externality levels will lead to a higher level of social welfare.

The model for demonstrating this is a neat and intuitive one which, beyond its prescriptive value, has the virtue of demonstrating a relationship between externalities and property distribution that had not previously been rigorously expounded. The idea is that, while the general public suffers from such externalities as air and water pollution, those who are profit claimants receive a possibly offsetting, concentrated gain from the profit that the polluting activity generates. If profit recipients determine the pollution level, either through their influence on the political process or their control of firms, then a higher pollution level will tend to be chosen the more concentrated are the profit claims, since such concentration causes the personal benefits to profit recipients to exceed their personal costs out to higher levels of pollution. By contrast, if ownership and exposure to externalities are distributed in the same way, owners' interests are exactly those of the public, so when owners determine the pollution level (once again, through either route), then only those negative externalities that are outweighed by material benefits for the average citizen will end up being endured.

While I find the model useful and attractive, I would also want to recognize that its conclusions are sensitive to certain assumptions. In particular, suppose that levels of pollution are determined by the political process, as the model assumes. If profit recipients use their wealth to dominate politics, the model's conclusions still hold; but if democracy functions more nearly as intended, with wealthy and non-wealthy citizens having relatively equal impacts, the thrust of the model's conclusions may be overturned. As non-owners, that is, ordinary citizens would be inclined to choose very low levels of pollution. When ownership is granted them, however, their tolerance for these externalities will increase. Pollution enthusiasts (if there are any) might therefore favor shareholding equality as a way of 'coopting the masses' into appreciating pollution's benefits, just as some enthusiasts of capitalism have advocated employee stock ownership plans and similar ways of spreading the equity as a means of widening support for that system.

Another problem with the externality argument, in the context of the essay's coupon proposal, is the fact that while profit shares become more equally distributed under that proposal, interest incomes do not. This means that conclusions about the impact of equalized profit claims on externalities hinge on the assumption that the switch from being big profit recipients to being big interest recipients radically alters the attitude of the wealthy towards externalities. If lenders have committed their funds before a pollution level is chosen, and if the probability of default on interest payments is a positive function of the allowed level of pollution, then the tolerance of the wealthy for pollution may be little affected by their switch from equity to credit positions. More generally, if technology and product preferences make pollution necessary to the vitality of industry, then the wealthy may continue to have a higher tolerance for pollution than do most non-wealthy counterparts.[16] What this suggests is that if the influence of the wealthy is as disproportionate as Roemer believes it to be, then it may once again be impossible to avoid a more direct attack on the distribution of wealth, if one wants to achieve the results that are desired here.

4 Distribution and Efficiency in the Coupon Economy

Although the redistributive achievement of the coupon economy may be fairly modest by the standards of some revolutionaries, one might nonetheless admire how much the proposal appears to accomplish without any redistribution of wealth and with no immediately apparent cost to efficiency. Control and profit rights in the economy's major firms have been evenly distributed without the slightest confiscation of assets, and there is the possibility, at least, that managers will continue to seek out projects in which resources can be combined to produce goods of high social (or at least market) value.

Yet can property rights really be this radically rearranged without seriously altering the incentives that underlie the economy's static and dynamic performance? That body of financial theory that stresses agency relations between owners and managers, and conflicts of interest between different classes of financiers, suggests otherwise.[17] The coupon economy proposal entails giving citizens a way to obtain control and residual rights without providing firms with real assets. Financing of the firm is therefore to come entirely from banks and other lenders. According to finance theory, however, firms in market economies are not found to be financed entirely by debt instruments because owners (including shareholders) have an interest in gambling with borrowed money if they do not have to repay in the event of bankruptcy. This is because while downside risks are shared by creditors, upside possibilities will benefit profit recipients only. The higher the proportion of debt in the firm's financial mix, the less owners themselves can lose in a risky project, and the higher the potential ratio of gains to money invested. Recognizing this conflict of interest, lenders will demand either a higher rate of return or some controls on the firm's activities as the price of providing credit to a highly leveraged company.

What, then, would be the consequences of imposing a 100 per cent leveraged structure on large firms as a matter of public policy? With 100 per cent leverage, controlling shareholders, who can diversify their portfolios of 1000 coupons over many firms, would be happy to see each firm gamble borrowed funds on relatively risky projects, since there is the possibility of a large gain with very little offsetting loss.[18] The efficiency effect would be a movement to possibly excessive risk-taking and an increasing number of bankruptcies. But there is also likely to be a first-order distributive effect, thwarting a central aim of the proposal. Lenders to 100 per cent leveraged firms would seek promises of higher interest payments. The outcome is complicated by the fact that, whereas the cost of credit to a nearly 100 per cent leveraged firm in the existing economy would be extremely high, the fact that all large firms would be 100 per cent leveraged in the coupon economy would deprive lenders of some of their bargaining power. Nevertheless, the price of borrowing can be expected to be higher than that facing a moderately leveraged firm in the existing economy, because lenders always have the option of simply consuming their funds, and they can also invest in zero or moderately leveraged small businesses either as equity holders or as providers of credit. Possibilities of moving funds to the non-coupon economies of other countries would further raise bargaining power. Even without foreign options, payments to creditors can be expected to be higher than otherwise, as a result of which the pure profit share of income in the economy would fall.[19]

In fact, there is a serious question of whether there would be positive expected profits to be had at all from large firm shareholding. In the existing economy, a firm issues shares as a means of raising investment funds. This gives it an interest in establishing a reputation for being efficiently managed and for repaying investors with some combination of value appreciation and dividends. The better the firm's reputation, the more funds it can obtain from a given share issue.

In the coupon economy, on the other hand, a firm may have little incentive to attract shareholders, since they bring no equity and perhaps then nothing of value to the firm. The essay's assumption that the coupon price of a firm's share will be used as a barometer of its performance suggests a reason firms would want to attract shareholders. Unfortunately, reasoning based on the barometer function in conventional capital markets breaks down if the evaluators see that a firm has no real reason to want a high coupon share price. If managers have no incentive to attract shareholders, they may also have no incentive to earn profits, or at least no incentive to have residual earnings that they will pay out to shareholders as dividends. Not only would creditors be asking for higher returns as a condition of financing highly leveraged firms, but firm managers would have less reason to resist such demands, in the absence of an incentive to please shareholders. The distributive goal of the proposal would therefore be undermined, with efficiency features also compromised by the fact that if there is no reason for shares to have positive net present values, share prices would tend to zero and would therefore have no informational content. The informational value of a stock market, which the proposal claims to preserve, would in fact be lost to the economy in this case.

Fortunately for the proposal, a reason managers would want to please shareholders is in fact provided: namely, assigning control rights to them. If shareholders can dismiss or financially punish managers who fail to earn and distribute adequate profits, managers will have reason to seek such profits, and this will in turn give some value to share prices as an indicator of management performance. What this discussion brings out, however, is the linchpin nature of shareholder control rights. If shareholders are not expected to be very active monitors of management, *a position with which Roemer expresses considerable sympathy*, then there is also less reason to expect firms to earn and distribute profits.

The conflict of interest between creditors and profit claimants means that a falling share price need not lead lenders to revise their judgment of management negatively. On the other hand, if lending banks are not only monitors but also effective exercisers of control – something that agency theory says they would seek, given their added exposure to risk – they will oppose much risk taking, and would have no reason to want managers to distribute, as opposed to reinvesting, any profits actually earned. To protect the distributive function of the proposal, in that case, there would need to be regulations requiring that a certain fraction of profits be distributed. Joining regulatory safeguards against 'cash cow' firms that pay out *too much of* the value of the assets in the form of dividends, which Roemer mentions, such *minimum* distribution requirements would limit responses to the changing investment possibilities facing firms, a factor that could not be entirely without efficiency implications.

Government regulations requiring firms to distribute profits, combined with government monitoring of profit levels, is a possible alternative to shareholder control of firms. The government could appoint firms' managers and evaluate them on the basis of profit levels, with some proportion of profits being distributed according to statute. The problem with this is that it is the government that would be the main monitor of firms, and governmental incentives to monitor firm performance are at least as questionable as are those of small shareholders.[20]

In summary, the rearrangement of property rights in the coupon proposal is likely to have implications that are not fleshed out in the essay. The proposal entails shifting large firms to a 100 per cent leverage basis, making the shareholder a residual claimant but not a supplier of equity. Creditors have reason to shun such leverage and may have to be compensated with higher returns and/or control rights. The first possibility means a diminution in the size of profits, which are the sole object of redistribution in the proposal. Giving too much control right to creditors could actually drive expected dividends and thus share prices to zero, eliminating both the redistributive benefits of the proposal and its retention of an informationally useful share price feature. Socially desirable risk taking would also be reduced. If shareholders retain effective control, on the other hand, the leveraged feature of firms could induce what might be socially *excessive* risk taking. Regulatory interventions to both prohibit 'cash cows' and assure that some profits are paid out would prevent some problems but not without reducing maneuverability and thus also affecting efficiency.[21, 22]

Other Remarks

There are a few other positions staked out in 'A Future for Socialism' on which I wish to comment briefly.

Blueprints and appropriability

While Roemer accepts the critiques of old-style socialist theory by thinkers such as Hayek and Kornai, he continues to embrace a view of capitalism as routinized and institutionalized, a view that would be rejected by a wide range of economists who embrace the spirit of the Austrian message. Thus, on p. 5, he describes large capitalist firms as 'centrally planned organizations', on p. 6 he states that '[t]he wealth of society is . . . reproducible, according to blueprints which are quite well understood', and later on the same page he says that 'mechanisms that have evolved . . . under capitalism that enable owners to control management can be transported to a socialist framework'. Although I agree that the market operates 'within the essential context of non-market institutions'[23] and that firms are somewhat analogous to centrally planned units, I think there is a danger of forgetting the influence of market forces upon firms.[24] More importantly, I would have to reject a cookbook view that activities can be replicated on the basis of known blueprints,[25] and I would be concerned to check proposals of institutional borrowing in view of the general equilibrium (and Darwinian) consideration that a part that functions a certain way in one environment may perform differently in another. None of this is to argue against efforts at social invention. Rather, it is to suggest undertaking such efforts with an extra ounce of Hayekian concern for the inherent unpredictability and complexity of economic phenomena.

The soft budget constraint and soviet-type economies

On p. 39, Roemer uses Kornai's 'soft budget constraint' idea in his discussion of the planner–manager relationship under centrally planned socialism. Although I find Kornai's approach quite useful for understanding the position of firms in reforming socialist economies that are making increased use of markets, I find it less directly applicable to the classical Soviet economy or to counterparts such as China in its pre-reform days. Because an objective of their brand of socialism was to replace market forces with planning and the dictates of profitability with the dictates of politics, prices were to play no role in allocative decision making, but were to serve an accounting function only.[26] In such a setting, adhering to budget constraints has no implication for efficiency and a government would be foolish to shut down enterprises simply because they showed no accounting profits. In this environment, the absence of incentives to reduce costs, and the presence of incentives to hoard inputs, give rise to the same investment hunger, as in that described by Kornai, but alternative descriptions of the problem (e.g., that of Nove[27]) strike me as more apt.

Yugoslavia and labor-managed firms

I agree wholeheartedly with the essay's argument that the Yugoslav 'labor-managed economy' proves the inefficiency of neither labor-managed firms nor market socialism.[28] Political interventions and peculiar property rights were too important there, and some outcomes can be attributed to the (then) country's level of economic development. I would stop short of confidently asserting that the outcomes had nothing whatsoever to do with labor management, however. For example, high levels of unemployment may have largely reflected rural–urban migration incentives and West German recessions exported in the form of returning Yugoslav 'guest workers', but I am not sure that we can rule out a partial influence of the predicted tendency of profitable LMFs to restrict employment.

The essay makes a number of favorable remarks about the

possibility of democracy in firms, but considers it to be a somewhat risky undertaking, the achievement of which is of secondary importance. At one point, the author suggests that, since models of labor-managed market socialism accept that firms must raise capital from non-members, this might compromise workers' control to such an extent that managerial and labor-managed proposals for market socialism would cease to differ. I agree that external finance would be more or less necessary for any capital-intensive LMF, but I question the view that such an LMF would be indistinguishable from a firm run by managers answerable to shareholders. For example, if financiers provided only credit finance and had no formal say in management, as is true of the financiers of large firms in Roemer's coupon economy,[29] then LMFs would certainly have to show financial prudence to stay on the good sides of creditors, but that would not prevent them from acting on workers' preferences with respect (say) to tradeoffs between wages, levels of rank-and-file participation in decision making, working conditions, and so on.[30]

In my view, there are potentially serious economic problems with labor-management that need to be looked at soberly.[31] But if equality of status and of opportunities for self-actualization are to be given their full place in a proposal for social change, democracy in the workplace deserves more attention than it receives in this proposal.

China's township and village enterprises

Roemer uses the rapid growth of rural enterprises owned by township and village governments in China (TVEs) as an example of market-socialist property. While the performance of these enterprises has been remarkable and is an intriguing subject for economists interested in economic institutions and their performance, they are not socialist if equal opportunities to participate in the political sphere (i.e., democracy) is a requirement of socialism. Although the TVEs are sometimes described as collectively owned, their control[32] rests in the local political structure, which is a non-democratic structure controlled by the Communist Party.[33] Would that this were not so and we had an example here of such economically dynamic community-run enterprises on so massive a scale!

6 Conclusions

'[A]s man perceives the extent of dehumanization,' wrote Paulo Freire, 'he asks himself if humanization is a viable possibility. Within history, in concrete, objective contexts, both humanization and dehumanization are possibilities for man as an uncompleted being conscious of his incompleteness.'[34] *A Future for Socialism* offers one vision of a society that, while answering economic needs to the satisfaction of those reasonably well off under capitalism, outperforms that system with respect to justice and equality of opportunity.

Roemer argues that equalizing rights to profits is more feasible than equalizing income from labor. Competitive markets are the only known satisfactory mechanisms for coordinating economic activity and unequal labor incomes play a crucial allocative and incentive function in market economies, whereas the distribution of profits is fairly arbitrary. He demonstrates the latter proposition by considering a hypothetical economy in which rights to profits are obtained with coupons which are distributed equally to all citizens. Although profit incomes are distributed relatively equally in the imagined economy, and although the market system could presumably function under such an arrangement, it is clear neither that the plan would be without consequences for efficiency, nor that it would achieve the author's distributive goals.

Shareholders who obtain claims on profits by using coupons offer nothing of value to firms. Except by the exercise of direct control rights, they can provide no incentive to managers to maximize their dividends. Providers of debt finance, on the other hand, will be wary of the 100 per cent leveraged structure of the revamped enterprises, and would therefore demand higher interest payments as a condition for their loans. If shareholder control is effective, a prospect that the author in fact discounts, enterprises will be more prone to risk than conventional firms are now. Less financing will flow into the large firm sector, and to some (perhaps small) extent, into the economy as a whole. However, to the extent that creditors exercise control, distributed profits will tend toward zero. Having already forgone that portion of redistributable capital income that goes to interest payments, the proposal therefore risks losing the gains from redistribution of profits too, whether because of higher debt payments or an absence of managerial incentives to earn and pay out profits. An imposed pay-out rule could partially solve the last problem but would itself carry efficiency costs.

Even if its redistributive benefits are small, Roemer argues, the proposal should have other advantages, the principal example of which is a reduction in the level of negative externalities chosen by firms. When the wealthy disproportionately influence these choices, a more equal distribution of profits and shareholding leads to a lower chosen level of externalities because the distribution of profits then more closely resembles the distribution of the noxious effects of the externalities. However, this benefit depends on continued wealth inequality and disproportionate influence of the wealthy, since if the level of externalities were determined democratically with equal citizen influence, a more equal distribution of profits would actually *increase* the chosen level of externalities.

In short, the coupon proposal succeeds in suggesting the compatibility of markets with equality of profit claims, but the assumption that it will have no efficiency effects may be unwarranted, and its attempt significantly to affect the distribution of capital income without directly redistributing wealth may prove a failure. While there are indeed daunting political obstacles to the outright redistribution of wealth, it is difficult to believe that the proposal's institutional experiment would be any more politically saleable. If and when a robust majority favoring a more egalitarian version of capitalism comes into being, it seems more likely that it would choose redistribution of wealth and maintenance of existing financial arrangements than that it would select non-redistribution of wealth and radical revision of those arrangements. In view of the potential costs of wealth redistribution for future saving, the moral legitimacy that many citizens attach to the holding of wealth obtained by various means, and its own positive impact on opportunity and quality of life, redistributing earnings potential through progressive education policies also deserves consideration.

In any case, movement toward a more egalitarian society, if it is to be accomplished democratically, will depend on a significant shift in preferences and perceptions.[35] Putting egalitarian capitalism (or 'socialism') on the agenda for discussion may be a necessary step towards such a shift, and proposals of the type presented by Roemer should play their part here. If the better society that such proposals seek is to be justified in terms of such higher goods as 'self-actualization', however, more attention needs to be given not only to income claims, but to other determinants of the quality of life and social interactions, including both education and the character of the work that occupies a substantial part of people's lives and is an important determinant of their self-esteem and personal development.

Notes

1. The most direct and explicit justification of Marx's value theory to be found in *Capital* seems to be in Engels' Supplement to Volume 3, where he asserts that 'the peasant of the Middle Ages knew fairly accurately the labor-time required for the manufacture of the articles obtained by him in barter. . . . Not only was the labor-time spent on these products the only suitable measure for the quantitative determination of the values to be exchanged: no other was at all possible. Or is it believed that the peasant and the artisan were so stupid as to give up the product of ten hours' labor of one person for that of a single hour's labor of another?' (Engels in Karl Marx, *Capital* Volume 3, *The Process of Capitalist Production as a Whole*, New York: International Publishers 1967 [1894], pp. 897–8). Without an explanation of why 'no other [exchange ratio] was at all possible,' and with no mention of bargaining power, the appeal appears to be to some primitive notion of fairness.

2. One might counter that Marx and other socialists want equality not as a good in itself but as a means of achieving the 'self-actualization' of humankind. As a higher stage on the path to that self-actualization, socialism will naturally be marked by greater equality. But here, in my view, one runs into the problems of (a) proving that a more equal society will support higher levels of self-actualization, (b) explaining *non-normatively* why self-actualization is good – a contradiction in terms! – and (c) the scientific unsupportability of assuming that history has an inevitable trajectory towards human improvement (see the quotation from Freire, below). In my view, we must, as members of society, make normative commitments, and this means getting over the modern tendency to be embarrassed about values.

3. This seems to be the tone, for example, of the passage in *Capital* where Marx contrasts the coordinated division of labor in the factory with the unplanned coordination of the market, for example: 'It is very characteristic that the enthusiastic apologists of the factory system have nothing more damning to urge against a general organization of the labor of society, than that it would turn all society into one immense factory.' (Karl Marx, *Capital*, Volume 1, *A Critical Analysis of Capitalist Production*, New York: International Publishers 1967 [1867], p. 356.)

4. Karl Marx, 'Critique of the Gotha Program', in Robert Tucker, ed., *The Marx–Engels Reader*, 2nd edn, New York: Norton 1978, pp. 525–41, quoted at p. 529.

5. While Roemer counts the Lockean source of this right as a reason for socialists to reject it, Marx himself seems to play on the widespread acceptance of this notion of entitlement as a way of gaining workers' sympathies with his indictment of capitalism. See also Gunnar Myrdal, *The Political Element in the Development of Economic Theory*; translated from the German by Paul Streeten (Cambridge: Harvard University Press 1954), which argues that Locke was the source of the labor theory in value in both Marx and Ricardo.

6. This issue is discussed at length in Louis Putterman, 'Why have the Rabble not Redistributed the Wealth? On the Stability of Democracy and Unequal Property,' paper presented at the International Economic Association Conference on Property Relations, Incentives and Welfare, Barcelona, June 1994.

7. Marx, 'Critique', p. 529.

8. In deriving an estimate for the value of the coupon dividend in the United States, in his Appendix, Roemer assumes that 'the present equity of firms in the corporate sector would be transformed into debt' (John E. Roemer, *A Future for Socialism*, Cambridge, MA: Harvard University Press 1994, p. 134). Of course, the right to a stream of profits could also be viewed as an asset, in which case moving to the coupon economy does entail redistribution of wealth as long as expected profit steams are not zero.

9. Lawrence Mishel and David Frankel, *The State of Working America*, Armonk, NY: Sharpe 1991, Table 3.3. No figure is given for 1983 in this source, but in view of

the stability of the data for adjacent years, the correct number was presumably close
to the $352 given for 1982.

10.   A figure on total net personal wealth is taken from James Smith, 'Recent Trends
in the Distribution of Wealth in the U.S.: Data, Research Problems, and Prospects', in
E. Wolff, ed., *International Comparisons of the Distribution of Household Wealth*,
Oxford: Clarendon Press 1987, pp. 72–89, at p. 79. This is combined with 1983 house-
hold wealth distribution data from Edward Wolff, 'Estimates of Household Wealth
Inequality in the U.S., 1962–1983', C.V. Starr Center for Applied Economics Research
Report #86–27, 1986, and with population data from US Bureau of the Census,
Current Population Reports. Note that wealth as defined here includes the value of
private but not that of public pension funds.

11.   Considering the influence that international financial institutions exert on post-
socialist policy making, the term 'remote' is probably more realistic than is 'small'.

12.   The highest return criterion can of course be questioned on social grounds
by considering income distribution, externalities, etc. But these objections to allocation
of resources by the market arise for labor as well, and are presumably to be met
by provisions for redistributing income, regulating externalities, setting appropriate
tax and subsidy rates, and so on, before we agree to a market system in the first
place.

13.   Putterman, 'Rabble'.

14.   See note 8, above.

15.   In Louis Putterman, *Division of Labor and Welfare: An Introduction to
Economic Systems*, Oxford: Oxford University Press 1990, I write about criteria for
judging economic institutions and point out the fallacy of supposing that by focussing
on efficiency alone, one can avoid dealing with normative issues.

16.   The special interest of an industry's workers in its right to continue polluting
activities would also merit attention in a more complete discussion of the problem.

17.   See, for example, Michael Jensen and William Meckling, 'Theory of the Firm:
Managerial Behavior, Agency Costs, and Ownership Structure', *Journal of Financial
Economics* 3 (1976), pp. 305–60. For other references and a review of related issues,
see Louis Putterman, 'Ownership and the Nature of the Firm', *Journal of Comparative
Economics* 17 (1993), pp. 243–63.

18.   The loss is not necessarily zero since, even if a coupon cannot be traded for
money, it has some opportunity cost, provided that it can purchase shares promising
income streams with positive net present values. If a coupon is invested in a company
that goes out of business with nothing to pay out to shareholders, it is (presumably)
forever forfeited by its original owner.

19.   Firms would also tend to compete with each other to obtain credit on better
terms by acquiring reputations for prudent management, i.e., less risk taking. In
equilibrium, it is reasonable to expect all three kinds of adjustments: less risk taking
by firms than if creditors did not respond to risk taking by demanding higher rates
of return, higher rates of return to creditors than if firms were less than 100 per cent
leveraged, and less credit flowing into the large firm sector and perhaps the economy
as a whole. After all such adjustments are factored in, however, the equilibrium
could nonetheless be expected to entail greater risk taking and higher interest rates than
in lower-leveraged firms controlled by equity-providing shareholders. The possible
reduction in capital formation could also be worrisome in the long run.

20.   See Louis Putterman, 'Exit, Voice, and Portfolio Choice: Agency and Public
Ownership', *Economics and Politics* 5 (1993), pp. 205–18.

21.   Simon's essay (this volume, chapter 2) mentions another efficiency problem of
the proposal which is related to the 'cash cow' issue, namely that firms might attempt
to run down assets to pay out dividends at different rates so as to appeal to investors
of differing ages. This danger could conceivably be addressed by requiring that individuals use their coupons to purchase firm shares only indirectly, by buying shares in
mutual funds, and that mutual funds be able to demonstrate the neutrality of their
holdings, in terms of Simon's concern, by having an age distribution of investors that

is within a narrow range of the age distribution of coupons in the general population. In order to meet the age distribution requirement, mutual fund managers would have to avoid a reputation for investing in firms with age-biased payout strategies, or else hold balanced portfolios of age-biased firms, eliminating firms' incentives to follow biased policies. Effective deterrence of *any and all* 'cash cow'-like behavior by way of regulation could render such restrictions unnecessary, but would conceivably be more difficult to enforce.

22. A possible way of remedying the problems discussed in this section is to revise the coupon proposal so that when a citizen uses her coupon to purchase stock in a firm, the government gives the firm a corresponding share of some kind of public capital fund. In this case, coupons would bring real equity to firms, which would no longer be entirely debt-financed. While managing a public capital fund in this way would avoid the fund allocation problems discussed in Putterman 'Exit, Voice and Portfolio Choice', determining the level and source of public funding could pose considerable political problems, possibly rendering the likelihood of public acceptance of the overall proposal even more remote. Whether the funded-coupon approach is on balance superior to the unfunded approach, perhaps amended to assure strong shareholder control rights, is thus difficult to decide.

23. Roemer, p. 3.

24. See my discussion of the debate over the autonomy of the firm from the market in 'The Economic Nature of the Firm: Overview', in Louis Putterman, ed., *The Economic Nature of the Firm: A Reader*, New York: Cambridge University Press 1986, pp. 1–29.

25. On the impossibility of replicating functioning organizations on the basis of blueprints, see Richard Nelson and Sidney Winter, *An Evolutionary Theory of Economic Change*, Cambridge, MA: Belknap Press 1982.

26. See, especially, Charles Bettelheim, *Economic Calculation and Forms of Property*, New York: Monthly Review Press 1975, who argues that to allow prices to influence resource allocation is to let choices over the use of scarce resources be tainted by the influence of an unequal distribution of income. He presents the socialist project as a matter of elevating political over economic choice, where the former means precisely choice based on resources and needs unmediated by price signals.

27. Alec Nove, 'The Problem of Success Indicators', *Economica* 97 (1958), pp. 1–13.

28. See John Bonin and Louis Putterman, *Economics of Cooperation and the Labor-Managed Economy* (Fundamentals of Pure and Applied Economics, volume 14), London: Harwood 1987, pp. 103–19. See also Janez Prasnikar and Jan Svejnar, 'Workers' Participation in Management vs. Social Ownership and Government Policies: Yugoslav Lessons for Transforming Socialist Economies', *Comparative Economic Studies* 33 (1991), pp. 27–46.

29. I am not inclined to think that such *fully leveraged* LMFs would be any less prone to difficulties than would the *fully leveraged* coupon firms in Roemer's model (see Putterman 'Ownership and the Nature of the Firm'), but I assume this form for the sake of symmetry and think a similar argument holds with some worker and even nonworker provision of equity.

30. Of course, with perfectly competitive labor and product markets, a formal worker voice may appear unnecessary, since workers' preferences are perfectly communicated through the labor market. Not only are real labor markets never perfectly competitive, but arguments can be made for worker voice even when they are. Thus, Jacques Dreze, 'Some Theory of Labor Management and Participation', *Econometrica* 44 (1976), pp. 1125–40, argues on mathematical and hedonic modeling grounds that worker preferences may not be identifiable from reservation wages if the number of job characteristics exceeds the number of jobs; and Richard Freeman, 'Individual Mobility and Union Voice in the Labor Market', *American Economic Review (Papers and Proceedings)* 66 (1976), pp. 361–68, argues that moving from an exit to a voice communication mechanism in the workplace changes the decisive opinion from that of the marginal to that of the median worker.

31.   See Louis Putterman, 'After the Employment Relation: Problems on the Road to Enterprise Democracy', in S. Bowles, H. Gintis and B. Gustafsson, eds, *Markets and Democracy: Participation, Accountability and Efficiency*, Cambridge: Cambridge University Press 1993, pp. 129–47.

32.   I refer here to those owned by township and village governments. There also exist some privately owned TVEs.

33.   Chun Chang and Yijiang Wang, 'The Nature of the Township Enterprise', unpublished, Carlson School of Management, University of Minnesota 1994.

34.   Paulo Freire, *Pedagogy of the Oppressed*, New York: Seabury Press 1970, p. 27. (and also the epigraph of my first book).

35.   Putterman, 'Rabble'.

9

Finance and Market Socialism

Fred Block

John Roemer's vision of coupon socialism represents a significant contribution to the reconstruction of socialist theory. By separating the idea of socialism from the historic goal of eliminating private property, Roemer has opened a broad terrain for debates about alternatives to existing forms of capitalism.

Roemer's framework is, however, vulnerable to two seemingly divergent types of criticisms. The first is that his vision of socialism does not do enough to expand the terrain of democratic politics. Roemer has repeatedly argued that increasing employee control of the workplace is not a necessary element of the socialist vision.[1] In his view, an egalitarian distribution of profits is far more important than democractic control of the workplace. The second criticism is that Roemer's vision of the operation of the financial system in coupon socialism relies too much on Kornai's famous critique of the destructive consequences of 'soft budget constraints' in state socialist societies. As a consequence, Roemer fails to confront some of the other major design issues in constructing a socialist financial system.

This essay begins with this second line of argument. It will explore the different ways that financial systems can fail. The purpose of this is to suggest several different design principles that need to be considered in thinking through the financial structure of market socialism. But several of these design principles lead directly back to the issue of employee power at the workplace. In short, I intend to show that a more systematic focus on the design of financial institutions in market socialism leads to proposals that place greater emphasis on the exercise of power by employees at the workplace.

Problems of Financial Intermediation

Any vision of market socialism begins with the idea that individual business enterprises will operate in the context of competitive product markets, labor markets and capital markets. Firms that are more efficient, and hence more profitable, should be in an advantaged position relative to other firms in going to the capital markets and receiving additional finance. This requires some institutional mechanisms of financial intermediation by which the savings of individuals and firms are funneled to profitable firms and other productive uses. In Roemer's proposal, firms raise capital either by selling shares to mutual funds or by borrowing from banks. But other market socialist proposals suggest other financing mechanisms and a wider or narrower range of different financial intermediaries.

To gain leverage on these design questions, it is critical to identify the financial dangers that one wants to avoid.[2] The first is the problem of soft budget constraints. The essence of Kornai's argument is that financial intermediaries in state socialist societies are unable to cut off flows of credit to inefficient firms because of the political costs of business failures.[3] Since the large state-owned enterprises employed thousands of people and often provided transfer payments to pensioners as well, their failure would have disastrous political consequences. Moreover, attempts by the financial institutions to monitor these enterprises to weed out ineffective managers were also bound to fail because of the difficulty of accumulating meaningful data about firm performance. One firm might appear to be efficient only because it produces a scarce commodity that has been assigned a generous price by the planners, while a firm that appears to be losing money might actually be managed quite effectively.

Kornai's argument produced two conclusions. First, firms must be subject to hard budget constraints, so that badly run firms will be allowed to fail; but, since bankruptcy should only be a last resort, it also follows that financial intermediaries should have the opportunity to monitor the performance of firms in which they invest resources. Such monitoring can discourage firms from pursuing undesirable strategies or lead to the replacement of ineffective managers. For such monitoring to be effective, prices have to be determined on markets and firms must make information available in accordance with accepted accounting practices.

However, if it is desirable that firms not face soft budget constraints, it is also a problem if the budget constraints become too hard. It is possible, for example, for financial intermediaries to impose harsh conditions on borrowers. The simplest case is when the interest rates on loans are pushed to levels where financial intermediaries are able to claim a substantial share of the borrowing firms' profit streams. These financial intermediaries are able to extract rents because potential borrowers have nowhere else to go. Another danger is that financial intermediaries engage in openly predatory activity; forcing firms to accept direction and control from those financial institutions. This has been emphasized in the Marxist literature on the domination of industry by 'finance capital'.[4]

Another critical aspect of brittle budget constraints is the withholding of credit from potentially creditworthy borrowers. Even mainstream economists now acknowledge that the financial markets are not balanced through the interest-rate mechanism.[5] On the contrary, credit is always rationed by financial intermediaries by withholding credit from borrowers who are perceived to not be credit-worthy. Since lenders tend to share the same criteria, this 'strategic non-lending' has been a major mechanism through which class power has been exercised. For example, the difficulty that worker coopera-tives face in borrowing capital has been important in discouraging their development.[6]

In theory, competition among financial intermediaries should always eliminate the dangers of brittle budget constraints. However, once problems of information in financial markets are recognized, it becomes clear why real financial markets often diverge from the neoclassical ideal. First, the ability of financial intermediaries to raise money depends critically on issues of trust and confidence. Neither households nor firms are likely to make their funds available to intermediaries who seem unlikely to make good on their promises. This creates a substantial 'first mover advantage' where the initial two or three financial intermediaries to establish themselves in a particular market are able to gain a major advantage in size and reputation. Moreover, since governmental regulations often play a central role in establishing and maintaining the soundness of financial intermedi-aries, it is quite common for the government's rules to privilege a few dominant institutions and to create obstacles to latecomers.

The second informational problem is the difficulty that financial intermediaries have in gaining accurate knowledge about potential borrowers. Even when borrowing firms operate within competitive markets and use common accounting standards, it is not easy to figure out the relative creditworthiness of firms. Financial intermediaries tend to respond to this difficulty by economizing on the expensive business of collecting and evaluating information and they rely instead on signals and conventions to evaluate creditworthiness. If all the relevant institutions use the same signals and conventions, then even a financial marketplace with a high level of competition could produce brittle budget constraints.

A third problem is that financial intermediaries operating within competitive markets face the continuous temptation to invest in riskier types of investments because they promise higher rates of return. In recent years, there have been repeated episodes in which financial intermediaries have poured huge sums of money into activities that seemed relatively safe at the time, but which ultimately proved to be quite risky. Such episodes in the US include excessive lending to Third World countries in the 1970s, excessive lending for commercial real estate projects by Savings & Loans in the 1980s, excessive purchases of 'junk bonds' to finance leveraged buyouts in the 1980s by a range of different intermediaries and, most recently, costly speculation in financial derivatives by mutual funds, banks and hedge funds.

Many of these episodes have rested on asset price 'bubbles' where continuing appreciations in the value of a particular asset has created the illusion that prices will continue to rise indefinitely. Real estate and stock prices in Japan and rents on shopping malls and commercial office space in the US followed this pattern. Financial institutions lent billions on the expectation that the bubble would continue, but when the inevitable decline in prices came, many of the loans could not be repaid.

There is a slightly different pattern when new categories of borrowers are willing and able to borrow at a premium over the standard interest rate. In the early period when those new borrowers are able to continuously increase their borrowing, they have no difficulty in maintaining interest payments. But over time, as the magnitude of the debt increases without corresponding increases in the debtor's productive assets, the borrowers find it increasingly difficult to service the debt. When new lending stops, the financial weakness of the borrowers becomes apparent, and large quantities of debt go into default. This was the pattern of Third World and Eastern European borrowing during the 1970s and some of the 'junk bond' borrowing to finance corporate restructuring in the 1980s.

There are two dangers when financial intermediaries become too involved with these more speculative types of investment. The first is that the financial intermediaries will waste large amounts of capital and will suffer huge losses that will put their very survival at risk. This, in turn, raises the troubling problem of 'soft budget constraints' for financial institutions. In the US, the system of Federal insurance of deposits at banks and savings and loans has created something very close to a soft budget constraint. Bankers in pursuit of higher profits can pursue riskier investments without fear because they know that the government will have to bail them out to protect the depositors. But even short of such catastrophes, there is a second danger: financial intermediaries will channel funds to less productive uses because they produce higher rates of return. Hence, when faced with the choice between lending a hundred million dollars to a hedge fund or lending the same amount to finance expansion at a hundred different medium-size firms, the former is the path of least resistance because it involves substantially lower transaction costs.

Above and beyond these other problems, financial intermediaries can simply do a bad job in allocating capital. Poor allocation encompasses several different types of problems:

A. Divergence between private and social rates of return

There are many circumstances where the positive or negative externalities of particular types of investment can create a significant divergence between the returns to investors and the returns to the society as a whole. A perfectly efficient capital market could easily finance vast investment in nuclear power plants, while withholding financing from a range of different solar technologies.

B. The time horizon problem

The specific organization of financial intermediation can influence the time horizon on which borrowers attempt to maximize returns. Much has been written about how the organization of finance in Japan encourages firms to develop long-term time horizons, while US firms are much more oriented to the short term.[7] The obvious advantage of the long term is that it encourages investments in intangibles such as research and development and human capital that have the potential of producing substantial future returns.

C. Ineffective monitoring of borrowers

As noted earlier, financial intermediaries face continuing pressures to economize on the collection of information about borrowers. Yet excessive economizing on information can lead to poor performance in differentiating between stronger and weaker borrowers.

For reasons noted earlier, there is no guarantee that this problem will be solved by competition among financial intermediaries. It is not difficult to imagine a circumstance in which the limited information gathered by creditors combined with certain shared preconceptions can lead to the systematic misallocation of capital.

Minimizing the Problems

This catalog of dangers suggests several design principles for organizing financial intermediation under market socialism. The first is the principle of political autonomy that is emphasized in Roemer's coupon socialism proposal. Each financial intermediary needs to be able to stand on its own feet within the financial marketplace. The intermediaries would be able to borrow funds from the central bank, but these borrowing rights would be contingent on effective performance. Insolvent financial intermediaries would be closed down by government regulators and their assets would be redistributed to their more successful competitors. By enforcing quite stringent definitions of insolvency, regulators would be able to discourage the managers of these intermediaries from believing that they could risk being careless about the quality of their loan portfolios. However, for regulatory threats to be effective, it is critical that any particular financial intermediary not be allowed to exceed a certain maximum size. In this way, one can avoid the 'too big to fail' problem where government regulators feel compelled to bail out an institution whose failure would have devastating macroeconomic consequences. The logical path would be to establish a normal procedure by which the most successful intermediaries would periodically divide themselves into two successor organizations.[8] This process of financial mitosis could create institutions with different kinds of specialties: a bank might, for example, divide between its large business accounts and its small business accounts. Moreover, this process occurring on an ongoing basis would assure that high levels of competition would continue among financial intermediaries.

A second design principle is the idea that financial markets should be segmented. In neoclassical theory, it is axiomatic that there should be the fewest possible obstacles in the way of moving capital to the activity with the highest rate of return. The policy implication of this axiom is that it is desirable to create the highest level of integration of capital markets within and between countries; but there are at least three different problems with this way of thinking. First, divergences between returns to investors and returns to society mean that greater financial integration makes it less likely that some socially valuable investments will be financed. Second, the greater the degree of integration of financial markets, the more funds are available to flow into certain types of speculative investments. This exacerbates the danger of speculative bubbles. Third, financial integration has the consequence of undermining the capacity of individual financial institutions to gather and analyze information about prospective borrowers. The simple logic of portfolio diversification means that a financial institution with opportunities to invest in a broad range of foreign or domestic assets will shift resources from the processing and assessment of loans to the analysis of these broader opportunities. In short, abstract financial information and analysis will tend to displace concrete knowledge about particular economic sectors or regions.

These problems can be significantly reduced by segmentation of the financial market, so that different financial intermediaries are constrained in terms of both the types of assets and the shares of different assets that they are allowed to hold. This means returning to a regime comparable to that in which Savings & Loans were largely restricted to mortgage financing, while commercial banks concentrated on business loans. It is critical to the idea of segmentation that there be vigorous competition among financial intermediaries in each segment, but competition across segments would be restricted.

For this reason, segmentation fits with the logic of the government using interest rate policies as a planning tool. In Roemer's model, the government would address the divergence between investor returns and social returns by establishing different interest rates for different activities. Hence, the costs of capital for business loans would be different from the cost of capital for mortgage loans. Furthermore, the government would manipulate these interest rates to keep parts of the economy from growing either too quickly or too slowly. With integrated financial markets, such policies are unlikely to be successful: there are too many ways for financial intermediaries to shift resources from one activity to another. With segmented markets, however, the regulatory tasks would be far more manageable.

Segmentation also provides a partial solution to the deposit insurance problem. Those segments where there is an explicit or implicit governmental guarantee of household savings would be subject to far more stringent rules on the riskiness of assets than those segments where such a guarantee was absent.

Moreover, the combination of segmentation with the government establishing different interest rates for different segments would also solve the strategic nonlending problem. One segment of the financial marketplace could be dedicated to financing non-traditional types of investment, such as employee cooperatives or local governments that wanted to launch productive enterprises. If institutions in this segment flourished, there would be expanding employment opportunities in nonhierarchical firms.[9]

The third design principle is that each financial intermediary should have strong incentives to invest in the development of specialized and concrete types of expertise. For example, an institution that is dedicated to funding public infrastructure projects needs to be able to identify poorly designed projects or incompetent environmental impact reports. Financial intermediaries who specialize in providing capital to high technology firms need to develop substantial technological expertise as well as the capacity to help technologically sophisticated managements solve their business problems.

The theoretical insight behind this principle is a criticism of neo-classical economics for placing far too much emphasis on allocational efficiency: on directing capital to activities with the highest rate of return. This has led to a systematic neglect of x-efficiency: the improvement in the output when specific quantities of capital and labor are brought together.[10] As Leibenstein emphasized, the gains from improving x-efficiency far outweigh those that can be expected from improvements in allocational efficiency. The primary task of financial intermediaries under market socialism would be to contribute to higher rates of x-efficiency by providing successful firms with more resources and by exerting pressure on less successful firms to improve their practices. But both of these require that financial intermediaries develop specialized expertise.

Segmentation is an important first step to encourage intermediaries to develop these specialized forms of expertise but, if the costs of obtaining solid information on potential borrowers remain high, intermediaries will continue to have incentives to economize on information gathering costs. Intermediaries would continue to rely on potentially flawed signals and conventions. In a segmented financial marketplace, this is highly undesirable because borrowers would have a smaller range of potential lenders. Another undesirable consequence of high information costs would be a continued emphasis on abstract financial expertise over concrete specialized knowledge.

If the cost of information gathering about potential borrowers could be reduced, financial intermediaries would be more likely to develop specialized expertise and to engage in effective ongoing monitoring of borrowers. Reducing information gathering costs can be accomplished by making borrowing firms more transparent, so that an outside observer could make a more rapid and more accurate determination of whether the enterprise, or a specific project, is well managed and well conceived. It is in this context that the idea of workplace democratization becomes relevant.

Under most circumstances, a firm's employees are able to provide useful information about the effectiveness of a firm's management and the soundness of particular projects. A knowledgeable interviewer can gain extremely important insights by talking to a firm's employees, but it is not practical for financial institutions to gain information by meeting employees in bars after work. This is expensive, and management also has legitimate concerns about industrial espionage and the passing of proprietary information.

Moreover, the quality of employee evaluations of a firm and particular projects will improve in direct proportion to the amount of information that employees are provided by management. The more that employees are able to place their understandings of day-to-day events on the shop floor in the broader context of the firm's strategy and economic performance, the more reliable will be their assessments of management's claims.

Hence, there are significant advantages for outside financial intermediaries if a firm has a democratic process through which elected employee representatives meet regularly with management and are provided access to data on the firm's performance. If representatives of the financial intermediaries were to meet on a regular basis with these employees, they would have an excellent means to verify or call into question management's definition of the situation.[11]

This is, of course, a minimalist design for workplace democracy. Giving employee representatives access to financial information and meeting with them regularly does not give them any formal power over the firm's decisions. However, for the representation election process to be meaningful, employee rights to free speech would have to be significantly expanded, and employees would have to be protected from retribution for disagreeing with management. This alone would expand the democratic space within firms. It seems plausible that these small steps would create an environment in which management would feel the need to gain employee consent for many of its initiatives. If employees wanted to press management on a particular issue, this limited democratization would significantly increase their leverage. However, more dramatic steps to workplace democratization such as electing employee representatives to the board of directors might work even better to make the firm transparent to financial monitors.

It also follows that if financial intermediaries are to be information-intensive organizations, they need a relatively flat organizational structure in which employees with specialized expertise have considerable influence over the firm's strategic direction. These employees need also to have a significant stake in the firm's success. This could be accomplished by placing ownership rights over these firms in a diversified board of directors. For example, both shareholders and employees could choose 35 per cent of the board members, and the remaining 30 per cent of the board would be 'public' representatives. One job of these public representatives would be to curb any tendency by these financial institutions to emphasize the short term over the long term or to engage in predatory activities.

Two other mechanisms could handle the problem of excessive accumulation of power and resources in the most successful financial intermediaries. First, the process of financial mitosis would keep any particular institution from becoming too big. Second, relatively high taxes on firm profits and employee compensation would allow the society as a whole to benefit from the successes of the most effective financial intermediaries.

Conclusion

It is to Roemer's credit that his work forces socialists to confront critical questions about the design of financial institutions under socialism. As Kornai's work has shown, the long neglect of these issues by socialist intellectuals has had dire consequences. Moreover, clarifying our theories about how financial institutions should work under socialism can also sharpen our critique of capitalism and even suggest promising paths for structural reform. But the main argument of this paper is that creating the most effective financial structures is inextricably linked to expanding opportunities for employees to exercise power and influence at the workplace. In a complex socialist economy, one of the central challenges is to improve the flows of information and raise the quality of decision making at the enterprise level. This requires new types of financial intermediaries and greater workplace democracy.

Notes

1. John E. Roemer, 'Visions of Capitalism and Socialism', *Socialist Review* 89:3 (1989), pp. 93–100, and *A Future for Socialism*, Cambridge, MA: Harvard University Press 1994.

2.   There is not a systematic literature on the ways that financial systems can fail. However, an excellent overview of weaknesses in the US financial system is provided by Gary Dymski, Gerald Epstein and Robert Pollin, eds, *Transforming the US Financial System: Equity and Efficiency for the 21st Century*, Armonk, NY: Sharpe 1993.

3.   Janos Kornai, 'The Soft Budget Constraint', *Kyklos*. 39 (1986), pp. 3–30, and *The Road to a Free Economy*, New York: Norton 1990.

4.   V.I. Lenin, *Imperialism: The Highest Stage of Capitalism*, New York: International Publishers, 1939. Rudolf Hilferding, *Finance Capital: A Study of the Latest Phase of Capitalist Development*, London: Routledge & Kegan Paul 1981.

5.   Joseph Stiglitz and Andrew Weiss, 'Credit Rationing in Markets with Imperfect Information', *American Economic Review* 71 (June 1981), pp. 393–410.

6.   Fred Block, 'Capitalism without Class Power.' *Politics & Society* 20:3 (September 1992), pp. 277–303.

7.   See Michael Porter, *Capital Choices: Changing the Way America Invests in Industry*, Washington DC: Council on Competitiveness 1992 and John Zysman, *Governments, Markets, and Growth: Financial Systems and the Politics of Industrial Change*, Ithaca: Cornell University Press 1983.

8.   It might be advisable to use the same procedure for all enterprises, as a means to avoid firms that are also 'too big to fail'. Hamilton and Biggart's description of enterprise organization in Taiwan seems to follow this model where firms continually spin off new enterprises rather than continuing to grow larger. See Gary Hamilton and Nicole Biggart, 'Market, Culture, and Authority: A Comparative Analysis of Management and Organization in the Far East.' *American Journal of Sociology* 94 Supplement (1988), pp. 552–94.

9.   Once they reached a certain size, employee cooperatives should also be able to sell shares to the mutual funds.

10.   Harvey Leibenstein, *Beyond Economic Man: A New Foundation for Microeconomics*, Cambridge, MA: Harvard University Press 1976.

11.   This type of arrangement could also be responsive to management's concerns about compromising company secrets. Management would have the opportunity to explain to employee representatives what information needed to be kept in confidence and what could be shared with other employees and financial intermediaries.

10

Would Roemer's Socialism Equalize Income from Surplus?

Frank Thompson

There are no doubt innumerable abstract entities, each of which, if presented to us, we could reasonably be persuaded to regard as a model of socialism. In the history of socialist thought only models in a minuscule subset of this realm have received attention and thus there is an almost limitless unexplored territory open for us to investigate. John Roemer has presented us with a model on the frontier of this territory, thereby creatively expanding our conception of what might count as a socialist and of how such a society might work.

I would like to attempt to focus some attention on what appears to be one particularly worrisome feature of the particular model of market socialism John Roemer is offering[1] for those of us who, like myself, find themselves in broad concurrence with his characterization of what socialists should strive for.

Loosely stated, the problem is this: to the degree that the equity of firms in this model is offset by debt, a corresponding portion of gross profits will be dedicated to debt service; that is, some profits will take the form of payments of interest. And to the degree that loanable funds are provided, via banks as intermediaries, by individuals, profits paid out as interest will take the form of income to individuals; but to the degree to which individuals' banked savings are unequally distributed, this flow of profits to payment of interest will also be unequally distributed to individuals.

Variations in each of these 'degrees' affects the degree of inequality in the distribution of profit income. If first, for example, enterprises are entirely debt financed, profits remaining to be distributed in an egalitarian manner as dividends to holders of equity shares (directly in firms or indirectly through equity mutual funds – derived from equally valued equity portfolios distributed to new adults), will only amount to, in the aggregate, the product of the difference between the average rate of gross profit and the interest rate times the aggregate value of firms. It is reasonable conventional economic thinking to believe that the nearer conditions of perfect competition are approached, the nearer this difference shrinks toward zero with all profits distributed as interest.

Second, if all funds loaned to firms originate from individual savings and banks serve only an intermediary role, then interest payments by firms from gross profits will terminate as income to individuals. Thus, it might be argued, with 100 per cent loan financing, perfect competition, and completely private savings, all profits will be distributed to individuals in proportion to the size of their savings accounts. (Of course matters are more complicated if, for example, there are spreads between interest rates paid by borrowers and received by lenders, enabling banks to make profits net of their interest payments to individual lenders, profits which perhaps might not be entirely distributed as interest payments to individual savers.)

Third, if the income elasticity of savings is increasing in income, savings will be more than proportionally concentrated toward the top of the income distribution. As a result interest payments will also be concentrated at the top and, thus, interest payments will further exacerbate inequality in the distribution of income.

One way to curtail these implications would be severely to curtail loan financing of production, an unattractive proposal for many reasons. Expansion of existing firms, not to speak of creation of new enterprises (especially those more capital intensive) would plausibly be strangled. Another way to avoid these implications would rely on alternative sources of loan capital for production. David Schweickart has been forcefully arguing for some time[2] for a version of market socialism in which firms operate with rented or borrowed *public* capital while paying charges on such capital, thus providing this supply of loanable funds. In Schweickart's conception, production by market socialism enterprises is in aggregate self-financed. Here individual savings from income play no role in providing capital; private saving is completely delinked from enterprise investment. Alternatively, although Schweickart is unsympathetic to this approach, taxes other than capital usage charges could be sources of loanable funds, among them income or consumption taxes on individuals. (Schweickart's proposal, based on labor-managed firms, arguably has its own problems of suboptimal investment demand from labor-managed firms and endogeneity in the capital rental rate or charge, which is de facto the rate of interest on investment.)

Let us consider further the distributional consequences of allocating the interest payments from enterprise profits in proportion to individual holdings of savings. There is certainly no reason to anticipate an egalitarian distribution of such holdings. (*Ceteris paribus* this inequality in savings might even be heightened by a prohibition on converting savings into equity holdings.) Even if coupon portfolios representing individual equity holdings (and entitling the holder to dividends from profits in excess of interest charges) are more or less equally distributed, financial holdings, that is savings, certainly will not be under remotely plausible assumptions. For labor incomes will presumably be unequally distributed, presumably more or less proportional to the economic value of labor supplied, and some fraction of labor income will be saved, thus creating differential claims on enterprise profits distributed as interest on debt.

If, in addition, not only variable abilities and proclivities to earn labor income are heritable – the offspring of those with higher (lower) labor incomes tend to have higher (lower) labor incomes – but also ownership of stocks of financial savings is heritable, there would seem to be no reason to expect this market socialist economy to engender a much more egalitarian distribution of income than a capitalist economy.

Disposing of this last point, let us take it as granted for this analysis that confiscatory death taxes (above some low if not zero deductible) are in place. There is of course presumably a macro-economic price to be paid for this policy; the average propensity to save would be reduced as almost everyone sought to arrange their lifecycle saving profile to end up with nothing (at least above the deductible) in the bank. Nor, taxation history warns, are estate and gift levies bureaucratically or politically inexpensively enforced.

Even if this prohibition on significant intergenerational financial transfers can be satisfactorily instituted (and I do not believe this is unachievable), the pattern of income distribution may still be open to profound egalitarian objections. Some such objections could be lodged even if the result were that distribution of interest income were in direct proportion to labor income. Then the portion of gross profits (society's surplus) paid out in interest would no longer be distributed in virtue of adult citizenship but rather, at least in part, in virtue of individual characteristics whose unequal distribution is surely morally arbitrary. Further, there is substantial reason to expect the distribution of interest income under such circumstances to be, even more objectionably, *more* than proportional to labor income.

As introspection about plausible preferences may suggest, and as relevant statistics arguably confirm, not only is individual saving increasing in income, it is increasing at an increasing rate.[3] That is, typically, individual savings increase faster than income. (Of course such statistics are themselves at best merely suggestive for this inquiry since they report on an economic system in which individual assets are freely shiftable between equity and debt and in which inheritance is relatively unimpeded.)

Insofar as this would remain true under market socialism the result is of course that profits which take the form of interest payments to individuals will not be distributed merely in proportion to labor income (and thus, arguably, in proportion to economic contribution), but rather such payments would even more disproportionally flow to those already *ceteris paribus* most advantaged. Under these circumstances, inequality of income due to inequality of labor income might not be mitigated by socialism but rather sharpened.

The effect on the total distribution of profit income – dividends via coupons and interest on savings – on income inequality would depend of course not only on the income elasticity of saving but also on how much gross profits exceeded debt service. But whether, given these details, the disposition of the surplus might worsen income inequality does seem to be a quite startling question to have to raise about a 'blueprint' for socialism. This question can be formulated more precisely with the use of some formalism, though a familiar price in lack of realism is paid for the use of a stylized model, as the Appendix shows.

Appendix

Suppose each individual i is conceived as having preferences over expenditure in two lifecycle periods, a and b, with preferences represented by a utility function u_i (a_i, b_i). In the first period an individual works and receives labor income, w_i, as well as an (equity) dividend payment, d_i. The dividend d_i is the same for everyone, $d_i = d$, but w_i varies in proportion to the value of labor supplied. In the second period an individual does not work, and second-period expenditures exhaust another dividend payment, d, plus accumulated savings $(d + w_i - a_i)(1 + r)$, where r is the rate of interest paid on individual savings. Thus each individual is to choose values of a_i and b_i to maximize u_i (a_i, b_i) subject to the budget constraint $b_i = d + (d + w_i - a_i)(1 + r)$. Or, substituting for b_i in the utility function, an individual can be seen as choosing a value of a_i to maximize u_i $(a_i, d + (d + w_i - a_i)(1 + r))$. The solution is then some a_i^* (w_i, d, r) such that $u_{ia}/u_{ib} = 1 + r$, i.e., a_i^* (w_i, d, r) such that the marginal rates of substitution and transformation of expenditure between the two periods are equal. (Optimal b_i^* is then simply $d + (d + w_i - a_i^*(w_i, d, r))(1 + r)$.) This is of course an instance of the simplest microeconomic theory of intertemporal choice.[4]

The concern here is the distributional aspects of this model. Individuals may receive income from three sources, dividends from equity, $2d$, wages from labor, w_i, and interest from savings, $r(d + w_i - a_i^*)$. The first is presumed to be distributed equally and the second, and, in consequence, the third, unequally. If we abbreviate savings as $s_i^* = s_i^* (w_i, d, r) = d + w_i - a_i^* (w_i, d, r)$, i.e., saving is first period income minus first period expenditure, then interest income is simply $rs_i^* (w_i, d, r)$. Total income for an individual is then the sum of dividend, labor, and interest income: $2d + w_i + rs_i^*$.

First to be noted is that the distribution of dividend income partially offsets inequality in the distribution of labor income rendering the distribution of the sum of these two more egalitarian than the distribution of labor income alone. The Lorenz curve for the sum of labor income and dividend income is unambiguously higher than the Lorenz curve for labor income alone. Lorenz curves are graphically reviewed in the section below.

To make this precise, let each of the population of n individuals be assigned a unique integer i (where $1 \le i \le n$) and thus as well a unique non-negative proper fraction $j = (i - 1)/(n - 1)$ (so that thus $0 \le j \le 1$) with the assignment satisfying the condition that y_i is non-decreasing, i.e., that $i \le k$, only if $y_i \le y_k$, where y_i is received by the individual assigned i.

Then the Lorenz curve is generated by the function

$$\lambda(j) = \frac{\sum_0^{j(n-1)+1} y_{j(n-1)+1}}{\sum_0^1 y_{j(n-1)+1}}$$

Here $\lambda(j)$ is the fraction of $\sum_i^n y$, e.g., of aggregate income, received by the lower jth of the population. Trivially $\lambda(0) = 0$ and $\lambda(1) = 1$. But an equal distribution would require that $\lambda(j) = j$ for all j, i.e., that the Lorenz curve coincide with the diagonal. For any unequal distribution $\lambda(j) < j$ for all j except 0 and 1.

One distribution is unambiguously more egalitarian than another if the Lorenz curve for the first is everywhere (except of course at 0 and 1) above the second. If neither of two distributions are unambiguously more egalitarian than the other, i.e., one Lorenz curve lies below the other for some i but above it for others, further criteria can be invoked to provide inequality rankings (but the usual procedure, ranking by Gini ratios, takes no note of where inequality is located in a distribution).

As stated, the Lorenz curve for the sum of labor income and dividend income is unambiguously higher than the Lorenz curve for labor income alone. For

$$\frac{\sum\limits_{1}^{i} 2d_i + w_i}{\sum\limits_{i}^{n} 2d_i + w_i} > \frac{\sum\limits_{1}^{i} w_i}{\sum\limits_{i}^{n} w_i}$$

where the LHS represents the distribution of the sum of dividend income and labor income and the RHS represents the distribution of labor income alone, reduces to

$$\frac{i}{n} > \frac{\sum\limits_{1}^{i} w_i}{\sum\limits_{1}^{n} w_i}$$

which holds if there is any inequality at all in the distribution of labor income.

If we allow ourselves to pretend that these distributions are differentiable, the same conclusion can be drawn by noting that the ratio of the sum of an individual's dividend and labor income to labor income alone, i.e, $(2d + w_i)/w_i$ is decreasing in i and thus, given d w_i/d $i \geq 0$, decreasing in labor income. The higher an individual's labor income, the smaller proportional income increase is provided by dividend income.

What is not obvious is the effect of the distribution of interest income on the distribution of total income including dividends. This effect depends of course on the prevailing values of d, w_i and r, and on the prevailing preference orderings of individuals. But there are arguably reasonable specifications of these parameters under which distribution from surplus would increase income inequality in what is presented to us as a model of market socialism.

The first question to consider is whether interest income worsens income inequality: does the Lorenz curves for total income lie below the Lorenz curve for total income minus interest income, i.e., dividend income plus labor income. This is the question whether the expression

$$\frac{\sum_{1}^{i} 2d_i + w_i + rs_i^*}{\sum_{1}^{n} 2d_i + w_i + rs_i^*} < \frac{\sum_{1}^{i} 2d_i + w_i}{\sum_{1}^{n} 2d_i + w_i}$$

where the LHS represents the distribution of total income (dividend, labor, and interest) while the RHS represents the distribution of dividend and labor income alone, an expression which simplifies to

$$\frac{\sum_{1}^{i} s_i^*}{\sum_{1}^{n} s_i^*} < \frac{i2d + \sum_{1}^{i} w_i}{n2d + \sum_{1}^{n} w_i}$$

holds for all values of i $(0 < i < n)$, a question which is equivalent to the question whether savings increases faster than non-savings income, i.e., whether the ratio of savings to non-savings income, $s_i^*/(2d + w_i)$, is increasing in i, or equivalently, given d w_i/d $i \geq 0$, whether the labor income elasticity of savings is sufficiently positive, i.e., whether

$$\frac{ds_i^*}{dw_i} \frac{w_i}{s_i^*} > \frac{1}{1 + 2d/w_i}$$

As is evident, the smaller the dividend level, the nearer is this criterion to the requirement that savings be relatively elastic in labor income.

To repeat, the question is: is there a plausible characterization of individual intertemporal preferences which, under these conditions, results in saving making the distribution of total income more unequal than the distribution of dividends plus labor income, i.e., condition [*] holds for all i?

Economists are fond of utility functions which rule this possibility out. For example, with constant elasticity of substitution (CES) preferences as standardly specified, the labor income elasticity of savings is sufficiently positive only if the rate of interest is negative.[5] But it is not difficult to find a prima facie plausible utility function representing preferences which require more saving to increase faster than labor income. Consider for example

$$u_i (a_i, b_i) = \min (a_i^2, b_i)$$

As income increases, optimal second period expenditure (and thus savings increases more than optimal first period expenditure. (The indifference curves associated with this function are L-shaped, i.e., the elasticity of substitution is everywhere zero, for tractability. But the same point could be made with utility functions with positive elasticities of substitution.) The optimum is thus where a_i^2 satisfies $a_i^2 = d + (d + w_i - a_i)(1 + r)$ and $b_i = a_i^2$.

With a bit of algebra these preferences yield

$$\frac{ds_i^*}{dw_i}\frac{w_i}{s_i^*} = \frac{2(d+w_i-s_i^*)w_i}{(1+r+2(d+w_i-s_i^*))s_i^*}$$

where s_i^* itself is available via the quadratic equation as an explicit function of d, w_i and r, and a bit more algebra demonstrates that the [*] condition indeed holds for all i.[6]

Given this specification of preferences, savings do in fact make the distribution of total income unambiguously more unequal than the distribution of dividends plus labor income. That is, the Lorenz curve is everywhere lower.

Finally, let us consider the combined effect of dividend income and interest income on the distribution of labor income. We have seen that dividend income unambiguously makes the sum of dividend income and labor income more egalitarian than the distribution of labor income alone, and that the distribution of interest income can, given a requisite characterization of intertemporal preferences, unambiguously make the distribution of total income, dividends, labor income, and interest, less egalitarian than the distribution of labor income and dividends alone. It remains to compare these opposed effects.

The answer, given again preferences rendering saving a 'luxury good', i.e., preferences under which the ratio of savings to income is increasing in income, is ambiguous in the sense that the Lorenz curve for total income is higher in some range than the Lorenz curve for labor income, and lower in another range. But the ambiguity takes a very simple form. These Lorenz curves cross only once. With a positive dividend and a positive rate of interest on savings, total income is more equally distributed than labor income in the lower portion of the distribution and less equally distributed in the higher portion, with the division point depending on the size of the dividend, the interest rate, and on the details of the preference relation. In particular, the lower the dividend and the higher the interest rate, the lower in the distribution at which the net result is to increase inequality. That is, the combined effect of distributing social surplus via both more or less equal dividends as well as interest on savings is

to diminish income inequality below, and increase income inequality
above, some intermediate level of income, relative to the distribution
of labor income.

In our formalism the question is what expression, among the
relational terms '>', '=' and '<', put in place of 'o' renders the following
true for what values of i, where the LHS represents the distribution
of total income and the RHS represents the distribution of labor
income.

$$\frac{\sum_{1}^{i} 2d_i + w_i + rs_i^*}{\sum_{1}^{n} 2d_i + w_i + rs_i^*} \circ \frac{\sum_{1}^{i} w_i}{\sum_{1}^{n} w_i}$$

Equivalent to this last is

$$\frac{i2d + r\sum_{1}^{i} s_i^*}{n2d + r\sum_{1}^{n} s_i^*} \circ \frac{\sum_{1}^{i} w_i}{\sum_{1}^{n} w_i}$$

and thus this question is equivalent to the question as to how non-
labor income (dividend and interest) varies with labor income, i.e.,
how the ratio of non-labor to labor income behaves.

Equivalently we want to know how the ratio of non-labor to labor
income $(2d + rs_i^*/w_i)$ varies with i, that is, what to put in place of 'o'
in

$$\frac{ds_i^* w_i}{dw_i s_i^*} \circ 1 + \frac{2d}{rs_i^*}$$

Where '<' is correct, the distribution of non-labor income is, at that
i, more egalitarian than the distribution of labor income, the Lorenz
curve of the former is above that of the latter. If '=', the Lorenz curves
coincide. If '>' is correct, the distribution of non-labor income is, at
that i, more unequal than the distribution of labor income; the Lorenz
curve of the latter is above that of the former. For the preference
relation described, these questions concern

$$\frac{2(d + w_i - s_i^*)w_i}{(1 + r + 2(d + w_i - s_i^*))s_i^*} \circ 1 + \frac{2d}{rs_i^*}$$

Another bit of algebra[7] shows that the change point comes when savings reach

$$s_i^* = \frac{2d\big((2+r)(d+w_i)+1\big)}{(r+1)(r+2d)+2d}$$

or, even less perspicuously, when labor income reaches

$$w_i = \frac{2d(2+r)(2d+r+dr)+\big(4d+r+2dr+r^2\big)\sqrt{d(2+r)(2d+r+dr)}}{(1+r)r^2}$$

That is, as income, and thus savings, grow with income, prior to this break point the distribution of non-labor income is more egalitarian than the distribution of labor income, the Lorenz curve of the former is above that of the latter. At the change point, the Lorenz curves cross, after which the distribution of non-labor income is more unequal than the distribution of labor income.

The change point is evidently increasing in the amount of the dividend and decreasing in the interest rate. Of course if there is no dividend income, the change point is at zero. On the other hand, as the rate of interest goes to zero, the change point goes to infinity. With zero interest no surplus is distributed in proportion to savings. (Of course if both d and r are zero, the Lorenz curve coincides with that for labor income.)

This analysis may provide some support for the quite unoriginal thesis that there are good reasons not to finance production from individual savings, since a positive real rate of interest on individual savings can have undesirable distributional consequences. If funds must come from individuals, taxing individuals need not have these consequences. The funding of production (however indirectly) from private voluntary saving (income minus consumption) is typical of some of capitalist development, but there are myriad exceptions. There is no evident reason not to dispense with it altogether under market socialism.

Endnote on Lorenz Curves

Lorenz curves graphically represent distributions with the cumulative portion of what is distributed on the vertical axis and the cumulative portion of the population (taken in an order non-decreasing in what is distributed) on the horizontal axis. Thus an equal distribution is represented by the diagonal and any inequality in distribution provides a Lorenz curve below the diagonal except at the end points (see Figure 1). If one Lorenz curve is below another everywhere except at the end points, it represents an unambiguously more unequal distribution (see Figure 2). But if two Lorenz curves cross, one is more egalitarian than the other in the portion of the distribution where it is higher and less egalitarian in the portion where it is lower (see Figure 3).

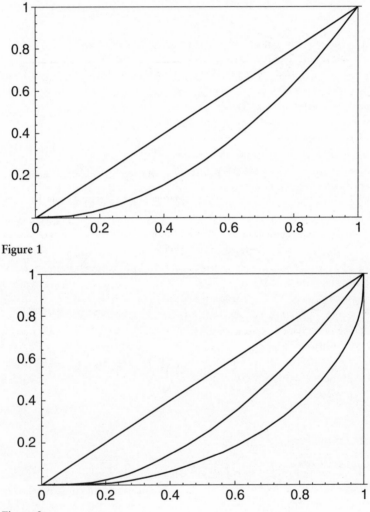

Figure 1

Figure 2

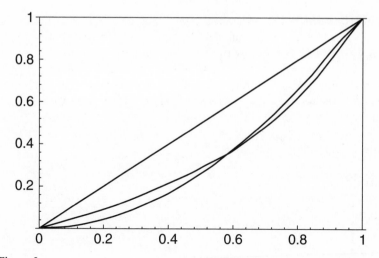

Figure 3

Notes

1. John E. Roemer, *A Future for Socialism*, Cambridge, MA: Harvard University Press 1994.

2. Most extensively in David Schweickart, *Against Capitalism*, Cambridge: Cambridge University Press 1993.

3. Arthur Kennickell and Janice Shack-Marquez, 'Changes in Family Finances from 1983 to 1989', *Federal Reserve Bulletin* (January 1992), pp. 1–18.

4. It will be noted that w_i is here taken as parametric. That is, we are here abstracting from an important subject of investigation, the (incentive) effects of surplus distribution on the value of labor individuals supply.

5. The general form of a CES utility function (where $1/(1 - \rho)$ is the elasticity of substitution) is

$$u_i(a_i, b_i) = \left(a_i^\rho + b_i^\rho\right)^{\frac{1}{\rho}}$$

Substituting in the budget constraint we have

$$u_i(a_i, b_i) = \left(a_i^\rho + \left(d + (d + w_i - a_i)(1 + r)\right)^\rho\right)^{\frac{1}{\rho}}$$

The optimal a_i^* is

$$a_i^* = \frac{\dfrac{2 + r}{1 + r} d + w_i}{1 + (1 + r)^{\rho - 3}}$$

Optimal savings is

$$s_i^* = \frac{\left(1-(1+r)^{1-\rho}\right)d+w_i}{1+(1+r)^{2-\rho}}$$

And the labor income elasticity of saving is then

$$\frac{ds_i^*}{dw_i}\frac{w_i}{s_i^*} = \frac{1}{1+\left(1-(1+r)^{1-\rho}\right)d/w_i}.$$

which exceeds $1/(1+2d/w_i)$ only if $r < 0$.

6. In outline, first the derivation of the elasticity:

$$\left(d+w_i-s_i^*\right)^2 = d+(1+r)s_i^*$$

$$2\left(d+w_i-s_i^*\right)\left(1-\frac{ds_i^*}{dw_i}\right)=(1+r)\frac{ds_i^*}{dw_i}$$

$$\frac{ds_i^*}{dw_i}\frac{w_i}{s_i^*} = \frac{2\left(d+w_i-s_i^*\right)w_i}{1+r+2\left(d+w_i-s_i^*\right)s_i^*}$$

Second, showing condition [*] holds:

$$\frac{2\left(d+w_i-s_i^*\right)w_i}{\left(1+r+2\left(d+w_i-s_i^*\right)\right)s_i^*} > \frac{1}{1+\dfrac{2d}{w_i}}$$

$$2\left(d+w_i-s_i^*\right)\left(\left(d+w_i-s_i^*\right)+d\right)-(1+r)s_i^*>0$$

$$2\left(d+w_i-s_i^*\right)^2+2\left(d+w_i-s_i^*\right)d-(1+r)s_i^*>0$$

$$2\left(d+(1+r)s_i^*\right)+2\left(d+w_i-s_i^*\right)d-(1+r)s_i^*>0$$

$$2d+(1+r)s_i^*+2\left(d+w_i-s_i^*\right)d>0$$

7. $$\frac{2\left(d+w_i-s_i^*\right)w_i}{\left(1+r+2\left(d+w_i-s_i^*\right)\right)s_i^*}=1+\frac{2d}{rs_i^*}$$

$$2r\left(d+w_i-s_i^*\right)^2-2d\left(d+w_i-s_i^*\right)(2+r)=\left(rs_i^*+2d\right)(1+r)$$

$$2r\left(d+(1+r)s_i^*\right)-2d\left(d+w_i-s_i^*\right)(2+r)=\left(rs_i^*+2d\right)(1+r)$$

$$s_i^* = \frac{2d\left((2+r)(d+w_i)+1\right)}{(r+1)(r+2d)+2d}$$

s_i^* can then be substituted out to solve for w_i using

$$s_i^* = d + w_i + \frac{1+r}{2} - \sqrt{\left(\frac{r}{2}\right)^2 + \left(d + w_i + \frac{1}{2}\right)r + 2d + \frac{1}{4}}$$

Normative Issues

11

Transitional and Utopian Market Socialism

Harry Brighouse

The rethinking embodied in Roemer's *A Future for Socialism?*[1] represents a healthy response to the current crisis of socialist politics. Even those who are less moved than Roemer by the collapse of what were once called 'actually existing socialisms' must be concerned by the apparent success of the Thatcher/Kohl/Reagan generation of politicians in driving not only socialist theory and practice, but even fondly remembered left-wing rhetoric, off the map of everyday politics. In the face of these phenomena socialists need more than a critique of the self-evident (and even the oblique) evils of capitalist society: they need to pose an institutionally viable alternative to capitalism which can plausibly be thought to avoid at least most of the evils of the no-longer actually existing socialist societies. The return to utopian and transitional model building, as long as it does not signal a thoroughgoing retreat into theory, is a valuable component in the revivification of the socialist project.

1 Liberal and Socialist Values

Roemer suggests that we should elaborate a defensible socialist political morality and then measure institutional proposals by both their feasibility and their tendency to promote the values embodied in that political morality. Socialist political morality is identified with some set of principles of equality: Roemer's own preferred equalanda are opportunities for welfare and self-realization, political influence and social status. He says nothing about their relative importance, because different strands of the socialist tradition have weighted these values differently, and will continue to do so (although I shall raise an objection to this omission later). It might seem ungenerous to object to this first part of his paper, and not just for this reason. There are other values, such as community and autonomy, which have been integral to some aspects of the socialist moral tradition, which Roemer may appear to neglect. But I take it that the notions of self-realization and social status, though they are both left undefined, are, between them, sufficiently flexible to accommodate concern with the apparently missing values. If one believes that valuable socialist lives will be autonomously led, or have to be shaped by as-yet-unexperienced community values in order to be fulfilling, then this will inform institutional design via either the requirement to increase equality of opportunity for self-realization or the requirement to diminish inequalities of opportunity for social status.

Having said that, these two notions of community and autonomy, at least insofar as they are distinct from equality of opportunity for political influence and of opportunity for welfare, are precisely those that have been neglected by the liberal egalitarianism from which Roemer takes his cue. If socialists fill out the notions of social status and self-realization in the perfectionist ways that would accommodate the apparently missing values, they depart to that extent from the contemporary framework within which liberal egalitarianism has been developed. The liberal egalitarian intellectual current from which Roemer takes his lead has tended to be committed to a principle of neutrality which says that the values which inform the design of state institutions should comment as little as is feasible on the content of the values by which people lead their lives. A stark economic egalitarianism passes a neutrality test, because it says nothing about how people should live their lives, commenting instead only on the relative resources that should be available to them in the pursuit of whatever goals and ideals they choose. But both socialist community or solidarity and the vision of self-realization Marx appears to endorse in the famous passage celebrating hunting, fishing, shepherding and critical criticism in the German Ideology,[2] fail the neutrality test: they comment on what a valuable life would be like and allow social institutions to be designed to encourage life of that kind or those kinds to be led. Insofar as they do that they violate liberal neutrality.[3]

Of course, this is not to say that there could not be a liberal socialism which mentioned these kinds of value. But the role assigned to perfectionist values would be different from that assigned to the neutral values. A liberal socialism could describe principles of socialist community and could predict that these values would be much more likely to be realized if institutions were designed in accordance with the neutral egalitarian principles. In other words, our neutral values should inform institutions, but in doing so our non-neutral values will be promoted, though the promotion of the non-neutral values is not the motivation for the use of the neutral values. Furthermore, in an egalitarian and liberal civil society, socialists could promote their non-neutral values (for example, through propaganda and the formation of voluntary associations) without any violation of neutrality (which is a directive about what values may undergird the design of involuntary institutions). Roemer's liberal socialism appears to have this structure but, if it does, either the ideas of self-realization and social status should not be expanded to accommodate other socialist values, or they should not be used to inform or to evaluate his institutional proposal.

The expansiveness of the notion of self-realization, combined with the fact that Roemer does not mandate a particular weighting of the different egalitarian principles, makes this work palatable to a wider range of socialists than it might otherwise. But it also makes it very hard to apply the method of evaluation which he proposes even in the speculative way that is available to us. If we object that his proposal pays insufficient attention to equality of self-realization, for example, he can reply that this is because the proper weighting of principles places less emphasis on that principle. Nevertheless, it is fairly clear that, of the principles described in the initial section, it is equality of opportunity for welfare which the proposal is likely to advance the most, by drastically reducing inequality of resources (which are major sources of opportunity for welfare) without restricting in any important ways juridical equality of opportunity. Equal opportunity for political influence is much less well advanced by the proposal. Roemer does not, for example, mandate any institutional changes in the structure of government or electoral systems, or discuss rules governing the access of political parties to the mass media. There is no discussion of proportional representation, the rights of minorities, or campaign finance reform to insulate political processes from residual background inequalities of income and wealth, and he specifically rejects the introduction of workers' control of the workplace, a demand which has played a major role in distinguishing recent socialist politics from liberalism and moderate social democracy.

This is not to say that the proposal does nothing to advance equality of opportunity for political influence. Major sources of inequality of influence in capitalist societies (perhaps the major sources of inequality of influence) are the vast inequality of control of capital and the correlative inequality of wealth. The rich, as those who control investment, have a bargaining advantage against any elected government that challenges them. They are also able to affect the outcomes of elections, without mentioning the bargaining advantage, by their disproportionate control of the means of communication and the mass media, as well as their ability to spend more money on political advertising. Insofar as it would redistribute resources (and hence control of investment) in an egalitarian direction, Roemer's proposal would increase equality of influence. However, central areas of economic life remain, under Roemer's proposal, governed by the market, and outside the reach of democratic processes. Moreover, it appears that there will be, under socialism à la Roemer, a distinct managerial class or caste, members of which, by virtue of their occupation, will have immediate access to skills and information which are likely to give them individually and collectively disproportionate political influence.

2 Evaluation of Transitional Proposals

As he anticipates, some socialists will be tempted to criticize his proposal on democratic grounds, and below I shall explore the appeal of that temptation. However, even if we regarded equal opportunity for political influence as somehow prior in importance to other egalitarian principles, as I shall argue that we should, such criticism might be said not to be pertinent. After all, regardless of what socialist values are, and regardless of how they are weighted against each other, that one of them is inadequately instituted by his proposal may not matter because the proposal appears to be essentially transitional in nature. When explaining why he does not include workplace democracy in his proposal he invokes the biological metaphor that 'an organism with one mutation is more likely to survive than one in which two mutations occur simultaneously', indicating that the financial restructuring he advocates is but the first step on the road. He goes on to say that he should not be taken as 'unequivocally endors[ing] introducing labor management as a second step after the first step . . . has been successfully completed', seeming to imply that his proposal is intended as an early stage in the transition. If it is the first step, we would not expect it to take us all the way: and its failure to implement a thoroughgoing liberal egalitarianism does not count against it.[4]

But what we should consider when evaluating transitional proposals is actually quite different from the factors involved in evaluating frankly utopian blueprints. If Roemer's is a transitional proposal what matters is not whether it implements some or all of the values which socialists espouse, let alone whether it accords the proper weight to those values, but whether it can reasonably be expected to establish a political dynamic towards a system which *will* implement those values adequately. In judging that question, it need not even be relevant whether the transitional system better implements some or other, or even all, of the ideals than the present system: we might, at least in principle, have to take steps backward before it is possible to make progress. This is not to say that the ends of a socialist society justify any means whatsoever in its pursuit: it may be that there are some limits which must be respected, and that those limits may be sufficiently important that if going beyond them were the only way of attaining socialism we should abandon socialism as an end.[5] But there is no reason to think that those limits prescribe that every change in the design of social institutions must make those institutions more nearly approximate those of the socialist utopia.

That this is so poses a difficulty for Roemer concerning his reluctance to offer a weighting among the socialist values he describes. Until models of feasible socialism are put forward, he says, 'arguing about differences in preference orderings of the three desiderata is of second order importance'.[6] However, because one criterion for judging a transitional proposal is how well it will effect a transition, we need to know something about the system which it is supposed to be a transition to. Different weightings of the different values will have quite significant implications for the character of the real socialism, and hence different implications with respect to whether any given transitional proposal is pointing in the right direction. If socialism gives priority to equality of opportunity for political influence, the proponent of a transitional model will have to explain how his or her model promotes the eventual implementation of radical democracy. If economic equality is primary, then the model must make provision for the ultimate priority of such equality. It seems that for different versions of the socialist utopia quite different transitional paths might be appropriate. While our different visions of ultimate socialism may not justify the mutual hostility which has frequently characterized relations between different strands of the socialist movement, deliberation about their relative merits cannot be put off as long as Roemer seems to hope.

A second factor involved in the evaluation of transitional proposals, which would trouble us less when considering utopian visions, is political feasibility. Since transitional measures purport to effect a transition from where we are to where we seek to be, when adjudicating between rival proposals we need to consider, among other things, which it is more possible to implement given the current or the foreseeable constellation of political and economic contingencies. In other words, the method suggested by Roemer, despite its relevance to the evaluation of frankly utopian projects, is not appropriate for evaluation of his own proposal.

3 Some Problems with Transitional Market Socialism

Agency

It is usually thought appropriate to ignore what we might call the question of rectificatory agency in discussions of political morality and even of the theory of institutions. After all, we are supposed to be talking about the institutional architecture of the society we want to see, and only when we have some idea of what it would look like can we discuss how to build it. However, Roemer's transitional proposal raises the question of agency in a sharp way. The problem is that while the proposal is self-consciously conservative by socialist standards, it is not so conservative that it does not require a radical shift of economic power and resources away from the currently existing capitalist class. In the short-to-medium term there is little prospect of Roemer's proposal finding favour internationally among the electable parties of the Left. The parties of Western social democracy are increasingly backing away from even more moderate social democratic goals, and their political approaches mimic those of the US Democratic Party. The Latin American Left has largely made its peace with international capital: the Mexican PRD has no radical reform proposals, and even the Brazilian PT poses itself as an anticorruption party of stability.[7] In the foreseeable future the mainstream international Left is unlikely to be in a position in which it can seriously put forward proposals like Roemer's and have any hope of being elected to implement them.

But the problem is not just that there is no agent to carry out the transitional proposal. A social agency which had acquired the capacity to bring about such a shift would likely have acquired the power to implement still more radical measures. The question that naturally arises, then, is why they would not claim more when they have the power to claim more?

The evolutionary metaphor

The reason Roemer would give them is signalled by the evolutionary metaphor. It is wiser, especially in the light of the dystopian experience of the Soviet-style societies, to experiment with one feature at a time: an organism with a single mutation is more likely to survive than one with multiple mutations. It is not unreasonable to be skeptical that such considerations will move people who are capable of doing more, even if they are superbly disciplined in ways that revolutionaries rarely are. Furthermore, the evolutionary metaphor is not generally apt for questions of institutional change. Biological evolution proceeds through the mechanism of random variance/natural selection.

Random variance is a shot in the dark, which the construction of socialist or presocialist institutions cannot afford to be for reasons which Roemer elegantly elaborates. The design and construction of such institutions are products of conscious and deliberate human activity. Very often institutional changes fail to achieve the desired results precisely because they are too conservative, failing to eradicate the mechanisms which will result in reversion to the prior status quo. Some argue that post-war social democratic reforms in Western Europe were of this kind. It is also sometimes argued, perhaps more plausibly, that the reforms of the Great Society and affirmative action in the US have failed to achieve what they were intended to because they were implemented while too many institutions that promoted poverty and racism were left intact. I notice these arguments not to endorse them, but to suggest that whether or not they are good criticisms can be established only by detailed attention to the empirical facts of the cases, and not by appeal to the evolutionary metaphor.

Effectiveness

There is a further worry, which concerns the ability of Roemer's proposal to effect the transition to the socialist utopia, regardless of the relative weights appropriately accorded to socialist values. Roemer's strategy is to assume the worst about people – that there is going to be no change for the good in human character – and set up institutions accordingly. But what if, contra Roemer, human character does begin to transform under his system? Should people become less competitive, less consumption-oriented, more interested in having leisure time and controlling the circumstances of their work life (the kinds of change in human character which we would like to see) there may be mere destabilization. There is no obvious mechanism providing for further change of the system, because the rationale for the system seems to be the expectation that the human traits that guide human nature under capitalism will persist. The worry, then, is that in assuming the worst we may be promoting the worst, and thus frustrating the possibilities for transition. A transitional proposal should provide mechanisms whereby, if desired changes in human motivation take place, further development towards the desired goal is likely to occur.

Does Roemer's proposal contain such a mechanism? It does not seem to. We might be tempted to respond on his behalf that this is a minor criticism, and that we should design and try to graft such a mechanism onto his proposal as it stands. But it is worth noting a pressure within Roemer's proposal against the eventuality of equality of opportunity for political influence and, in particular, workplace democracy. Under his scheme there is bound to emerge a distinct managerial class or layer possessing extensive knowledge and understanding of the workings of the firms and the economy. Things being as they are, we cannot expect the operation of market mechanisms to deprive them of disproportionate political and economic power, and they would be liable as a class to attempt to accumulate and retain their power. In all likelihood, even without transformations in human character, a mitigated class struggle would persist. If transformations in human character were to occur, or struggle for the next stage of socialist change (suppose that it is labour management) occurs, we want some reason to believe that things are weighed in favour of the right change.

Roemer could deflect much of the criticism I have advanced so far by treating his proposal as frankly utopian, rather than as a transition. He could say that it is, if not the end of the road, at least the furthest that we can see. As such we should directly evaluate it in terms of the three egalitarian/socialist values properly weighted, because no significant further steps are expected or hoped for. The agency problem is then irrelevant: no longer should we see the project as one of rectificatory justice. Rather we would see it as an institutional description towards which rectification should be pursued. There are parts of the essay – especially in the responses to the putative left-wing and democratic critics – in which Roemer indeed seems to be thinking of this much more as a utopian proposal and much less as a transitional one.

4 Market Socialism as a Utopian Blueprint and the Value of Democracy

Considered as a utopian proposal, Roemer's market socialism seems to reflect a commitment to the priority of distributive material equality over equality of opportunity for political influence or democracy. In particular, workplace democracy, which has played an important role in some strands of socialist theory and agitation, is explicitly rejected. I shall briefly make a prima facie case for regarding democracy as a value at least as central as equality of opportunity for welfare and self-realization, alongside which case I shall explain why specific democratization of social institutions would likely serve well as an element of any transitional proposal. It should be borne in mind that I have no alternative institutional proposal to Roemer's and the value of these comments is circumscribed by this. Finally I shall explore the significance of a particular set of arguments for workplace democracy, and shall suggest, despite my advocacy of the priority of equality of opportunity for political influence, that Roemer would be on firmer ground if he simply denied the moral basis for workplace democracy, rather than hold it out as a more distant goal.

Pat Devine has recently argued against market socialist proposals in general that they retain the depoliticized and impersonal character of economic life under capitalism: ' . . . in my view, instead of seeking to depersonalize interdependence, socialists should be seeking to democratize it, as part of the process of moving toward a governing society based on conscious uncoerced cooperation.'[8] Although very different in other respects, Roemer's proposal is like familiar versions of market socialism in the respects to which Devine objects. While I shall explore the case for democratization, it is worth heading off the comment about the impersonal character of economic life. It seems to me that modern economic life is by its nature impersonal, and that this is no vice. We interact with vast numbers of people in morally significant ways, and the virtues of personal relations are both inadequate and inappropriate for the governance of those interactions. That we do not know, like or care about the strangers whose relations with us are mediated both by democratic and market processes reflects the complexity of modern societies and insuperable limits of human nature. What is important is that these relations, which are of necessity impersonal, are justly governed. Devine should be read as saying that thoroughgoing democratization of those relations will contribute to their eventual just governance. This is one of the questions taken up below.

The case for democratization comes in two parts. The first part advocates democracy as a central element of our political morality, and hence as a fundamental principle by which we should evaluate utopian blueprints. The second part notes the likely value of democratizing measures in facilitating transition.

First, it could be contended that democracy, or equal opportunity for political influence, appears to give expression to mutual obligations among strangers that are more central than those expressed by equality of opportunity for welfare. If our opposition to capitalism is based on our commitment to equality as expressed in Roemer's egalitarian principles, the realization of which is impeded by capitalism, then we need to look behind the principles at the reason for holding them. Why should we endorse a principle of equal opportunity for political influence? One natural answer is that ensuring that others have institutionally available to them equal control over our shared circumstances is a fairly natural requirement of the deeper moral principle that we accord them equal respect. The idea is that democratic procedures play an ineliminable role in the communal recognition of the equal moral worth of persons.

Think about how equal respect is expressed within some affective associations; for example, a group of friends. We express equal respect by consulting all who wish to assert their preferences in making decisions about where to go out to eat or which movie to go and see. If having consulted them we ignore their expressed preference in making the decision, that is usually a sign of disrespect. The requirement of equal respect is more stringent, of course, in involuntary associations, and especially among strangers: those who (unlike our friends) have yet to prove to us that they are inappropriate objects of our respect.[9]

It might be objected that equal opportunity for political influence is too weak a principle to capture what is required by political equality. For example, in one sense of opportunity, as long as citizens have equal resources and equal votes, vote buying is consistent with equal opportunity for political influence. If each had, at the age of majority, the opportunity to retain their vote and to buy as many others as everyone else had the opportunity to buy, they would each have equal opportunity for future voting. Yet this is incompatible with our normal intuitions about the propriety of making the right to vote inalienable, and hence with democracy as we normally conceive it. For this reason it might be better to call the principle supported by the notion of equal respect 'equal availability of influence', which prohibits such foreclosure on future influence, and requires that institutions be designed to facilitate the relatively easy re-entry into influential participation of long-term abstainers.

While it is easy to find a case for equal availability of political influence from the deeper moral principle of equal respect, it is more difficult to make a case for equality of opportunity for welfare (or self-realization or social status for that matter). There do not appear to be similar micro-cases within affective associations where respect (or any other value) is realized by providing strictly equal opportunities for welfare, especially if welfare is conceived as actual preference satisfaction. This is not to say that equality of opportunity for welfare is not valuable, but it does seem, prima facie, to express less central impersonal obligations than does equal availability of political influence.[10]

The second part of my case shows there are three reasons for thinking that specific democratization will be a valuable element of a proposed transition. The first two hold, however Roemer's egalitarian values are weighted; the third relies on the idea that democracy will be a central element of the socialist society we hope to achieve.

The first reason is that, because democracy is a much more widely shared value in contemporary societies than is material egalitarianism, a proposal giving it a central place has more chance of being adopted. Democracy is widely valued partly because it can be argued for from a range of different moral and political perspectives (including many which are false but nevertheless widely believed), and because it at least appears to impose less extensive mutual obligations among citizens than, for example, material equality. As noted above, despite Roemer's concentration on anticipating objections from the Left, his own proposal is far beyond the bounds of respectable political debate in the US and many other industrialized countries. In other words we should not let the complaints of some that it is insufficiently extreme obscure the fact that it is nevertheless extreme.

The second prima facie reason for favouring transitional proposals focussing on democratization is instrumental. Assuming that egalitarian principles are true and rationally acceptable, appropriate increases in democracy will make it easier for socialists to argue successfully for those principles. It will also, by increasing the power of most citizens over collective circumstances, including social institutions, increase their ability to reform or revolutionize those institutions in the ways that socialists support. As long as we can persuade a large number of people of the correctness of socialist political morality, increased equality of opportunity for political influence will better enable people to secure (and maintain) the institution of that morality. A good increased democratization proposal will be able to invoke this fact as a mechanism by which further transition can be effected.

Finally, whereas market socialism relies for its success on material incentives and rewards, and hence both relies on and reinforces economically self-interested behaviour of the kind which capitalist markets similarly rely on and reward, radical democratization of the right sort, albeit in a different sphere, rewards rational deliberation about the good of society as a whole. As such it is more likely than a market socialist proposal to train and develop the kinds of motivation which, ultimately, will make possible full socialism (on the assumption that full socialism includes significantly different motivations and human characters than does capitalism).

In the absence of a reasonably well developed democratizing institutional proposal, of course, these considerations are far from conclusive, and anyway they argue for a supplement to, rather than a replacement of, Roemer's proposal (as long as his is taken as transitional). Nevertheless they suggest the desirability of more rather than less emphasis on equalizing the availability of political influence, and raise the question (which it is not possible for me to answer) whether more democracy could be injected into a modification of Roemer's proposal without undermining it. Certainly, if Roemer's proposal turns out to be incompatible with radical democracy, the work he has done has shifted a burden onto radical democrats to describe feasible radically democratic institutions.

That said, there is an argument against premature democratization which we should take seriously, and which may appear to support Roemer's against as yet unconstructed democratizing proposals. This is that until people have transformed their consciousness, democratization will tend to allow for discrimination and oppression by personal and political means (rather than by impersonal non-political means). Yet being discriminated against by the state, consciously, may have a much worse effect on the opportunities for self-realization of the victims than the impersonal discrimination of market forces. Why? Because it may be much more detrimental to our self-respect. When the normal operation of market processes disfavors us, at least those of us who understand what kinds of process are at work can console ourselves by saying 'well, that's just the way things go: it could have happened to anyone.' But when we are disfavored to exactly the same degree by democratic processes we have to say: 'This was the foreseen or intended result of deliberate action on the part of my peers: I suffered either because they intended it or because their advantage mattered more to them than my disadvantage.'

While this concern needs to be taken seriously, I doubt that the consequences of democracy will be as the argument suggests. In fact democracy at the national or community level is as impersonal in many ways as the market, at least as long as it is not required to resolve very severe conflicts, such as longstanding tribal rivalries.

Furthermore, under capitalist markets, at least, few people are sufficiently cool about their own situations that they are able to attribute
their own disadvantages to the arbitrariness of market processes, and
hence insulate their own self-respect. So I doubt there will be much
difference between market and democratic allocations in terms of the
self-respect of those disadvantaged by the outcomes.

However, the objection to premature democratization has more
power when applied to institutions in which affective and personal
ties play a significant role in governing interactions. For example, in
smaller workplaces, where the collective life of the work force is
infused with affective ties and personal interaction, democratization,
at least prior to the kinds of transformation in human character of
which Roemer is skeptical, may give rise to conflicts and oppressions
within the workplace which constitute barriers to self-realization of
some at least as severe as those constituted by the domination at the
point of production experienced under capitalism as we know it. Now
I shall turn to the question of whether there are principled reasons for
trying to institute democracy in the workplace.

5 Workplace Democracy

As I have suggested already, one feature of Roemer's proposal which
socialists are likely to want to modify, especially if it is considered
as a utopian blueprint, concerns the organization of the workplace.
Roemer explicitly rejects labor management or workplace democracy,
a demand which has characterized at least one central strand of recent
socialist thought and of recent Western socialist practice. Would an
adequate model of a socialist utopia include labor management or
democratization of the workplace? This question can be answered
through the answer to a slightly different question: is there a right to
workplace democracy? If there is such a right, then any proposal
which failed to ensure that every worker could work in a democratic
workplace or firm would fail to be just and hence be unacceptable
as a utopian model. If there is no such right then Roemer's failure to
provide such assurance yields no justice-based reason for rejecting his
model as a utopian proposal.

I understand a right to workplace democracy as follows. Like a
right to democracy at the national or community level, it is a right
borne and exercised by individuals. The right protects a claim to
be able to work in a workplace or firm within which all employees
have an institutionally guaranteed right to participate as equals in the

decision making. It includes the requirement that any who have more institutionally facilitated power over decisions be elected by and accountable to a body in which all members have an equal number of equally weighted votes, and which includes at least all the employees of the workplace or firm. While this claim must be balanced against claims protected by other individual rights, such as freedom of conscience, and freedom of association, it can only be thought of as a right if we think that it should be upheld even if upholding it has significantly deleterious effects on productivity both in the workplace and in the economy as a whole.

What might be the moral basis for a right to workplace democracy? I shall consider three arguments.

First, one might appeal to Roemer's principle of equality of opportunity for self-realization, and argue that democracy in the workplace ameliorates alienated labour in ways essential for widespread access to self-realization. In fact this (usually in combination with the idea that workplace democracy enhances productivity) is probably the standard argument for workplace democracy within the Marxian political tradition. In his early writings, Marx characterizes labor under capitalism as alienated in the sense that the worker has control of none of the following aspects: the decisions about what she produces; the process by which she labors; and what happens to the fruits of her labor once they have been produced.[11] The contrast, it is fairly evident, is with some forms of pre-industrial and early industrial artisanry in which the laborer would have as much control of at least some of the above factors as market or quasimarket relations would allow.

Of course the model of the artisan does not in itself support any argument for workplace democracy based on the ideal of unalienated laboring. Given that model the most natural argument would be for a society of free and roughly equally endowed individual producers. The argument for a right to workplace democracy becomes relevant when it is acknowledged either that such a society is unfeasible in modern conditions or that it is undesirable on other grounds.[12]

If that is acknowledged, then it is thought either inevitable or desirable that most production be carried out collectively. In such conditions workers will not, of course, be able to have full control over the three factors over which capitalist norms of productivity deprive them of any control. But workplace democracy can provide them with partial control over those factors: it provides each with control equal to that of each of their workmates, and hence ameliorates the condition of unalienated laboring equally for all. Thus it is required by the principle of equal opportunity for self-realization.

I doubt that such an argument for a right to workplace democracy would be compelling. First, there are different kinds of work. Some kinds, especially intellectual and very complex manual labor, may afford a great deal of self-realization when they are unalienated, and very little when they are alienated. But for other kinds of work the gap will be much smaller; if it exists at all. Many kinds of work will be as fulfilling as they can be as long as the worker has the time, materials and permission to do the job properly. But this does not require that they have full control of the process, only that they not be impeded from doing the work as it ought to be done. Some forms of work, it might be argued, are not going to be very rewarding intrinsically, regardless of how much control the laborer has. Furniture removal, for example, affords limited scope for self-expression. A bad furniture remover is likely to be very frustrated and unhappy, but an excellent furniture remover is likely to get most of her self-realization from her non-working activities, even when she has full control of the work process, from beginning to end.

In fact, it is reasonable to dispute the speculation about human nature that most people could get significant self-realization from the process of work itself. But even if it were possible for human character to change in such a direction it is not clear what reason there would be deliberately to encourage that change through the design of transitional institutions. Rather than encourage humans to change into beings which find labor rewarding it might be preferable, if possible, to encourage them to find their solitude and their relations with one another rewarding, and to promote technological changes which diminish the amount of time they have to spend working to provide themselves with desirable material comforts.

Second, the principle of equal opportunity for self-realization does not disaggregate potential sources of self-realization in a way that would be needed to support the right to workplace democracy. What it requires is that each person face a diverse set of life activities which afford reasonable expectations of self-realization, and that that set is equal for each person. If Julian has the opportunity to work in a democratic workplace and Sandy does not, but nevertheless faces an array of options liable to afford him as much self-realization as Julian's options are liable to afford him, Sandy has no complaint emanating from the principle. In other words, even if workplace democracy is generally conducive to self-realization, this does not make it something anyone has a right to independent of considering what other opportunities they have for self-realization.

A second possible argument for the right to workplace democracy is that it is directly implied by the principle of equal availability of political influence. But while that principle does require that the economy as a whole be placed within the domain of democratic decision making, I doubt that it implies a right to workplace democracy. Some firms have a substantial impact on our shared circumstances while others do not, and this difference is not directly correlated with the size of the firms. If we tried to implement equal availability of political influence primarily through workplace democracy we would fail to equalize because of this difference. Furthermore, even under socialism, some persons (for example, those with severe and irremediable disabilities) will not be able to work, but will still be properly part of the democratic polity. Finally, we share our circumstances with far more people than our workmates, and while much of what is important in the workplace can be controlled through democratically determined national regulation, much of what is important outside the workplace cannot be achieved through workplace decisions. Yet if we see workplace democracy as a less than central means for achieving equal availability of political influence it is not properly seen as a right in itself but merely as a mechanism which we may or may not employ to implement something which is a right.

One might think instead that the case for a right to democracy in the workplace is, if not a direct implication of it, at least a natural extension of the case for a right to democracy at the national or community level. This is Cohen's view, as expressed in the following argument, which he calls the parallel case argument:

> The best justification for the requirement of democratic governance of the state is that a political society is a cooperative activity, governed by public rules, that is expected to operate for the mutual advantage of the members. Anyone who contributes to such an activity, who has the capacity to assess its rules, and who is subject to them has a right to participate in their determination. But economic organisations are cooperative activities governed by rules, and they are expected to operate for the advantage of each member. Workers in such enterprises contribute to the cooperative activity, have the capacity to assess the rules that regulate it, and are subject to them. So they have a right to determine the regulative rules of their workplaces.[13]

In fact, of course, this is only one of several possible parallel case arguments. The content of a parallel case argument for workplace democracy depends on the content of whatever you take to be the best case for democracy at the national or community level. So, for example, Richard Arneson does not recognize democratic rights as intrinsically just, but argues for them on the grounds that democracy is the best available system of governance with respect to guaranteeing other more fundamental individual rights.[14] A case for democracy which is less liberal than Arneson's and Cohen's might argue that meaningful engagement in the determination of collective affairs is an essential component of any truly valuable life, and so democracy is mandatory on the grounds that everyone be provided with the opportunity to live well. The parallel case to the Arneson argument would be that we have fundamental rights that might be breached in the workplace but for the presence of direct democratic accountability. The parallel case for the non-liberal argument would be that, because a large part of one's life is spent in the workplace, a full opportunity to live a valuable participatory life requires that democracy be available in the workplace.

So what argument is there against there being a right to workplace democracy? Arneson has argued against it on the grounds that it violates a neutrality constraint on state action. Widely mandated workplace democracy would, he presumes, have significant material costs. These costs and the correlative benefits of participation would be assessed differently by different people, presumably depending on how much they enjoyed participating. But state neutrality 'forbids the use of state power to confer special benefits on some citizens merely because they have tastes of a sort that are favored or deemed more admirable than the tastes of others'.[15] Hence state mandated workplace democracy would be unacceptable, since it would indeed confer its benefits and disbenefits differentially.

Arneson uses this argument against the parallel case for his own argument for democracy (that democratic rights tend to protect other more fundamental rights). However, it in fact impugns only the non-liberal parallel case argument, which singles out a particular way of life as more worthy, and hence to be given more institutional support, than others. Neither Cohen's or Arneson's arguments for democracy deem participation as uniquely valuable or even as a particularly good thing, and nor do the cases parallel to their arguments. In both cases the requirement that participation be available is not a function of the distinctive value of the participatory life, but rather of the fact that making it institutionally available fulfills obligations we have towards others.

It is true that mandated workplace democracy would violate a different neutrality constraint. We might accept, contra Cohen, that justice does not require that workplaces be democratically organized, and also believe that neutrality of a different sort constrains democratic decisions; namely, that the state should do nothing which makes it easier to fulfill some conception of the good life than others. Then, noting that mandating workplace democracy would have this effect, we might reject it as an impermissible democratic decision. But neutrality conceived this way is an extremely strong constraint on democratic decision making. The constraint would have the effect of making it impermissible for the state to provide most public goods, most of which have differential effects on different individuals' pursuits of their ways of life. So minimal a state ill fits the ambition of socialist morality and leaves little to democratic discretion. As such, I think this constraint should be rejected.

Alternatively, the scope of neutrality could be reinterpreted to call into question both the liberal arguments for workplace democracy, by understanding it as requiring that no possibly controversial values inform the design of social institutions. I think this gives neutrality an implausibly wide scope. Furthermore, on this understanding of neutrality, the liberal cases we have considered for democracy at the national or community level would have to be rejected: the value of interpersonal respect which appears to underlie Cohen's argument, and of fundamental individual rights which inform Arneson's argument, are non-neutral in the relevant sense. So, unless we are willing to give up altogether on the idea that there is a right to democracy, neutrality will not serve as an adequate basis for principled opposition to mandated workplace democracy.

However, most defenders of capitalism as we know it, even if they are friendly to democratic governance, will attempt to block the parallelism by retorting that there is a suppressed premise in both of the liberal cases for democracy at the national level. What makes the case for democracy at that level so powerful is that citizens generally have no realistic option of exit. In other words, the involuntary nature of the association is what makes democracy obligatory. For voluntary associations, from which members do have a realistic option of exit, the case is much less clear: non-Catholics do not find the undemocratic nature of the Roman Catholic church one of its objectionable features, while non-Chinese do generally find the non-democratic nature of China an objectionable feature.

But, the defender of capitalism without workplace democracy will say, workers are simply not in the same situation. They are free to choose where and whether to work, and can quit if they do not like the regime at their workplace. The labor contract is a voluntary contract for mutual benefit, and having entered into it freely and with full knowledge the worker has no grounds for complaint.[16]

Socialists (even of Roemer's kind) are certainly liable to respond that the freedom of contract for the worker is at best limited and at worst illusory under capitalist property relations.[17] So the case for workplace democracy under capitalism may remain strong. However, under a welfare state, or at least under socialist economy, the case immediately weakens, because if something like universal basic income grant is available,[18] it may be much more reasonable to consider the contract genuinely free. After all, if working is optional, then which workplace you work in is also optional in the relevant sense.

As such it may be reasonable to think of workplaces as more like voluntary associations, and hence the case for democracy at that level is less compelling. On the rights protection argument for democracy, this is because the option of exit from the workplace gives the worker other ways than participation of protecting her rights. In the Cohen argument, it is because the voluntary nature of the association robs the argument for democracy of an essential premise.

The proponent of a parallel case argument might respond to this that in fact the non-voluntary nature of political society is not really relevant to the case for democracy at the national level. After all, most democrats will be reluctant to admit that if we were to open the borders, and provide massive material compensation to potential immigrants so that the otherwise enormous personal costs of emigration were genuinely offset, there would be no obligation to maintain democratic institutions at the national level.

But opening the borders and providing massive compensation are not analogous to providing something like an unconditional basic income grant. A basic income grant allows the option of not being in any workplace and hence not being subject to any workplace rules at all. But open borders only give people a realistic choice between sets of rules, not a choice of living under no rules at all. Such a choice is the choice of not living in a society, and as such it is not possible to compensate someone meaningfully in such a way as to make it a realistic option. The non-voluntary nature of living in a political society is hence an ineliminable feature, and it is not clear to me that there is a coherent thought experiment which enables us to detach it so the case of democracy at the national level can be made genuinely parallel to that of workplace democracy in an economy with a basic income grant. It is reasonable, nevertheless, to think that the case for a right to workplace democracy is at best much weaker in a socialist society than in a capitalist society.

Notice that the considerations invoked here, unlike those invoked in the earlier argument expressing mere unease about democratizing small workplaces, do not rely on there being no transformation in human character. That argument could have been defeated by showing, for example, that human beings were much more tolerant, reasonable and altruistic than we currently suspect, and therefore the predicted conflicts would not arise. Workplace democracy would then be unwise in transition, but would be a proper part of the utopian blueprint. But consideration of Cohen's argument raises the question of whether there is a case for workplace democracy even in the utopian blueprint, regardless of whether human character transforms.

In other words, once egalitarian economic relations have been achieved, the case for a right to workplace democracy seems to fade somewhat, at least if it is modeled on liberal cases for democracy at the level of the community and the nation state.

Showing that there is no right to workplace democracy does not mean that workplace democracy should never be introduced in a socialist society. If, as some argue, democratic practices in the workplace often have productivity enhancing effects, then policies favoring it would presumably be selected as appropriate by either the managers of firms or by the democratic process within a market socialist society. Of course, whether workplace democracy enhances productivity will depend partly on the nature of the work, and also on the structure of the background economic institutions. For reasons about which he is very clear, Roemer's proposal makes it particularly unlikely that workplace democracy will enhance productivity. But there would only be principled reasons for seeking background institutions which made it more likely if there were a right to workplace democracy. And only if there is a right to workplace democracy should a utopian blueprint be faulted for leaving it out of the institutional design.

6 Concluding Remark

Some of my comments in Section 4 will identify me as among Roemer's democratic critics. I believe that socialism requires dramatically increased democratic control over our collective circumstances, and it is evident that I suspect that Roemer's proposal does too little, whether as a transitional proposal or as a utopian blueprint, to advance this. It could be that Roemer simply believes that recent history has given us reasons to be extremely skeptical that increased democratic control over our collective circumstances is achievable, at least with morally acceptable consequences. It will be evident that I disagree, but that is not the point. The aim of my paper is to urge socialists to give serious scrutiny to Roemer's socialist principles, and to investigate the question of what weight should be accorded to each. Proper evaluation of his proposal, and of any other proposed transition or utopia, requires resolution of this question, which he deliberately leaves unresolved.[19]

Notes

1. John E. Roemer, *A Future for Socialism*, Cambridge, MA: Harvard University Press 1994.

2. See Karl Marx, *The German Ideology*, New York: International 1970, p. 53. I say only that he appears to endorse it because he strictly says only that communist society makes this opulent life possible, and not that this is a or the reason why we should choose communism.

3. Both Ronald Dworkin and Richard Arneson appear to be committed to such a view of neutrality. See Dworkin, *A Matter of Principle*, Cambridge, MA: Harvard University Press 1985 and Arneson, 'Neutrality and Utility', *Canadian Journal of Philosophy* 20 (1990), pp. 215–40. Joseph Raz, *The Morality of Freedom*, Oxford: Oxford University Press 1986, elaborates a defence of liberalism which is clearly non-neutral, but which also is not egalitarian.

4. Roemer, p. 93.

5. Ibid., p. 13.

6. For a discussion of the limits on what socialists may do to advance socialist ends, see Norman Geras, 'Our Morals: The Ethics of Revolution', *Socialist Register* (1989), pp. 185–211.

7. The PT has done this with such success that *The Economist* magazine regularly praised its former presidential Candidate Lula. See, for example, 'Lula on the Road', *The Economist*, March 12th 1994, p. 47.

8. Pat Devine, 'Market Socialism or Participatory Planning', *Review of Radical Political Economics*, vol. 24, nos. 3 and 4, (1992), pp. 67–89.

9. I develop the argument of the previous three paragraphs in much more detail in 'Egalitarianism and Equal Availability of Political Influence', *Journal of Political Philosophy* (forthcoming).

10. Notice that on this explanation of the centrality of the value of democracy, the democratic principle is not a maximizing one. The ambition of a principle of political equality is to ensure that people have available equal influence over some appropriately determined sphere. Rights of privacy, for example, lie outside that sphere, and a principle of political equality has no ambition to increase the total amount of political influence by allowing democratic interference in the so-called private sphere.

11. It is also usually thought that the fragmented nature of work under the division of labor within capitalism contributes to alienation. I neglect this feature, because democracy in the workplace would do nothing to guarantee its elimination. For Marx's account of alienated labor see Karl Marx, *The Economic and Philosophic Manuscripts of 1844*, New York: International 1964, pp. 106–19.

12. I ignore here the possibility that the objectionability of alienation might press us to redirect the development of our technology in less alienating ways.

13. Joshua Cohen, 'The Economic Basis of Deliberative Democracy', *Social Philosophy and Policy* 6, no. 2 (1987), pp. 25–50 at p. 27.

14. Richard Arneson, 'Democratic Rights at National and Workplace Levels', in Copp, Hampton, Roemer, eds, *The Idea of Democracy*, Cambridge: Cambridge University Press 1993, pp. 118–48.

15. Arneson, p. 143.

16. Arneson also points this out and draws what are ultimately similar conclusions from it.

17. G. A. Cohen, 'The Structure of Proletarian Unfreedom', *Philosophy and Public Affairs* 12 (1983), pp. 3–33.

18. Philippe Van Parjis, 'Why Surfers Should Be Fed: A Liberal Case for an Unconditional Basic Income', *Philosophy and Public Affairs* 20 (1991), pp. 101–31 and Andrew Levine 'Fairness to Idleness', *Economics and Philosophy* (forthcoming) both argue for a basic income grant.

19. I'm grateful to some of the other contributors to this volume as well as Daniel Wikler, Daniel Hausman, and Lynn Glueck for discussions of previous versions of this chapter, and to Randy Blumenstein, Noel Carrol, A. J. Julius, David Pagac and Kirk White for discussions of the section on workplace democracy.

12

What Do Socialists Want?

Richard J. Arneson

Discussions of the ethics of socialism have tended to focus more on the scholastic issue of what Karl Marx really thought than on the substantive issue of what socialists ought to affirm. For the past several years John Roemer has brought to bear the techniques of contemporary theoretical economics on the latter issue, with illuminating results.[1] In *A Future for Socialism* he characterizes the socialist project in terms of commitment to the goals of 'equality of opportunity for (1) self-realization and welfare, (2) political influence, and (3) social status'.[2] As he recognizes, each of the terms in this sketch calls for interpretation. In these comments I do some preliminary spadework toward clarifying these proposed ideals and revealing their mutual tensions. Although I criticize Roemer's tentative affirmation of principles of equality of opportunity, at the end of this comment I strongly endorse Roemer's call for articulate clarity about the relationship between plans of economic and political reconstruction that might reasonably march under the socialist banner and the moral principles that would justify such plans in specified circumstances.

Equal Opportunity for Political Influence

It is readily shown that the affirmation of these three abstract goals, far from having the quality of truism, is highly controversial and indeed probably incorrect. To illustrate, consider the single ideal of equality of opportunity for political influence. This phrase has a nice radical democratic ring to it. The socialist, one might suppose should not be contented with merely formal democratic citizenship rights, which are compatible with the control of politics behind the scenes by fat cats. 'Equal opportunity for political influence' announces a substantive ideal of democratic equality in the sphere of citizenship. But under examination the ideal shows itself to be not quite what we had in mind and not truly an ethically desirable goal.

Let us say that equality of opportunity for political influence obtains among the citizens of a society – just in case, if any two citizens were to put forth equal effort and sacrifice toward influencing in the same direction a policy choice by the government or by the voters, each would have the same prospect of exercising the same degree of impact on the outcome. Equality of opportunity so defined is not violated when Smith has more political influence than Jones, provided that if Jones were to exert herself to the same degree that Smith does, she could have the same influence as he. Suppose, in contrast, that Smith has inherited great wealth and so is far wealthier than Jones, and that in other respects they command similar resources for influencing political outcomes. Since Smith could have greater political influence than Jones by putting forth less sacrifice, equal opportunity for political influence is violated in this case. So far, so good.

Suppose that Lenin is more intelligent than I, has a greater capacity for insight into public affairs, and has a greater ability to marshall clear and cogent arguments and articulate them persuasively. Given the political culture of the society we inhabit, these intellectual capacities tend to give their possessor access to political influence. Then, other things being equal, these differences between Lenin and me will bring it about that he will have more political influence than I, and the factors that give him greater political influence also produce a violation of the norm of equal opportunity for political influence. But no ideal of equality worth upholding is violated in these imaginary circumstances. For all that has been said so far, the society in which Lenin has greater opportunity for political influence than I might be an ideal deliberative democracy in which only the force of the better argument prevails and political policies are chosen by a consensus of voters all seeking conscientiously and reflectively to determine where the common good lies.[3]

It might seem that my argument has gone off the track by assuming a plainly incorrect account of how equal opportunity for political influence should be understood. Try this instead: equal opportunity for political influence obtains among the citizens of a society just in case, if any two citizens were to put forth equal effort and sacrifice toward influencing in the same direction a policy choice by the government or by the voters, and if the two equally striving citizens had the same intellectual capacities for political reflection and persuasion, each would have the same prospect of exercising the same degree of impact on the outcome. By this revised conception, in the example described above, Lenin and I have equal opportunity for political influence, because our unequal ability to make an impact on public affairs results from differences in our political talent, and such differences do not destroy equality on this revised conception.

Notice the disparity between this conception of equal opportunity and Roemer's characterization of the equal opportunity idea as it operates in the context of concern for self-realization and welfare: 'equality of opportunity requires that people be compensated for handicaps induced by factors over which they have no control.'[4] But surely my lack of political talent arising from my genetic endowment and early socialization experiences is a factor beyond my control, hence a factor that should be counterbalanced if equality of opportunity in the same sense that is operative in the self-realization and welfare sphere is to be applied in the sphere of political influence. Thus it seems that we must invoke different and opposed conceptions of equal opportunity in the two spheres. The question naturally arises why this should be.

I would venture the hunch that we should not seek equality of opportunity for political influence construed so that politically talented and politically untalented alike have the same prospect of influencing political process outcomes because we should want the political process to be set so that it is as likely as possible to produce good political outcomes: good in the sense that they improve the prospects that people will lead rich and satisfying lives and that distribution of these prospects is equitable.[5] Setting up the political process so that talented and untalented alike have the same access to levers of political power is a manifestly poor strategy for producing good outcomes in this sense. One powerful argument for political democracy is that, over the long run, majoritarian political procedures structured by freedom of expression and other civil liberties tend to do better than less democratic procedures at selecting qualified and conscientious political rulers. (For this argument to succeed, it is not necessary to show that democratic procedures work well, just that they are less bad than feasible alternatives.)

The opportunity for political influence is a mode of power over the lives of other people. In general, one does not have a right to power over the lives of others unless the expectable outcome of one's exercise of that power is better for those affected than what would be produced under alternative distributions of power. This is true even of the democratic franchise, which is a small lever giving the possessor of the vote a small bit of power over the lives of those affected by the decisions reached by democratic votes. For this reason there is no moral presumption that if the distribution of political intelligence and other aspects of political talent takes the form of an arbitrary natural lottery, then everyone should be entitled to equal opportunity for political influence regardless of one's share of talent, which must be undeserved.

The ideal of equal opportunity for political influence is vulnerable to criticism from another direction. The ideal could in principle be fully met in a society in which only a small subset of people participate in political affairs and have an influence on political policy making. There is equal opportunity, but very unequal exercise of the opportunity. The political process is then formally democratic but in practical terms elitist.

Equal opportunity for political influence might then be contrasted with the ideal of politics as a deliberative democracy in which citizens equally participate in public reflection with a view toward achieving a consensus on the common good. This ideal might be embraced either as intrinsically desirable or as desirable for the expected consequences for human lives of organizing politics this way. Equal opportunity for political influence is neither necessary nor sufficient for the existence of deliberative democracy. Not necessary because in an ideal deliberative democracy, where the force of the better argument determines the choice of political policy, not all citizens have equal access to the force of the better argument, so not all have equal opportunity for political influence. Not sufficient because equal opportunity for political influence, as described above, could be satisfied even if few exercise the opportunity to exert influence, but the ideal of deliberative democracy requires that all citizens participate in the deliberative process, not merely that all have the opportunity to participate.

Equal opportunity for political influence does not capture the ideal of political democracy. Moreover, it is unclear whether or not the ideal of political democracy, however it is conceived, should be regarded as morally desirable for its own sake besides as a possible means to further good goals.

Equal Opportunity for Social Status

Karl Marx detected class hierarchy within the formal equality of market trading relationships, so that when the subject of his analysis shifts from the circulation of commodities to the production of surplus value, the economic agents significantly change their demeanor: 'He, who before was the money owner, now strides, in front as capitalist; the possessor of labour-power follows as his labourer. The one with an air of importance, smirking, intent on business; the other, timid and holding back, like one who is bringing his own hide to market and has nothing to expect but – a hiding.'[6] One would suppose the socialist, whatever her other aspirations, would be committed to the abolition of the indignity of hierarchical social status.

The phenomenon of status involves at least the following elements: (1) a ranking by each of the members of a group of all the rest along some dimension of worth; plus (2) the further fact of sufficient agreement among the individual rankings to generate a social ranking. We should add that (3) occupying a position at the top of the social ranking induces significant desired behavior from group members and occupying a low position attracts significant undesired treatment. Status so characterized could be momentary or longlasting. It might be based on ascribed or earned characteristics. Notice also that the ranking by each of the members of a group can involve deference by individuals to rankers deemed authoritative, as when all members of society prize scientific achievement but the rankings of elite scientists determine everyone's rankings. We should also distinguish the one-dimensional status that accrues from scoring high on one such rating and all-things-considered status, which exists among the members of a group when (1) each member constructs an overall ranking of all the rest of the members by assigning weights to each person's score on all significant one-dimensional status rankings and summing the scores, and (2) there is sufficient agreement among the individual overall rankings to generate an overall or all-things-considered social ranking.

To simplify, let us confine our attention to overall social status. Let us say that equality of opportunity for social status obtains in a society just in case any member of society could achieve the same likelihood of obtaining the top overall status if she sought high status with effort and sacrifice equivalent to that associated with the striving for status of the individual who currently has achieved the top likelihood of occupying the top position. In other words, given that an element of luck enters the determination of status, equal opportunity for status obtains when anyone could gain the same prospect of top status as the person whose prospect of top status is highest, if one was willing to work for status as hard as the person who is now most likely to gain it. (Do not worry that equal opportunity for status so understood is utopian. If the ideal were desirable but unattainable, it might be worthwhile to strive to achieve it to the greatest feasible extent.) But is equal opportunity for social status a desirable social ideal?

Notice that the society of equal opportunity for status might be a society in which overall social status is highly salient in social life, conditioning one's treatment by others in all social encounters. The society is organized around competitive jostling and jockeying for position in one big social ranking, and this endless competitive striving for advantage conditions all of social life. In this imagined society, one's place in the pecking order matters a great deal, and much of social life is given over to ritual deference and acceptance of deference by persons occupying lower and higher rungs of the social hierarchy. In all social encounters some persons strut with an air of importance, smirking, intent on business, while other persons slink behind, diffident and obsequious. But unlike what occurs in capitalist and other class-divided societies, in our imagined society everyone has equal opportunity to attain the top status positions which confer the privilege of smirking.

For that matter, a society which exhibited equality of social status might also be a society in which much of social life is dominated by jockeying and jostling for status position, and by making and accepting gestures of deference. For example, the society of equality of status might be divided into Walzerian separate spheres, with a rigid pecking order determining the quality of social interactions in each sphere, but with different persons attaining the top status positions in the various spheres, so that everyone's overall status ranking is approximately the same.[7] This could come about in two ways: either all members of society agree in the weightings they assign to different dimensions of status, and everybody's overall status orderings rank everyone about the same, or the members disagree in the weightings to be assigned to different dimensions of status, so that even though there is overall inequality of status according to everyone's overall rankings, the individual members' rankings do not agree sufficiently to determine an overall society-wide status ranking. In either case a society could exhibit equal opportunity for status or even equality of status yet be thoroughly shaped by status-conscious behavior conditioned by recognition of significant hierarchy.

These examples suggest that alongside the ideals of equal opportunity for status and equality of status one should also consider the distinct ideal of statuslessness or freedom from status consciousness. This ideal could be attained if social rankings of individuals along dimensions of worth either ceased to exist or ceased to play a significant role in determining the character of social interaction. The latter half of this disjunct coincides with failure of condition (3) for the existence of status to obtain. In the society marked by freedom from status, either there are no pecking orders or one's place in the pecking orders that do exist does not significantly condition how one treats others and is treated by them. There might be social rankings, but no smirking.

I conjecture that once the ideals of equal opportunity for status, equality of status, and freedom from status consciousness are distinguished, the first two will appear more problematic and less attractive once they no longer benefit from the halo effect emanating from the third ideal.

Rather than view this last comment as a criticism of Roemer's views on socialist ethics, I take myself to be following up Roemer's explicit statement that his list of fundamental goals is provisional and in need of further analysis. Moreover, I view it as entirely an open question whether or not any of the ideals of equal opportunity for status, equality of status or freedom from status is intrinsically morally desirable (as opposed to desirable as possibly effective means toward some other goal). Perhaps status competitions of some types, in some circumstances, are on the whole desirable.

No doubt social life provides many examples of debilitating status competition. Society upholds an unworthy standard such as getting one's livelihood by unearned rather than earned income, and people waste their lives trying to outdo each other according to the false standard. This sort of example does not show the badness of status competition, just the badness of status competition organized around an unworthy standard. But one can conceive worthy standards. Imagine that people are competing for status by striving to achieve excellence according to the standard of virtuous public service directed toward the common good. Even if the standard that determines status is worthy, one might worry that focussing people's attention on their relative standing with respect to this standard rather than on their absolute level of performance or satisfaction of the standard is bad. But why? Why is it inappropriate to wish to be best, or better than most, and appropriate to wish to be good or excellent? For many activities in which humans engage, the standards of good performance are essentially comparative, so there is no saying what is good performance without having an idea of how people on the average tend to perform. And even if one's conception of good in some sphere is not parasitic on one's notion of better, still, what is wrong with wanting to be better?

Another thought that suggests the undesirability of status hierarchy is that it may induce wasteful or unprofitable competition. But this criticism applies to particular forms of status competition, not to status competition per se. Surely competition for status along some dimensions of worth is socially useful. If excellence in playing basketball is desirable, then upholding basketball excellence as a goal worthy of pursuit is probably desirable, and inevitably the Michael Jordans of the world will be esteemed above their fellow athletes. Perhaps in some contexts status can serve as a cheap reward motivating people to socially useful action; if medals could sometimes substitute for cash prizes, the resources saved could be put to alternative good uses. Perhaps it is the idea of competition for all-things-considered or over-all status that is felt to be meretricious. Whether this is so or not would seem to depend on the difficult issue of whether or not it is good that there should be sufficient agreement among the values of the members of society about the comparative value of the goods that serve as dimensions along which status is measured to permit society-wide overall rankings.

The desire for high status might be derogated as essentially com-petitive, necessarily producing losers as well as winners. If all want to be best, all but one individual (except in the case of ties) must be frustrated. But of course, since most valued goods are in scarce supply, even when the goods are not essentially competitive in character, it is often contingently the case that your desire for a good can be satisfied only if other people's desires for that good are frustrated. It may simply be a fact about the world we inhabit that many goods worth having are either essentially or contingently the object of competitive striving. Moreover, even if many want to be best and only one can win, perhaps the nature of the competition is such that the gains of the winner over-balance the losses of the losers (who do not much care about losing). And again, we often judge status competition to be invidious when the competition generates aggregate negative total utility; the losses of the losers outweighing the gains of the winners (here I assume cardinal interpersonal utility comparisons can be made). But this objection does not tell against all status competitions, just against those that generate aggregate utility loss.

A clue that may be worth seizing is the distinction between the class-less society envisaged by Marx and the society free of status distinctions envisaged by some as a generalization of Marx's concerns.[8] Class and status are of course different ideas. Your status is determined by how other members of society regard you, but your class membership is determined by the extent of your control over means of production, whatever the attitudes of other people toward you might be. But in-sofar as Marx is concerned with status, what concerns him are status distinctions arising from class relations. Perhaps something could be done with this. Perhaps status distinctions arising from certain sorts of economic relationships should be singled out and opposed on principle. I suspect that opposition to status distinctions should be limited to some types rather than directed toward the abolition of all types, but it is not obvious that economic status singles out a universally obnoxious variety.

In the light of these various considerations, a plausible position is that status distinctions and competition for status are intrinsically neither desirable nor undesirable, but can be either depending on their effects on people's life prospects. If it is feasible to abolish a particular realm of status, and doing so would tend to make people's lives better on the whole or bring about a more equitable distribution of chances to lead rich and worthwhile lives, then one should support that abolition, otherwise one should not.

Equal Opportunity for Self-realization and Welfare

This norm to my mind cuts much closer to the heart of the matter than the two norms just reviewed. After all, the traditional socialist critique of capitalism targets the extremes of wealth and poverty that a market economy based on private ownership continuously generates and perpetuates. Intellectually sophisticated attempts to characterize these great disparities as morally deserved may impress us with their cleverness but ultimately appear unconvincing.[9] As we will see, within the socialist critique several different objections are jostling for attention. We may object to the magnitude of the gap between the living conditions of the poor and the wealthy or to the disproportion between the ratio of the deservingness of the rich to that of the poor and the ratio of the wealth of the rich to that of the poor. On the other hand, we may find most objectionable the avoidable bad quality of the lives the poor can anticipate. Marx suggests yet another objection when he observes that for a given state of technology, the time at the disposal of society 'for the free development, intellectual and social, of the individual is greater, in proportion as the work is more and more evenly divided among all the able-bodied members of society, and as a particular class is more and more deprived of the power to shift the natural burden of labour from its own shoulders to those of another layer of society.'[10] I hear in this comment an appeal to a norm of reciprocity: To the extent that everyone shares in the benefits of social cooperation, those who are able should reciprocate this benefit by putting forth (to an equitable extent) effort aimed at contributing to the cooperative pool from which these benefits are drawn.

One plausible interpretation of the moral norm underlying the socialist critique of capitalist inequality is equality of life prospects: all members of society should have equal opportunity to lead good lives.

Roemer asserts this norm and decomposes the idea of a good life (meaning a life that is good from a self-interested standpoint for the person who lives it) into two components: welfare, which is having one's personal preferences satisfied; and self-realization, which Roemer, following Jon Elster, glosses as the development and exercise of the powers and abilities of the individual in ways that are observable by others and that admit of public evaluation.[11] Roemer like Elster finds the affirmation of self-realization construed as essential to human good expressed in the writings of Marx.

Given Roemer's understanding of what welfare is, it is not surprising that he does not take welfare to be all there is to the good life. I would go further. Sometimes welfare as Roemer conceives it makes no contribution at all to the goodness of someone's life. Consider preferences based on confused reasoning or false belief. Imagine that my older sister devotes her entire life to constructing monuments to my virtue (which she supposes to be of high caliber). This is overwhelmingly her most cherished personal preference and it is satisfied abundantly. At her deathbed the landscape is dotted with massive monuments to my virtue. However, my virtue level is nothing special, but well below average. Given that her personal preferences are overwhelmingly satisfied, my sister obtained a high level of welfare-as-construed-by-Roemer, but her life was a tragic waste. The problem here is not that 'self-realization' was lacking. We can add to the story the detail that my sister strained her talents to the limit in constructing her grotesque pointless statues, which were thoroughly evaluated and judged worthless by the public. The problem is that her preferences were ill-considered and based on cognitive error; hence their satisfaction does not significantly contribute to her welfare, if we are to understand welfare as what makes someone's life go better, what adds intrinsically to one's flourishing. Since preference satisfaction per se does not always enhance the quality of a person's life, preference satisfaction is a poor candidate for the role that Roemer assigns it – one of two fundamental elements that together determine the goodness of a person's life.

To figure out what is really meant or should be meant when we assert that someone's life goes better or worse is to plunge into deep and incompletely charted water. In the previous paragraph I appealed to the idea that what makes a person's life go well is determined by the judgments that she herself would make about what is valuable for her for its own sake, if she were to make these judgments without suffering from cognitive defects such as false belief or confused reasoning. In other words, each person's good is determined from that very person's evaluative perspective, as formed by her own experiences and dispositions, but it is her evaluations not as they are but as they would be if she were suffering from no cognitive errors that settle the standard by which her quality of life is to be measured. This proposal encounters puzzles and difficulties which I cannot enter into here. My point is limited and simple. I do not believe that welfare-as-construed-by-Roemer is rightly viewed as a fundamental component of a person's good.

To my mind, if we had a more adequate conception of welfare than Roemer's in place, we would be less tempted to suppose that some other element such as Elster-style self-realization must be added in order to capture what makes a person's life go well. (Let's call the whole of which preference satisfaction and self-realization are claimed to be the parts 'well-being'.) Roemer is persuaded that preference satisfaction is not all there is to well-being by considering the example of Tiny Tim, the Charles Dickens character who is crippled, but very cheerful, and has many easily satisfied preferences.[12] Tiny Tim is happy and enjoys a far-above-average level of welfare (that is, preference satisfaction), but we are still inclined to suppose that Tiny Tim is badly off, not well off, and according to egalitarian norms of distributive justice is entitled to compensation that alleviates his handicap, such as a state-of-the-art wheelchair or mechanized crutches.

If welfare is not preference satisfaction as Roemer thinks but satisfaction of well-considered judgments about what would be valuable for oneself, the example looks less puzzling, and the identification of welfare and well-being looks less problematic. The Tiny Tim story might be elaborated in two significantly different ways. In the first version, Tim's evaluations and preferences simply fail to register the extent of the loss that being a cripple entails. If this cognitive deficiency were repaired, his evaluations and preferences would place a high premium on the mobility he lacks, and he would not qualify as having high welfare despite his cheerfulness and obliviousness. In the second possible version of the story, Tim's character and dispositions are such that, even if his evaluations and preferences were formed without any taint of cognitive error, he would still count as nothing the satisfactions that lack of physical mobility denies him. Playing chess rates high in Tim's well-considered preference ordering and traipsing around the countryside or the shopping malls and the like rates very low. In this second version of the story, if it is plausible to suppose that Tim has the opportunity for a high level of satisfaction of well-considered judgments of what would be valuable for himself, it is ipso facto plausible to suppose that Tim has the opportunity for a high level of well-being (a good life).

Let us set aside the concern voiced in the previous paragraph and assume for the sake of the argument that Roemer is correct that welfare-construed-as-satisfaction-of-one's-actual-preferences is one element of well-being. Does adding Elster-style self-realization to Roemer-style welfare produce a satisfactory and complete notion of well-being (what makes a person's life go well)? No, I think not. Whereas it is very plausible to suppose with Roemer that there are some things which are objectively valuable for individuals and enhance the quality of their lives whatever their attitudes toward these things may be, it is very implausible to identify the set of objective goods with exercise and development of talents in a way that admits of public evaluation.

The point that worries me is not that there are trivial talents and abilities, such as building houses of cards, the development and exercise of which contribute little if anything to well-being: I suppose that a full account of self-realization would include a norm that distinguishes trivial from significant human talents and forms of excellence. My worry is that there are many important human goods which have just as much title to be classified as objectively valuable as the development and exercise of talents in ways subject to assessment. In this category of valuable goods other than talent exercise I would include taking enjoyment from passive consumerist experiences (such as lying on the beach and eating ice cream), having intense aesthetic experiences (such as seeing plays, reading books, listening to music, perhaps taking mind-altering drugs), having relations of friendship and love, and so on. It is plausible to suppose that these experiences can enhance the quality of a person's life, even if having them does not contribute toward one's preference satisfaction. A religious ascetic in the grip of a misguided religious doctrine may attach no value to having carnal pleasure and may not want it, but still, getting such pleasure would do him good. The various putative goods listed above either do not involve any exercise or development of talent or do not involve it in a way that admits of public assessment.

I conclude that on the assumption that equal opportunity for having a good life is a plausible rendering of the norm underlying the socialist critique of capitalist inequality, Roemer's proposed decomposition of the idea of a good life into the elements of welfare and self-realization is not successful.

Equality of Opportunity versus Equality of Outcome

Why should a just society concerned with equality be concerned to provide individuals with equality of opportunity for valued things rather than equality in the resultant shares of the valued things that individuals ultimately gain from whatever opportunities are provided? Why have equal opportunity rather than equal outcome?

Speaking specifically of equal opportunity for welfare, Roemer has a sensible answer: 'Were equality of welfare the goal rather than equality of opportunity for welfare, then society would be mandated to provide huge resource endowments to those who adopt terribly expensive and unrealistic goals.' In contrast, equality of opportunity for welfare 'puts some responsibility on [the individual] for choosing welfare-inducing goals that are reasonable.'[13]

Several different thoughts might be expressed by this answer. In my judgment none of these thoughts ultimately generates a defense of the idea that a society's fundamental principles of justice should be concerned with opportunities not outcomes.

One thought is that the announced commitment by society to guarantee all citizens equality in the distribution of some value would give rise to horribly perverse incentives. Roemer provides the example of a cultivated expensive taste. If Smith cultivates modest goals and hence can reach a high level of satisfaction with modest resources, but Jones cultivates grandiose ambitions which cannot be satisfied without enormous expenditures by society, it does not seem fair to deal with Smith and Jones in such a way as to induce equal welfare for them. For that matter, why should I get out of bed in the morning if society is committed to guaranteeing that I will reach exactly the same level of welfare overall as anyone else in society, no more and no less, whether I exert myself vigorously on my own behalf or pull up the covers round my head and vegetate?

This line of thought appears to offer a pragmatic objection against the announcement of a commitment on the part of society to sustain equality of outcome along some dimension. The objection seems to be that such a commitment would cause an enormous welfare loss, so that even if the commitment is met and equality is achieved, this will be equality at a low level of welfare compared to what is feasible. Suppose in the light of this worry we amend equality of welfare so that it becomes a principle that requires equality of welfare at the highest feasible level for all. The objection then can be revised to target this new principle: if society undertakes a public commitment to ensure equality of welfare at the highest feasible level of welfare for all, this public commitment will be self-defeating in the sense that equality at a higher feasible level of welfare could be obtained in the absence of this commitment.

The objection appears to be pragmatic rather than principled. That is to say, the objection seems to locate a problem not in the principle of equality at the highest feasible level but in the untoward consequences of the public adoption of the principle by society. The conclusion then should not be that the principle is false or morally unacceptable. Rather the conclusion should be that public adoption of the principle is unlikely to be the best means of satisfying it to the fullest possible extent. Perhaps public adoption of equal opportunity would better secure equality at the highest feasible level than would public adoption of the revised equality principle itself. This finding would be interesting but would not suffice to show that anyone should believe that equal opportunity is the better candidate for the role of fundamental principle. For one cannot justify a proposed fundamental principle by observing, even if correctly, that adopting it would be an efficient means to the achievement of some further, different principle.

This point can be put another way. If one is concerned that implementation of a principle of equality would give rise to perverse incentives, this indicates that one's ultimate concern is oriented to the final outcomes that perverse incentives would worsen. This line of thought cannot provide grounds for affirming an equal opportunity principle except as an instrument for obtaining better final outcomes.

Another possible line of thought in defense of equality of opportunity invokes the responsibility of an individual to exercise reasonable prudence in the conduct of her life. How exactly do we get from the supposition that the individual is responsible for behaving with reasonable prudence to the different thought that if the individual fails to exercise reasonable prudence and as a result he is threatened with harm, no one else is responsible for taking effective steps to avert the harm or for compensating the person for the harm if it becomes unavoidable? Let us say that to be responsible for an outcome is to be obligated to bring it about that the outcome fall within an acceptable range. In this sense the fact that Smith is responsible for outcome X obviously does not preclude others also being responsible for outcome X. If a small child is drowning in shallow water at a public beach in plain sight of a hundred nearby adults, each individual may be responsible for the outcome, obligated to save the child provided that no other adult has saved her. From the fact that the individual has primary responsibility (obligation) for acting prudently to safeguard her own welfare, it does not follow that society does not have a back-up responsibility (obligation) to act charitably to forestall harm if the individual acts imprudently and harm threatens her. One responsibility obligation need not crowd out another; both may coexist.

Exactly the same point holds true if responsibility is understood as answerability. Given that it is within Smith's power to influence which outcome within a certain range occurs, we may hold Smith responsible for the outcome, meaning she is answerable for its quality, liable to praise or blame depending on its quality. But holding Smith responsible in this sense is compatible with holding others responsible as well for the same outcome. We may hold Smith responsible for a drowning that she could have prevented and also hold Jones responsible for the same drowning, and we may hold the individual responsible within limits for the quality of life she secures for herself while also holding society responsible for the quality of life of the same individual. (I believe these points broadly support generous policies of income support to poor people in capitalist democracies, policies different in spirit from what is currently in favor in the US.)

Another line of thought lurking in the neighborhood of the expensive tastes worry is that the responsibility (obligation) of society to cater to the welfare of any individual may be limited in stringency in the sense that those bound by the obligation are only required to fulfill it if the sacrifice they must incur in order to fulfill it is below some threshold value. Imagine that Smith needs help in order to attain a decent level of welfare, but every time we offer help, he squanders it, over and over again. At some point in this cycle, given our limited responsibility, our obligation to help gives out. Perhaps the same goes for expensive tastes, at least voluntarily cultivated ones. Given the assumption that the responsibility of society with respect to the maintenance of tolerable levels of welfare for all members of society is limited in stringency, it remains an open question whether within the limits deemed reasonable, the responsibility (obligation) we do have is oriented to welfare outcomes or to opportunities for welfare.

If the responsibility were oriented to provision of opportunities as their ultimate concern, then it would seem that our limited obligation to provide opportunities would not diminish or cease just because we happen to know that provision of opportunities in this case is pointless because the opportunities will certainly not be utilized. Imagine that Smith and Jones live on separate islands, and that they can interact in only one way: knowing that the island she inhabits is rich in resources and that the island Jones inhabits is barren by comparison, Smith can provide Jones with extra resources by placing them in a boat that will drift with the tides to the shores of Jones's island. On some views of distributive justice, Smith is obligated to help Jones by transferring resources to Jones in the example as so far described. Now suppose that Smith knows the further fact that any resources she sends Jones will certainly be left to rot on the beach (perhaps Jones has strict religious scruples against profiting from a gift or perhaps Jones will just procrastinate endlessly and fail to move the goods from the beach). The opportunities Smith is providing Jones are just as much opportunities, just as rich in potential welfare, whether they are used or wasted, so if the ultimate obligation of society is to bring about equality of opportunity for welfare, it is hard to see why the obligation should lapse in this example. If you think the obligation does give out here, and that Smith is not responsible for making sacrifices to supply Jones pointless opportunities, my conjecture is that you are valuing opportunity provision just insofar as that is a means to ethically desirable outcomes, rather than as ethically desirable for its own sake.

An equal opportunity norm tolerates leaving an individual in a worse condition if she conducts herself imprudently through her own fault, than the condition she would have reached had she been prudent. A finegrained equal opportunity principle is formulated so that it respects the maxim that people should be held responsible only for what lies within their control. According to the finegrained version of the principle, two people do not have equal opportunities (for self-realization and welfare, say) if they could reach the same level of the target goods if they behaved in a perfectly prudent way, but one would have to exert herself to a greater degree or resist temptation to a greater degree or the like in order to achieve this perfect prudence. According to the finegrained version of equal opportunity, the responsibility of the individual must be tailored to her particular choice-making and choice-following deficits. Make the heroic assumption that we can make this determination and hence can determine when any two individuals truly enjoy equal opportunity for self-realization and welfare. We might think that once the members of society enjoy equality of opportunity understood in a finegrained way, it is better that society allow any member's level of attainment of self-realization and welfare to be determined by her own choices in the circumstances she faces. Given that finegrained equality of opportunity has been achieved, it is morally preferable that people who behave imprudently through their own fault should tend to do worse than people who are prudent. An equality of opportunity principle tolerates this outcome, and hence is morally preferable to any equality of outcome principle, we might be inclined to think.

This inclination is wrong. At least, the intuition that the extent to which people attain the target goods with which distributive justice is concerned should be allowed to vary with the quality of their personal conduct does not uniquely favor an equality of opportunity principle. The problem is that even finegrained equality of opportunity will forbid providing further opportunities to someone who already has enjoyed an equal share of opportunities and squanders them, but in some circumstances the refusal to tender more aid is unfair.[14] Consider Bert, a young adult who enjoys finegrained equality of opportunity, but then behaves imprudently in a way that is unequivocally his own fault: he rides a motorcycle fast on a deserted terrain without protective headgear and without insurance. Suppose a crash occurs and Bert could be restored to good health if society provided surgery: if not Bert will become a vegetable for the rest of his life. Since Bert has already received his fair share of opportunities, he should not get more according to equal opportunity, but this seems cruel. The problem seems to be that Bert's 'punishment' exceeds his 'crime'. He is imprudent, but he is also very unlucky, so that one act of imprudence threatens to ruin his entire life. Given that Bert has behaved imprudently and costs must now be paid, it is perhaps morally appropriate that he should suffer for his imprudence, but equal opportunity imposes excessive suffering.

An equal opportunity principle is blind to results once equal opportunities have been provided. A more outcome-oriented view that respects the intuition that the truly undeserving should be permitted to suffer the costs their conduct causes might include a presumption in favor of equality of outcome (equal self-realization and welfare for all) but would qualify the presumption by a norm that fault forfeits first: when truly faulty conduct generates unavoidable costs, it is better other things equal that these costs be imposed on less deserving individuals (those whose true fault is greater) than on more deserving individuals (those whose true fault is less). Applied to the Bert case, the norms of equality of outcome qualified by fault forfeits first would hold that Bert should be given the operation that will restore his health, to prevent his self-realization and welfare levels over the course of his life from falling far below average; if possible, however, the costs of the operation and similar restorative measures necessitated by faulty conduct should be imposed on the faulty in proportion to the true faultiness of their conduct.

I conclude that, even if one does not challenge the conceivability of obtaining sufficient information about individuals to implement, even in thought, a finegrained equality of opportunity principle, this principle is still shown by the Bert case to be too punitive in its implications. The motivating idea that seemed to support equality of opportunity makes a better fit with the norm of fault forfeits first. Moreover, the equality of opportunity norm has been shown to be unsupported by reflection on our concepts of responsibility and vulnerable to the pointless opportunities objection.

Why Equality?

Not all political egalitarians favor equality as a moral ideal. That is to say, some who favor redistributionist, traditionally left-wing policies (involving transfers of resources and opportunities to worse-off members of society for the purpose of bringing about improvement in their life prospects) support these policy preferences without appealing to any principle of distributive justice that holds it to be intrinsically morally desirable that everyone should have the same in some respect. Let us say that a *true egalitarian* is one who does take some form of distributive equality to be significantly morally desirable; be it equality or equal opportunity with respect to welfare, some mix of welfare and self-realization, primary goods, some other measure of resources, functionings, functioning capabilities, achievement of excellence according to a perfectionist measure, or some other equalisandum.[15] Then not all political egalitarians are true egalitarians. Some see equality or equality of opportunity as at most, in some circumstances, a useful means to the attainment of other, genuinely important moral goals.

In other writings Roemer himself has expressed agnosticism as to whether true egalitarianism is the correct line for political egalitarians to embrace.[16] I agree that there are grounds for doubt. For example, if your sole principle were, say, equality of resources, even if you qualified the principle as Roemer suggests by stipulating that the equality to be sought is equality of resources for all persons at the highest possible level, you would still have to favor wastage of resources that could be used to improve people's lives in some circumstances. If George has more resources than others, and there is no way to transfer resources from George to the others, and no way to bring the others up to the resource level of George, then equality of resources at the highest possible level must hold that George's extra resources should be destroyed in order to create equality. But many have found it a hard saying that it is better to make George worse off in resources without making anyone else better off in resources, just in order to ensure that everyone's resource holdings are the same.

One might respond that perhaps sustaining relations of equality in people's resource holdings, even when achieved by destroying rather than transferring resources, might make people's lives go better, for example, by reducing envy and fostering communal fellow feeling. But to respond in this way is to suppose that equality of resources is valuable as a means. If what really matters is how people's lives go, the well-being levels they reach, then the question would become: is equality of well-being intrinsically morally important? A version of this worry would again be relevant. If one's ultimate aim is to achieve *equality* of well-being at the highest possible level, then if George has had a nicer life so far, it should be morally desirable to give George's life a nasty turn, so his overall well-being level decreases, even though hurting George in this way does no good to anyone else. There is nothing incoherent in this doctrine, but to many of us it seems inhumane. I suspect that commitment to equality for its own sake is more often attributed to the Left by right-wingers intent on discrediting their rivals than unequivocally affirmed by left-wingers.

In order to cast some doubt on the supposition that political egalitarianism requires true egalitarianism for its defense, I sketch here an alternate principle that would generate justification of political egalitarian policies in many circumstances. This principle helps itself to the assumption that cardinal interpersonal measurements of well-being are possible. Of course, even if this large assumption is granted, measurability in principle does not guarantee measurability in practice. The justification of political egalitarianism that relies on the alternate principle I shall describe also requires the assumption that at least rough interpersonal comparisons of well-being are feasible in societies as we know them, with existing limited technologies relevant to the assessment of well-being.

The central idea of the proposed rival of true egalitarianism is that the strength of the moral reason to bring about a small gain in well-being for a person varies inversely with the person's cardinal level of well-being before receiving this benefit (on the assumption that the level exceeds zero). In other words, the less well-being a person enjoys, the greater the moral value of bringing about a small improvement in the person's well-being. The overall moral value of bringing about a small improvement in anyone's well-being then varies directly with the size of the gain and inversely with the person's previous well-being score. Building on this approach, the doctrine holds that institutions and policies should be set so that moral value so measured is maximized. The position has been called the weighted well-being view.[17] It will turn out in many possible circumstances that more moral value is created by giving a dollar to a person who is badly off in well-being than by giving a dollar to a person who is well-off in this respect, even if the receipt of the dollar would produce a greater increase in well-being for the already better off person (who may be an efficient transformer of resources into well-being). Such a position quite obviously has an affinity for political egalitarian policy measures.

Further discussion of weighted well-being is beyond the scope of this discussion. The aim of the present discussion is limited to arguing for the following claim. True egalitarianism in distributive justice (the position that holds that equality in all persons' shares of some target good is morally desirable for its own sake) encounters objections which do not attach to at least one rival moral doctrine (weighted well-being) which, like true egalitarianism, offers broad support to political egalitarianism. Asked to choose between a norm of equality of outcome and a norm of equality of opportunity, one should perhaps reject both.

Conclusion

Unlike John Roemer, Karl Marx eschewed discussion of first principles of ethics, at least in his published writings. Insofar as Marx's writings contain ethical condemnation of capitalist institutions, the principles that ground the condemnation are not the focus of attention. I think it is fair to say that Marx tends to assume that those readers who can be brought to accept the empirical characterizations of capitalist society that he is at pains to establish, would overwhelmingly converge, from a variety of commonsense perspectives, on the judgment that the society truly characterized in these ways is ethically indefensible beyond the pale.[18] One could say that Marx's approach to moral issues is political not metaphysical. He does not try to justify communism or condemn capitalism by appeal to first principles of ethics; rather Marx implicitly appeals to a wide range of plausible mid-level principles that have the property of converging in support of the political assessment and proposals that he is concerned to advance.

Moreover, leaving Marx's example aside, I note that the term 'socialism' is used to refer to a family of proposals for reconstructing the economic and political organization of society that center on the idea of public rather than private ownership of the major means of production. For clarity's sake one might well wish to resist Roemer's reidentification of the socialist project with commitment to a set of egalitarian first principles and to a pragmatic orientation to the issue of how these principles might best be achieved. Invoking the authority of Marx, one might suspect that agreement on first principles of ethics is neither necessary nor sufficient for achieving a consensus in society on a political program that is morally continuous with the socialist and communist tradition.

Nevertheless I strongly agree with Roemer that socialist theorists today are well advised to be explicit about the moral underpinnings of their institutional critiques and proposals. Theorists should not merely invoke principles but should try to motivate their acceptance. The reason that Marx's example in this regard should not be followed is simple. Contrary to what Marx supposed, his criticisms of capitalism rely on highly controversial moral claims, not on obvious commonsense truisms. The work by Roemer and others, that traces Marx's critique of exploitation back to egalitarian moral principles, definitively shows that Marx's 'political not metaphysical' moral opinions are revisionary and controversial or at least that, when one deletes certain false social scientific claims from Marx's analyses, to support his criticisms of capitalist society as he modeled it one must appeal to moral claims that may be true but are far from obvious.[19] Hence there is no getting around the need to be clear about the claims and about how they might be best supported by sound principles. If you cannot assume a prior moral agreement with your audience you have no choice but to try to create a new consensus by moral argument. In this larger context, although I might disagree with this or that ethical formulation that Roemer proposes, I strongly endorse his broad strategy of redefining socialism in terms of basic ethical commitments and keeping an open mind about the political and economic arrangements that would be required to fulfill these commitments so far as is feasible. Socialism on this reconstruction becomes a variety of liberal political morality not a rival to it.

Notes

1. Several of these essays have been collected in John E. Roemer, *Egalitarian Perspectives: Essays in Philosophical Economics*, Cambridge: Cambridge University Press 1994. See also his books *A General Theory of Exploitation and Class*, Cambridge, MA: Harvard University Press 1982 and *Free To Lose: An Introduction to Marxist Economic Philosophy*, Cambridge, MA: Harvard University Press 1988.

2. John E. Roemer, *A Future for Socialism*, Cambridge, MA: Harvard University Press 1994, p. 11.

3. On deliberative democracy, see Jürgen Habermas, *Communication and the Evolution of Society*, tr. Thomas McCarthy, Boston: Beacon Press 1979; also Joshua Cohen, 'Deliberation and Democratic Legitimacy', in Alan Hamlin and Philip Pettit, eds, *The Good Polity*, Oxford: Basil Blackwell 1989, pp. 17–34.

4. Roemer, *A Future for Socialism*, p. 12.

5. See Richard J. Arneson, 'Socialism as the Extension of Democracy', *Social Philosophy and Policy* 10, no. 2 (Spring 1993), pp. 145–71; also Arneson, 'Democratic Rights at National and Workplace Levels', in David Copp, Jean Hampton and John E. Roemer, eds, *The Idea of Democracy*, Cambridge: Cambridge University Press 1993, pp. 118–48.

6. Karl Marx, *Capital*, vol. 1, tr. Samuel Moore and Edward Aveling, New York: Charles H. Kerr 1906, p. 196.

7. On separate spheres of distribution, see Michael Walzer, *Spheres of Justice: A Defense of Pluralism and Equality*, New York: Basic Books 1983. See also David Miller, 'Complex Equality', and Richard Arneson, 'Against "Complex Equality"' both in David Miller and Michael Walzer, eds, *Pluralism, Justice, and Equality*, Oxford: Oxford University Press (forthcoming).

8. The idea that Marx is concerned to eliminate inequalities of class hierarchy rather than all manner of social inequalities is explored in Allen Wood, 'Marx and Equality', in John E. Roemer, ed., *Analytical Marxism*, Cambridge: Cambridge University Press, pp. 283–303.

9. See Robert Nozick, *Anarchy, State, and Utopia*, New York: Basic Books 1974; also David Gauthier, *Morals by Agreement*, Oxford: Oxford University Press 1986.

10. Marx, *Capital*, vol. 1, p. 581.

11. Jon Elster, 'Self-realization in Work and Politics: The Marxist Conception of the Good Life', *Social Philosophy and Policy* 3, no. 2 (Spring 1986), pp. 97–126.

12. The Tiny Tim example is drawn from G. A. Cohen, 'On the Currency of Egalitarian Justice', *Ethics* 99, no. 3 (1989), pp. 906–44.

13. Roemer, *A Future for Socialism*, p. 12.

14. I borrow this point from Marc Fleurbaey.

15. On the issue, what sort of equality is intrinsically morally important, see Amartya Sen, *Inequality Reexamined*, Cambridge, MA: Harvard University Press 1992.

16. John E. Roemer, 'The Morality and Efficiency of Market Socialism', *Ethics* 102, no. 3 (April 1992), pp. 448–64.

17. See Paul Weirich, 'Utility Tempered with Equality', *Nous* 17, no. 3 (September 1983), pp. 423–39.

18. This point is explored in Allen Wood, 'The Marxian critique of Justice', *Philosophy and Public Affairs* 1, no. 3 (Spring 1972), pp. 244–82.

19. See Roemer, *A General Theory of Exploitation and Class*; also Roemer, 'Property Relations vs. Surplus Value in Marxian Exploitation' and 'Should Marxists Be Interested in Exploitation?', both reprinted in his *Egalitarian Perspectives*, pp. 37–64 and pp. 65–96; also Richard Arneson, 'What's Wrong with Exploitation?', *Ethics* 91, no. 2 (January 1981), pp. 202–27; and Will Kymlicka, *Contemporary Political Philosophy: An Introduction*, Oxford: Oxford University Press 1990, ch. 5.

Saving Socialism and/or Abandoning It

Andrew Levine

I confess to a deep ambivalence about *A Future for Socialism*.[1] On the one hand, it is plain that much of what Roemer says about socialism, both critically and constructively, is on target. Anyone committed to retrieving what remains vital in the socialist tradition cannot fail to appreciate the importance of this contribution to socialist theory. On the other hand, it is hard to resist the conclusion that socialism after Roemer is hardly socialism at all; that in order to save socialism, he found it necessary to abandon it. My aim in these remarks will be to articulate this ambivalence and to try to move beyond it. To this end, I shall take issue mainly with Roemer's claims about what socialists want.

Roemer thinks that socialists, whether they knew it or not, have always wanted what contemporary liberal egalitarians want: equality construed in roughly the way(s) that have emerged in the ongoing 'equality of what?' debate.[2] Roemer's aim is to show how equality, so conceived, can be achieved or at least approximated without sacrificing economic well-being. His central claim is that socializing property relations, through a radical transformation of control and revenue rights in non-labor productive assets, is instrumental and perhaps indispensable for realizing equality, and that market mechanisms are instrumental and almost certainly indispensable for economic well-being. *A Future for Socialism* is mainly devoted to developing and defending these theses.

What I will suggest is that those of us, like Roemer, who want the socialist tradition to develop and flourish risk being led astray by Roemer's account of what socialists want. Socialists do want equality and efficiency, though perhaps not quite, as Roemer assumes, in the sense(s) that have come to dominate contemporary academic discourse. They also want peace, sound environmental policies, the end of racial, sexual and ethnic oppression and many other laudable objectives that most liberals want too. But at least some socialists, those whose political and theoretical positions derive from Marx, want something that liberals do not and that liberal theory cannot properly accommodate: they want *communism*.[3] My quarrel with Roemer's account of socialism's future therefore has to do, in the first instance, with what his vision of socialism leaves out and the implications of these omissions for the moral philosophical underpinnings of socialist politics. However, the ambivalence I will go on to exhibit has to do mainly with the politics *A Future for Socialism* suggests or, more precisely, with the implications of Roemer's prescriptions for the strategies of political movements that aim to continue the tradition(s) of nineteenth- and twentieth-century socialism. In short, I am dubious that in the absence of a political vision that transcends the liberal egalitarian horizon, Roemer's proposed reforms, whatever their merits, can help to get us from where we now are to where socialists ultimately want to be.

The Marxist tradition has made a virtue of undertheorizing communism.[4] A democratic commitment to the 'self-emancipation' of the working class and a corresponding opposition to social engineering partly account for this reticence. No doubt there are less principled explanations as well. This is not the place to attempt what Marx himself forswore. But even if I can offer no 'recipes for the cookshops of the future' to contrast with liberal egalitarian visions, I can draw on the understanding of communism that for decades has directed socialist practice. Communism implies a form of community that supersedes market society. It does not follow from this observation that socialism is incompatible with markets. Indeed, Roemer may be right to insist that any feasible socialism must rely on market mechanisms. But, if we are not to abandon socialism in order to save it, we must do so in a way that does not block the way towards the realization of a genuinely communist social order, *beyond* market society. In market societies, individuals' behaviors are not directly coordinated at the societal level; what occurs in the aggregate emerges as an unintended consequence of voluntary bilateral exchanges, motivated by self-interest. In contrast, under communism, coordination at the level of the whole society is achieved directly and democratically; as in the just state of Rousseau's *The Social Contract*, 'the whole people rule concerning the whole people'. But, again following Rousseau's lead, when the whole people rule, they are not motivated, as in market societies and also in mainstream understandings of democratic collective choice, by self-interest. Their votes do not register preferences for alternative outcomes in contention, but opinions as to what is best for the collective entity they freely constitute. In other words, under communism, individuals view themselves as indivisible parts of collective entities, and they make the interests of these collectivities their own. In Rousseau's terms, they place themselves 'under the supreme direction of the general will', that principle of volition that aims at the interest of the whole community. Thus individuals' behaviors are coordinated in consequence of a consensus on ends around communal interests. Under communism therefore there exists a form of community that even the most radically egalitarian liberalism cannot contemplate. It is this vision, along with equality and other objectives socialists and liberals share, that has sustained generations of socialist militants. To fail to accord it pride of place or even to acknowledge it at all is to misrepresent what at least Marxist socialists want.

To establish the legitimacy of this concern, I will begin by venturing some thoughts about the place of A Future for Socialism in the trajectory of Roemer's own intellectual and political evolution. To do so is also, unavoidably, to reflect on its place in the theoretical and political tradition inaugurated by Marx. Roemer has been a central figure in the 'analytical Marxist' movement, an intellectual current that once promised, and may yet deliver, a reconstructed Marxist theory (or theories). But it may also appear with historical hindsight that analytical Marxism provided a way to abandon Marxism or rather to collapse what is living in it into what Marxists would once have called 'bourgeois' social science and philosophy. Since the future of Marxism is relevant to the future of socialism, a brief look at how Marxist socialism stands after nearly two decades of analytical investigations, focussing especially on Roemer's own contributions to the subject, is an apt starting-point for reflecting on A Future for Socialism.

Marxism after Roemer

Non-Marxists and even anti-Marxists used to concede, following Schumpeter's account in Capitalism, Socialism and Democracy,[5] that there was a hard core of good social theory in Marx's work, interspersed with many bad, politically motivated 'prophesies'. But then it was claimed, following Schumpeter again, that virtually all of what was worthwhile had passed into the mainstream intellectual culture. I think there is much to fault in these observations. The claim that some of Marx's ideas have been assimilated into received understandings of the ways societies work is beyond dispute. Among these assimilated notions is the concept of capitalism itself; another, the idea that social-ism is capitalism's historical alternative. For many decades, it was not just Marxists who held these views; (nearly) everybody did. Now, however, the old consensus is gone. *A Future for Socialism* is in part a reaction to this situation, in part a contribution to the dissolution of the old assumptions.

I can only report on these transformed understandings from my own, very parochial vantage point. When I say 'we' and 'us', I mean Western (indeed American or, at least, English-speaking) leftist academics of the generation of 1968 plus or minus one or two. Analytical Marxism was one of our creations. In contrast to most other intellectual currents that have identified with Marxism, it was always a product of a university culture, with hardly any connection to political parties or even to social movements. From its inception, analytical Marxism has been, for better or worse, an intellectual tendency without a political constituency. Nevertheless, its under-standings of socialism and capitalism were largely shared by the socialist Left throughout the world. In any case, this is the context of Roemer's ongoing engagement with Marxist theory and socialism.

Like everyone else, we all used to know what socialism was, whether or not we identified expressly with analytical Marxism. Under socialism, the means of production (at least the important ones) were socialized. We were not always of one mind about what 'social-ized' meant; some thought it meant 'democratized', others did not. But since we all knew that capitalism was the historical alternative to socialism, and since we were sure that under capitalism the principal means of production were privately owned, we were inclined to identify socialism with the absence of private property in (important) means of production. Even those of us who thought that this was not sufficient, perhaps because democracy was indispensable, agreed that the abolition of private property was necessary for socialism, and were sure that we understood what that meant. Analyses of private and public ownership were therefore off the research agenda; there was no need to investigate what was clear enough. Nowadays, of course, these understandings no longer pass muster, and it is widely assumed that the demise of 'actually existing socialism' somehow explains this change. But in retrospect it is incomprehensible that the old under-standings were ever secure.

For one thing, it was a commonplace long before 1989 that ownership is a bundle of rights to control assets and to benefit from them and that what we call private property designates a fairly diverse set of bundles. It was also a commonplace that ownership rights are constantly evolving and frequently contested. Yet when we thought about socialism and capitalism, we tended to focus on extreme positions: unrestricted rights to benefit and control, on the one hand, and state ownership, on the other. To be sure, there are many things that individuals own privately from which, according to prevailing law and custom, they may rightfully benefit absolutely and use as they please (so long as they do not harm others). But this paradigm of private ownership seldom applies to anything that might be considered a principal means of production. And it is far from clear, in any case, that state ownership is its antithesis.

It is also puzzling why the end of (big-C) Communism had such a momentous impact on current understandings of socialism. Some of us were persuaded that the economic system in place in the Soviet Union was 'state capitalist' or, in any case, not socialist. However, most of us probably did believe that 'actually existing socialist' societies were indeed socialist, even though their socialism was hardly what we wanted. They were socialist because they had abolished private property in (principal) means of production, replacing private property and markets with state property and central planning. Many of us questioned the wisdom of relying on plans instead of markets, but we were remarkably uncritical of the Soviet form of public ownership. However much we reproached the Soviet Union, and this was, after all, the pivot of left politics, we never questioned the idea that public property was necessarily state property.

We might have been led to a more critical attitude had we reflected more on the existence of state property in the capitalist world. But this was the occasion for yet another theoretical aporia. It has never been clear, in any case, just how, if at all, state ownership challenges capitalism. Those of us who worried about this issue used to say that state-owned enterprises in capitalist societies were not islands of socialism, even as we identified public ownership with state ownership, because the state only took over firms that were failing in capitalist markets and/or because these enterprises interacted with private firms in market transactions in just the way that private firms would and/or because they had internal organizations that were not significantly different from those of privately owned firms. But these defensive claims, whatever their merits, hardly vindicate an uncritical identification of socialism with state ownership of major productive assets.

In view of our understanding of property rights, our various attitudes towards the Soviet Union, and our experience with state property in capitalist economies, it is remarkable that we were once so sure what socialism and capitalism, public and private property were. The pressing question, however, is what they actually are. This has been a central focus of Roemer's recent work. *A Future for Socialism* reflects the advances in understanding he has made. For our purposes now, what matters in Roemer's view is that private property becomes public property at the point at which revenue rights in major productive assets are distributed across large sectors of the (relevant) population.[6] Under socialism, therefore, revenue rights help to equalize income and not, as under capitalism, to generate inequalities. This understanding of public property and, by extension, of socialism itself helps to motivate Roemer's account of what socialists want.

So too does Roemer's view of the connection between Marxism and moral theory. Just as we once thought we knew what socialism was, there was a time when we were confident about 'their morals and ours'. Or at least we were sure about theirs. Since some of us thought, following Marx himself, that it was politically otiose to launch moral arguments for socialism (because the 'laws of motion' of capitalist societies rendered such arguments unnecessary), since we knew that 'the ruling ideas' (including the moral assessments) of any period are just the ideas of the ruling class, and since Marx and Marxists disparaged moralizing repeatedly, more than a few of us were officially hostile to 'morality' and defensive about moral theory. These hesitations waned throughout the 1970s. But the conviction that their morals were not ours nevertheless lingered. They had bourgeois values and ideas, but what did we have? Alienation, perhaps; but some of us (in the grip of Althusserian 'theory') disliked this concept, with its neo-Hegelian flavor and its position on the wrong side of 'the epistemological break'. So we focussed on exploitation, a concept with an impeccable Marxist pedigree that, among other things, appeared to have superseded the 'alienation' of Marx's early writings. In addition, exploitation provided a point of contact with the theory of justice, and therefore with mainstream social and moral philosophy after Rawls. Thus we could remain in the academy with a good conscience, and without marginalizing ourselves or being marginalized. But then, alas, Roemer maintained that we were wrong to be concerned with exploitation.[7] At best, the idea was a proxy for injustice, and it wasn't a perfectly reliable proxy at that. Not everyone agreed, for reasons that I cannot pursue here, but, partly thanks to Roemer's influence, exploitation began to diminish as a distinctive normative concern. Our morals began to look increasingly like theirs.

Our distinctiveness in the social sciences was quickly fading too.

Not long ago, to us they were vulgar (albeit technically sophisticated) economists, while we (in their eyes) were 'minor post-Ricardians'. In sociology, the differences were even clearer: they were 'abstracted empiricists'. Most of us, they insisted, were not sociologists at all but pseudophilosophers, proponents of this or that obscurantist methodology. Then, at some point, it came to be thought that we were dealing with 'incommensurable' paradigms and, for more than a decade, Marxism and 'bourgeois' social science contended on this understanding. However, by the late 1970s, what was ostensibly incommensurable had already been compared. In economics, thanks in part to Roemer's own reconstructions,[8] it became clear that the difference between Marxist positions and neoclassical ones were in fact resolvable, and not unequivocally in favor of the Marxist side. Marxist positions were intelligible, though often cumbersome and sometimes untenable. Class analysis could contribute to sociology, but it was, at most, a distinct field within the broader discipline, not a new methodology. Thus Marxist social science too was collapsing into theirs. Just as everybody once knew what socialism was, everybody used to know what a Marxist was. Today it is far from clear.

There is yet another consequence of the analytical turn in Marxist theory that bears importantly on the concept of socialism. No doubt, Marx did hold something like the theory of history reconstructed and defended by Cohen in *Karl Marx's Theory of History*, the book that gave analytical Marxism its feet.[9] In any case, it was a version of this theory that became canonical for Marxists, after the founding of the Second International, with implications for the broader intellectual culture (as Schumpeter observed). In particular, the theory's concepts of capitalism and socialism (or post-capitalism) helped shape received understandings of private and public property. Even orthodox Marxists knew this was not the whole story. In retrospect, they did not have much useful to say about socialism (or post-capitalism). But they did at least keep alive Marx's conviction that history finally ends with communism – a society that transcends the form of community endemic to societies organized through commodity production. Cohen's work, because it succeeded so brilliantly in its own domain, helped to blind many of us to the possibility of a communist future. By focussing so enthusiastically on Marx's theory of history's structure and direction, a theory that ends, as it were, with capitalism's demise, we lost sight of the end of history itself. In effect, a part of Marx's account of capitalism's future, the part that involves the end of private property in external means of production, came to stand in for the whole story. Thus the very idea of communism lapsed.

In taking historical materialism on board as we did, we effectively broke with our 'erstwhile philosophical consciousness', following the more worthy precedent of Marx himself in *The German Ideology*. The Marxisms we knew first, whether neo-Hegelian, existentialist or structuralist, evinced a deep, though seldom acknowledged, hostility to historical materialism. Whatever complicated (and unformed) relations we had with one or another aspect of these diverse strains of theorizing, most of us, I think, shared this hostility. But, by the end of the 1970s, these European imports were increasingly overtaken by events and overcome by internal exhaustion. 'Western Marxism' was fast becoming as 'academic' as analytical Marxism always was. As such, much of it stood revealed as obscurantist posturing. But in its place, after Cohen, there was at hand a defensible (or at least plausible) account of history's structure and direction that connected us to Marxism's (pre-Bolshevik) Golden Age, a theory in which private and non-private (public) property played a decisive role, but in which communism played virtually no role at all.

The development of analytical Marxism, after Cohen, severed even this connection to traditional socialism. It is worth remembering how Roemer once joined his work on exploitation with historical materialism.[10] The epochal historical divisions historical materialism identified were marked by the progressive elimination of historically specific forms of exploitation or, what came to the same thing, by successive deprivatizations of real property relations (first in other persons, then in alienable means of production). When it still seemed that exploitation mattered, movement along the historical materialist trajectory could therefore be regarded as morally progressive. At each stage along the way, there were qualitatively fewer forms of exploitation remaining. So long as what remained did not, as it were, rise up to fill the void, we could infer that there was less exploitation overall. Since we were all critical in varying degrees of 'actually existing socialism', we concluded that post-capitalist 'status exploitation' had more than taken up the space left vacant by the elimination of capitalist exploitation. But we remained confident that socialism could be, and 'normally' was, normatively superior to capitalism, even if the balance sheet between existing socialisms and existing capitalisms tipped in the other direction.

In time, Roemer came to regard even this conviction as problematic. With historical materialism 'reconsidered' almost to oblivion and the normative force of exploitation demolished, there were no longer distinctively Marxist grounds for preferring socialism to capitalism. If socialism is superior to capitalism, therefore, it can only be because it can be expected to get what liberals want better than capitalism can. In retrospect, the picture of socialism implicit in *A General Theory of Exploitation and Class* was the last gasp, from an analytical Marxist vantage point, of the old, formerly secure understandings. This is not the place for me to explain why I think the old Roemer was more on track than the new. But even those of us who resist following Roemer into the liberal camp must concede that the special purchase we thought we had qua Marxists on the future of socialism is anything but secure. Unless, of course, we bring communism back in.

What Do Socialists Really Want?

Roemer's position, again, is that equality (or rather equality of opportunity) for self-realization and welfare, for political influence and for social status is what socialists have always wanted. Socialists therefore wanted socialism, deprivatization or socialization of the principal means of production, only as a means to these ends. Now it would indeed be odd and arguably even unreasonable to want a form of property relations for its own sake. Thus it must be true that socialists never cared about socialism per se; that socialists were socialists because of what they believed about socialism's effects on what they did care about intrinsically. Roemer claims that what socialists have always cared about intrinsically is equality; therefore, socialists are egalitarians, not more, not less.

Needless to say, we could press a similar claim against equality itself. Why, after all, should we care about the equal distribution of this or that distribuand for its own sake? An up-to-date response, owing to the latest turn in Rawls's work, is that we want equality for the sake of 'social unity'.[11] But this justification is, I would hope, too liberal for anyone who identifies with socialist politics to abide, even one who believes that socialists and liberals ultimately want the same thing. For, however much times may have changed, it is surely still the case that to identify with the socialist tradition politically is to endorse a style of politics that aims at changing the world radically, indeed at revolutionizing it. On the other hand, Rawls's emphasis on consensus suggests, even if it does not strictly imply, a politics of continuity with existing arrangements; a suggestion corroborated by the celebration of American constitutional principles that pervades his recent writings. In any case, it would be profoundly ahistorical to imagine the institutional reforms Roemer proposes installed by ordinary constitutional means. Because they are so radical, they

would almost certainly require something very like a social revolution
to put in place. If only to maintain consistency therefore between
politics and political philosophy, it will be better to take recourse in
the more standard view (since Kant), according to which equality (of
the right distribuand) implements 'impartiality' or equal respect for
persons which is, in turn, intrinsic to morality. The question, 'Why
equality?', therefore devolves into deep but familiar questions about
the moral order, and becomes tractable to the degree that fundamental moral philosophical issues can be satisfactorily resolved. However,
at this point we might wonder how deep justifications must go before
we can give a satisfactory accounting of what socialists want. Whatever we make of his politics, there is surely something right-headed
in Rawls's insistence that political philosophy be political, not
metaphysical. I suggest we take Rawls at his word in this regard and
also, at the risk of appearing disingenuous, that we appropriate (or
misappropriate) an aspect of Roemer's account of what egalitarians
(and therefore socialists) want, the better to reflect politically on what
socialists really want.

In other forums, it would be appropriate to take issue with
Roemer's intervention into the 'equality of what?' debate, but not
here. For one thing, the remarks in the first chapter of *A Future for
Socialism* are only stage-setting for the reflections on institutional
arrangements that follow. For another, the position he endorses is
more or less a composite of the most sensible things others have said.
I will therefore only register the view that I am dubious of the scheme
to fuse welfarist and perfectionist concerns, as Roemer does when he
claims that socialists want equal opportunity for self-realization and
welfare. I would also question the claim that egalitarians need always
be proponents of equal opportunity in contrast to straight equality.
But I shall not pursue these objections. I shall instead reflect in a non-
Roemerian spirit on the third of the distribuands Roemer claims
socialists want equally distributed: social status.

Equality of social status could mean just equality of citizenship:
(formal) equality before the law, one person one vote, and so on.
Socialists have always been partisans of equality in this sense (albeit
with some reservations about the rights of former exploiters in post-
revolutionary societies) but so has virtually everyone since the French
Revolution. It was, in fact, this idea of 'political emancipation' that
Marx criticized incisively, not to deny its merits but to reveal its
limitations, in his early writings. It is therefore true but uninformative
to say that socialists want equality of social status in this sense. At the
other extreme, equality of social status might mean the end of 'status

exploitation' as Roemer conceived it, an end to individuals' rights to benefit differentially from the incumbency of positions in hierarchically structured institutions.[12] Even more radically it might mean the end of hierarchy itself. The abolition of hierarchy as such is plainly utopian, as even Marx would probably have acknowledged.[13] Marx himself seems to have regarded the abolition of status exploitation as a utopian aspiration too; in any case, he relegated far-reaching measures aimed at advancing toward this goal to the remotest communist future. Roemer accordingly maintained that status exploitation (along with skills exploitation) survives the transition from capitalism to socialism, that is, to the early, 'transitional' phases of history's final 'mode of production'. It is only with the greatest hesitation, therefore, that even the Roemer of a decade ago could have maintained that socialists want the end of status exploitation. This leaves a third sense of status equality to be teased out, not too disingenuously, from some of Roemer's remarks on status equality. On this understanding, what socialists want (in addition to formal political equality) is the end of one kind of status inequality, the kind that follows from class divisions. In other words, what socialists want is a classless society, a society that does not sort individuals into social class (even if it does allow individuals to benefit differentially from the incumbency of positions in hierarchically structured organizations). This understanding of status equality points us back to communism. For a necessary condition for general will coordination of individuals' behaviors is the absence of systemic social divisions of a sort that render a real consensus on ends unachievable. Marx plainly thought that class divisions were the deepest and most salient obstacles in the way of communist community. In his view, the end of class society was certainly a necessary condition for communism. Indeed, a reader of Marx's more exuberant political writings, *The Communist Manifesto* for example, might conclude that Marx thought it a sufficient condition as well. This is not the place to examine further the connection between classlessness and communism. It is enough to note that classlessness can fairly serve as a proxy for communism. Thus there is a sense in which even some of Roemer's own reflections on what socialists want can be enlisted in support of my contrary contention.

Again, I am attaching meanings to Roemer's remarks on status equality that he almost certainly did not intend. *A Future for Socialism* ignores communism. It even relegates its proposed successor, the full realization of liberal equality, to an indefinite future that socialists need not dwell upon as they concoct schemes for reforming existing institutions. It is tempting to accede to this advice. In dark moments, it does seem dangerously rigid and anachronistic to retain faith in a future so remote and so out of line with current thinking. But I would insist nevertheless that the current crisis of socialist theory and practice can be satisfactorily addressed only if we resist this temptation and resolutely bring communism back in.

Why Communism Matters

Like Roemer's assertion that socialists want what liberal egalitarians want, the claim that socialists want communism is, in part, a historical observation and, in part, a political recommendation. Since the issue is socialism's future, not just its past, the repertorial and political aspects of these competing claims overlap. What is in contention is the legacy of the socialist tradition and its (possible) futures.

Were communism an impossibly utopian aspiration or, worse still, an incoherent ideal, the heirs of the socialist tradition ought indeed to abandon it. Liberal equality would then be a suitable, second-best goal. Whether or not socialists or their heirs should remain socialists, whether they should continue to seek the socialization of property rights in (important) means of production, would then depend solely on socialism's efficacy and feasibility for implementing liberal objectives. Thus there is a sense in which, on Roemer's view, what distinguished socialists from other liberals historically was only their view about the consequences for equality of socializing property relations. Again, I think this way of looking at the matter is wrong-headed. Socialists have always wanted more than equality. But if communism is not a viable ideal, then perhaps liberal egalitarianism is indeed all that can be retrieved from the socialist tradition. Roemer's concern in *A Future for Socialism* is to defend this much of the old ideal against strategies for the Left that are not socialist at all. In contrast, I am suggesting that even in the present political conjuncture the heirs of the socialist tradition would be well advised to declare themselves unabashedly its continuators.

Nowadays, the consensus view about what is utopian stops far short of communism. It stops virtually at the systems in place in the Western democracies. Thus Adam Przeworski has suggested that 'what died in Eastern Europe is the very idea of rationally administering things to satisfy human needs'.[14] This assessment was made in sadness. Throughout our intellectual and political culture, a similar judgment is celebrated. Everywhere, we are told that attempts at rationalizing economic and social affairs directly are bound to fail, and that the consequences of trying are almost always disastrous. Some on the right maintain that individual optimizing is all the rationality we need or can (safely) obtain. Accordingly, they would have us rely on market mechanisms exclusively and forever. Liberals counter by identifying market incompetencies and arguing for public-sector remedies. Who cannot be affected by this revolution of diminishing expectations! In a world in which even the affirmative state liberalism we all used to deride has come to seem impossibly left-wing, communism is off the political agenda altogether.

I would once again assert that communism is materially possible, humanly desirable and consistent with real-world historical tendencies.[15] Of course, communism is not likely to be on the immediate political horizon any time soon, a fate it shares with Roemer's proposals. In any case, this is not the place to marshall arguments in defense of communism if only because they are orthogonal to the 'short-run' focus of *A Future for Socialism*. I would, however, venture some thoughts on why such a very long-range and ostensibly 'unrealistic' goal matters, even in the time frame that is Roemer's principal concern.

First, communism matters politically because without it left politics risks devolving into a motley of good causes, void of any guiding vision. What we have without communism is what we have increasingly on the Left today: liberalism with a vengeance. Even when it is motivated expressly by egalitarian aspirations, as liberal politics seldom has been, the liberal style is to muddle through, to identify issues and contrive policies to address them but not to seek to implement a vision of a qualitatively different and better social order, except as one might emerge as an unintended consequence of cumulative, small-scale improvements. Liberal politics is a politics bereft of overarching purpose. Indeed, for so-called 'political liberals', the absence of a purpose is liberalism's defining characteristic and principal virtue.[16] Without communism or some functionally equivalent end in view, liberal politics would win by default, and the Left would have no genuine alternative around which to mobilize opposition to existing institutional arrangements. It would devolve instead into what it is already fast becoming: a collection of aimless do-gooders.

A Future for Socialism stands in a contradictory relation to this prospect. On the one hand, it expressly endorses liberal political philosophy; thus it evinces an affinity with liberal politics. At the same time, it proposes reforms of prevailing property relations too far-reaching for any imaginable liberal politics to sustain. This is why Roemer's proposals, despite their official modesty, have a utopian flavor. Paradoxically, the way to a greater 'realism' is to abandon the attempt at moderation. A more equal distribution of resources is part of what socialists want. But the main thing is to transform human life qualitatively; above all, in its communal dimensions. The end of (big-C) Communism is hardly an occasion for abandoning this goal. In time, it may even prove instrumental for its resurrection. If only as a focus for discussion, the prescriptions advanced in *A Future for Socialism* can help to promote a renaissance of socialist theory. More importantly, since efficiency does matter, Roemer's design for society may well find a place in the socialist polities of the future. But there will be no future for socialism if socialism's objectives are set aside. For there would then be no idea capable of mobilizing the political support necessary for breaking away from received practices and institutions. For *A Future for Socialism* to be part of socialism's future, it is crucial that its radicalness not be diluted by liberal politics but instead be unequivocally embraced.

The possibility that Roemer's prescriptions may be integral to the socialism of the future suggests yet another reason for bringing communism back in. Whoever wants to transcend market society, even if only as a distant goal, must look to the consequences of social institutions on individuals' characters; for institutions, whatever else they may be, are always also educators. Market socialists therefore need to correct for the educative consequences of the market mechanisms on which they rely. A deep ideological commitment to the longstanding objectives of socialist politics can provide a corrective. Indeed, there may be no other way to prevent an economic system with market mechanisms from developing into a full-fledged market society, the antithesis of what socialists want. Even if Roemer is right to insist that, for the foreseeable future, socialists must accede to the incentive structure capitalism has generated, their paramount task is to discourage the indefinite prolongation of market mentalities, the raw material out of which market societies are built. Without the idea of communism, they are disarmed from doing so. What socialists want would therefore remain forever elusive.

Socialism versus *A Future for Socialism*

Because communism is so undertheorized in the Marxist tradition, it is not at all clear how to identify advances towards it. But there are difficulties too in identifying progress towards the realization of liberal egalitarian objectives. To gain a deeper, political understanding of *A*

Future for Socialism, it will be helpful to reflect on the implications of some of these difficulties. It will emerge that Roemer's market socialism, insofar as it is only a means for obtaining what liberal egalitarians want, is almost certainly a poor substitute for social democracy, a prospect that bodes ill for its role in reviving socialism's future. This consideration adds further support to the contention that *A Future for Socialism* can be part of socialism's future only if its institutional recommendations are liberated from the liberal egalitarian profession of faith in which they are presently framed.

How are we to know if we have moved forward in implementing what liberal egalitarians want? For now, let us assume away vexing and possibly unsolvable problems in the way of combining the egalitarian distribuands Roemer lists. Imagine, for example, that we can say in a principled way that this much loss in opportunities for welfare and that much gain in equality of political influence represents an overall gain (or loss) for equality. There is still the problem that, for these distribuands, all but very gross changes are difficult, if not impossible, to detect. Social status (with its attendant ambiguities) apart, we do not have good cognitive access to welfare levels, to opportunities for self-realization or to political influence. This is why throughout the 'equality of what?' debate, whenever questions of practical implementation arise, the recourse is always to proxies for one or another egalitarian distribuand (or collection of distribuands). Thus it is fair to observe, even as 'the equality of what?' debate continues to unfold, that in practice liberal egalitarians all want the same thing: equality of income and wealth.

To the extent that this proxy is reliable, we can tell when we are headed in the right direction. This is why it is reasonable to expect that the transformed stock market Roemer envisions would enhance equality. A Roemerian coupon economy would diminish inequalities of wealth (assuming no new mechanisms for generating wealth inequalities take the place of the one that is eliminated) and therefore significantly diminish inequalities of income based on inequalities of wealth.[17] But, if the point is only to equalize incomes, 'social democratic' redistributive taxation and national (or international) wage policies would be at least as efficacious as the alterations in property rights that Roemer proposes.

Roemer does advocate joining social democratic measures wherever possible to his proposals for transforming property rights. But we might wonder why, insofar as he is only intent on equalizing income and wealth, Roemer is not a social democrat *tout court*. There are two answers that can be gleaned from *A Future for Socialism*. Neither is satisfactory, but the less unsatisfactory answer at least suggests the understanding of status equality that rejoins Roemer's institutional prescriptions with genuinely socialist aims.

The more unsatisfactory answer is that, as the world economic system has developed, further advances in social democracy have become politically unfeasible, even in those parts of the world where social democracy has, to date, advanced the farthest. But, as I have already suggested, feasibility is hardly the strong suit of Roemer's own proposals. Insofar as it is intended as a political intervention, *A Future for Socialism* is addressed mainly to the Left of the former Second World. But, as such, it is suspended in that brief interval between the collapse of 'actually existing socialism' and the headlong rush of formerly socialist countries to imitate, with truly horrendous consequences, the worst features of existing capitalist societies. Perhaps for a few months the constraints on historical agency in Eastern Europe were less overbearing than such constraints typically are. But that moment has definitively passed. Roemer also suggests that his proposals may be feasible somewhere in the Third World, perhaps in Brazil. This is equally doubtful. Thus, even if his gloomy prognostications for social democracy are sound, a social democrat could fairly reply *tu quoque* to Roemer's complaint. A social democrat could also point out that social democracy has a long record of working well in many historical contexts, while Roemer's version of market socialism has no record at all.

However, Roemer does have another reason for not proposing a strictly social democratic strategy for the Left. From its inception, social democracy has been based on a class compromise that effectively disarmed workers from challenging the profit positions and power of the capitalist class. Roemer's coupon economy, on the other hand, eliminates Big Capital at the outset. It goes without saying that socialists have always been anti-capitalists. But having (justifiably) blurred the distinction between socialism and capitalism, Roemer cannot simply assume that socialists want Big Capital gone, even for instrumental reasons. Ingeniously, however, he does provide a way to retrieve this aspect of historical socialism: he demonstrates that capitalist power, if not capitalism itself, should be diminished in order to lessen the incentives capitalists have to generate public bads. However, in this respect too we are entitled to wonder why social democracy is not enough. All social democrats favor social democratic measures for their ameliorative effects. But left-wing social democrats have also defended social democracy for its likely consequences in altering the balance of power between capital and labor, to a point where a peaceful transition beyond capitalist domination, a self-liquidation of Big Capital, comes on to the political agenda. This objective does not quite connect social democracy to socialism in the Marxist sense, but it does make social democracy at least tendentially anti-capitalist. Left-wing social democrats distanced themselves from Marxist socialism for reasons different from those that motivate Roemer's rethinking of socialism's future. But it is far from clear that the futures they envisioned are in any significant respects different from the future implicit in Roemer's design for society.

Were I persuaded that we must abandon the kind of socialism that aims at communism, I would question the need to stray from social democracy's tried and true (though admittedly problematic) path. I would even be tempted to turn against Roemer's own proposals the 'conservative' rationale that Roemer himself invokes to rebut critics from the Left: that the more untried and radical the proposed changes, the less feasible they are and the less likely they are to succeed. But of course I am not persuaded that the old socialist ideal is finished. Roemer defends his proposals, not always compellingly, against latter-day social democrats (like Joshua Cohen and Joel Rogers, Fred Block and others) who are even more 'moderate' than he declares himself to be. Political feasibility is the pivot of their disputes. But, in this case as in so many others, the best defense is a good offense. Insofar as the issue is not what is now on the political agenda but what kind of political agenda we can and should create, there is no 'pragmatic' reason to forbear from the vigorous pursuit of genuinely socialist aspirations: for a future free from systemic class oppression, where genuine liberty and equality are achieved in conditions of real community ('fraternity'); where, as *The Communist Manifesto* famously maintains 'the free development of each is the condition for the free development of all'.

I leave it to others to refine Roemer's institutional recommendations. Allowing that his scheme or some emendation of it is cogent and workable, there is little doubt that it would represent an improvement over the status quo. But from the vantage point I think socialists ought to adopt, institutional changes should be assessed not just for their ameliorative consequences but also, mainly, for their long-run dynamic implications, for their efficacy in moving humankind toward a communist future. My worry is that erstwhile socialists will be tempted to mobilize behind a program that collapses socialism into (left) liberal politics, just as Roemer would officially collapse socialist (normative) theory into liberal egalitarianism. It may be wise in the present conjuncture for socialists to advance only minimal agendas.

But all reforms relevant to socialism's future, including the ones Roemer proposes, should be assessed in the light of communism, not just in comparison to existing capitalism. We socialists must never lose sight of where we want to go. If we are to revive and continue the socialist tradition, we must not do what *A Future for Socialism*, in its zeal to save socialism, comes perilously close to doing: we must not abandon socialism in order to save it.

Notes

1. John E. Roemer, *A Future for Socialism*, Cambridge, MA: Harvard University Press 1994.
2. See, among many others, Amartya Sen, 'Equality of What?' in S. M. McMurrin, ed., *The Tannner Lectures on Human Values*, vol. 1, Salt Lake City: University of Utah Press and Cambridge, Cambridge University Press 1980, and *Inequality Reexamined*, New York: Russell Sage Foundation and Cambridge, MA: Harvard University Press 1992; Ronald Dworkin, 'What Is Equality? Part 1: Equality of Welfare', *Philosophy and Public Affairs* 10 (1981), pp. 283–345, and 'What is Equality? Part 2 Equality of Resources', *Philosophy and Public Affairs* 10 (1981), pp. 655–69; Richard Arneson, 'Equality and Equality of Opportunity for Welfare', *Philosophical Review* 56 (1989), pp. 77–93; and G. A. Cohen, 'On the Currency of Egalitarian Justice', *Ethics* 99 (1990), pp. 906–44.
3. Needless to say, throughout what follows, (small-c) communism should not be confused with (big-C) Communism, the economic, social and political system formerly in place in the erstwhile Soviet Union and elsewhere.
4. I elaborate upon and defend the claims advanced in this paragraph in Andrew Levine, *The General Will: Rousseau, Marx, Communism*, Cambridge: Cambridge University Press 1993.
5. Joseph Schumpeter, *Capitalism, Socialism, Democracy*, New York: Harper and Row 1942.
6. As we shall see, it is always possible in principle to achieve similar and even more radically egalitarian distributional outcomes by keeping private property intact and redistributing revenues collected through taxes. Thus, in Roemer's view, it is not distributional outcomes per se that matter for defining socialism, but rather property relations.
7. Cf. John E. Roemer, 'Should Marxists Be Interested in Exploitation?', *Philosophy and Public Affairs* 14 (1985), pp. 30–65, and *Free to Lose*, Cambridge, MA: Harvard University Press 1988.
8. John E. Roemer, *Analytical Foundations of Marxian Economic Theory*, Cambridge, MA: Harvard University Press 1981.
9. G. A. Cohen, *Karl Marx's Theory of History: A Defence*, Oxford: Oxford University Press and Princeton: Princeton University Press 1978.
10. John E. Roemer, *A General Theory of Exploitation and Class* and 'New Directions in the Marxian Theory of Exploitation and Class', *Politics and Society* 11 (1982), pp. 253–87; reprinted in John Roemer, ed., *Analytical Marxism*, Cambridge: Cambridge University Press 1986, pp. 81–113.
11. See especially John Rawls, *Political Liberalism*, New York: Columbia University Press 1993.
12. Cf. J. Roemer, *A General Theory of Exploitation and Class*.
13. There is, to be sure, Marx's celebrated vision of people hunting in the morning, fishing in the afternoon and criticizing at night (without being hunters, fishermen or

critical critics). But the examples Marx chooses leave the interpretation of this picture indeterminate. The most charitable construal of what Marx had in mind is a world in which individuals pass effortlessly from one position to another. It is of course compatible with this (dubious) idea that positions in complex organizations continue to be hierarchically structured.

14. Adam Przeworski, *Democracy and the Market: Political and Economic Reforms in Eastern Europe and Latin America*, Cambridge: Cambridge University Press 1991, p. 7.

15. I elaborate upon and defend these claims in Levine, *The General Will*.

16. Cf., among many others, Bruce Ackerman, *Social Justice in the Liberal State*, New Haven: Yale University Press 1980, 'Political Liberalisms', *The Journal of Philosophy* vol. xci (1994), pp. 364–86; and John Rawls, *Political Liberalism*.

17. However, if we are to achieve economic well-being as well as greater equality from Roemer's reforms, we must acknowledge what Roemer does not expressly admit: that this equalizing mechanism must be held in bounds. Roemer cannot allow income inequalities generated through stock ownership to diminish very far. Coupon holders have to care about their dividend incomes if they are to serve their appointed role in promoting the efficiency of firms. But they won't care enough, given what Roemer assumes about human nature, unless dividend incomes are high enough to make a significant difference in their lives.

14

Socialism as an Attitude
Julius Sensat

In an effort to avoid utopianism in his investigation of future possibilities for socialism,[1] John Roemer seeks to develop models of egalitarian economies driven by familiar, largely egoistic or personal forms of motivation. While I agree that socialists and egalitarians should try to avoid utopianism, I question the effectiveness of this strategy. In my view, what is required is something Roemer attempts to do without: a fairly deep exploration of the range of motivational possibilities and their relation to social structure.

For Roemer, proposed social arrangements are utopian if they would require too much altruistic or impartial motivation on the part of the people living under them. He tries to avoid this pitfall in the same way the classical utilitarians did. To the objection that utilitarianism demands too much in expecting people always to be motivated by a desire to enhance the general welfare, Mill replied that this was to confuse the criterion of right with the motive of action. 'No system of ethics,' he said, 'requires that the sole motive of all we do shall be a feeling of duty; on the contrary, ninety-nine hundredths of all our actions are done from other motives, and rightly so done, if the rule of duty does not condemn them . . . the motive has nothing to do with the morality of the action. . . .'[2] While the utilitarian tradition has occasionally countenanced impartial moral sentiment as a limited and slowly cultivatible source of motivation for compliance with the institutions of justice and property, the major focus has been on institutional mechanisms that would produce morally optimal outcomes from non-morally motivated actions. Bentham's position provides an extreme example. Since he endorsed both utilitarianism in ethics and egoistic hedonism in motivational psychology, he viewed the problem of institutional design as the problem of creating a system of incentives that would motivate those who seek only their own pleasure to do what collectively maximizes social welfare. As

Thomas Nagel points out, he placed great importance on his 'Duty and Interest junction principle', which would sanction such measures as tying income to effectiveness on the job.[3]

I will speak somewhat tendentiously of Roemer's response to the challenge of utopianism as Benthamite, because even though his conception of the good is not utilitarian but rather places value on various kinds of equality of opportunity, he envisages people being directly motivated largely by personal aims. It is the function of well-designed institutions to channel the pursuit of these aims so as to bring about morally good results. He defends his market socialist proposals by establishing the existence of economic equilibria for them that have certain egalitarian features and by arguing that equilibrium behavior can be motivated by material incentives and legal enforcement mechanisms similar to those in place in contemporary capitalist economies. These incentives and mechanisms are designed to bring about a 'junction' of duty and interest, so that, for the most part anyway, specifically moral motivation need not be relied upon. My characterization is tendentious insofar as Roemer might envisage non-egoistic, non-hedonistic forms of personal motivation and even some moral motivation in the voting booth (though he does not probe this possibility), thereby departing from a strictly Benthamite approach.

In order to assess this response, it is necessary to conceive of utopianism somewhat more broadly than we have so far. A reform proposal should be thought of as utopian not only for requiring too much impartiality of people, but for failing adequately to address any serious threat to the proposed arrangement's attainability or stability with respect to the values it is supposed to realize. One problem with Roemer's strategy is that utopianism in this sense threatens even Benthamite proposals. We can illustrate the point with a simple example. One can easily model an economic environment and a laissez-faire, private-ownership market economy in which the initial distribution of wealth (including property rights in firms) is fairly equal and whose corresponding Walrasian equilibrium has some nice equality properties. But it would be unwarranted to expect such egalitarian features to be sustained over time were the initial parameters of the model satisfied in reality. Because of changes in supply and demand as a result of innovations, changes in preferences, business startups and failures, etc., one should expect the distribution of wealth and income to become increasingly unequal over time, at least up to a point. Thus even if no one's motivations are strained in an impartial direction by the rules of the system, it would none the less be utopian to propose the system as a way of implementing egalitarian principles, even leaving aside the question of attainability.

Similarly, with Roemer's models (his model of market socialism with a stock market, for example), even if we assume that obeying the rules does not require anyone to be motivated by a sense of justice or the common good, we should expect that some firms will be more successful than others, some portfolio purchases will turn out to be more lucrative than others, and that consequently the distribution of property income will depart from equality. Also, the possibility of borrowing money on one's stock as collateral, for instance to start up small private businesses (something the model is designed to encourage) provides a way around some of the protections of equality the prohibition on selling stocks for money is supposed to provide. Though all of this behavior is system-conforming and driven by material incentives, it can reasonably be expected to lead to inequalities of the opportunities the system is supposed to equalize. The basis would then be laid for successful and quite legal efforts on the part of the more advantaged to modify the system so as to strengthen their position. Moreover, if there are any incentive incompatibilities in the system itself, then in the absence of moral motivation one could expect role-violating behavior that could well work in an inegalitarian direction.

We can bring out another limitation of the Benthamite approach by considering the question of legitimacy and its relation to socialist principles. Let us say that society embraces an ideal of legitimacy when it is true and common knowledge that everyone is concerned to deliberate and act in a way that everyone can freely accept on due reflection, on the basis of what all can recognize to be sufficient, publicly acceptable reasons. Let us say further that society realizes this ideal to the extent that it follows procedures and practices that answer to this concern. Roemer claims that socialists want equality of opportunity for welfare and self-realization, political influence and social status. Assuming for the moment that this is correct, we still need to ask about the importance of legitimacy in this scheme. That is, is it important to the ideal of socialism itself that these values be realized with legitimacy, or is the proper role of legitimacy a more instrumental and contingent one?

There should be no doubt on this score about the Marxian conception of socialism, which envisaged the consensual, joint deliberative regulation of economic and political affairs by the members of society. The role of legitimacy in this vision is not simply that of a means for achieving egalitarian ends. Rather, it is viewed as a requirement of rational agency itself in certain social contexts, since independent deliberation in those contexts, especially by agents engaged in the capitalist production of commodities, tends to result in reification or alienation, a form of agency in which agents unwittingly confer on their own actions an alien dynamic that escapes their deliberative control.[4] Legitimacy becomes necessary for people to assume rational control over their own lives.

But if socialism must be based on legitimacy, then the Benthamite solution is not capable even in principle of achieving the necessary kind of stability, since it does not draw on the relevant kind of concern. The stability of socialist principles, procedures and practices must be based on a reasoned allegiance to those principles, procedures and practices, and the Benthamite solution does not draw on such allegiance.

It may seem that a legitimacy requirement would only make the utopian pitfall loom larger for socialism. But in fact the opposite might be true. Depending on the availability of principles and procedures that meet it and help to reproduce it, a concern for mutual justifiability of action could be a potent source of egalitarian motivation, and thus a key element of a stable egalitarianism. Consequently, proposals that do not seek to develop and to tap this source of motivation might be more vulnerable to utopianism than others that do. In fact, insufficient concern for the legitimacy of procedures and decisions may have played a more important role in the failure of socialist ventures stemming from the Bolshevik Revolution than the absence of innovation driven by market competition – the cause cited by Roemer. If a certain apathy, cynicism and indifference infected economic performance, perhaps this had as much to do with the absence of legitimacy as it did with the absence of markets.

There are passages in which Roemer seems implicitly to acknowledge concern for legitimacy as a source of motivation. For example, when he speculates that the belief that people 'have earned, in the moral sense, what they receive through selling their talents on the market' may limit social-democratic redistribution because 'an economic mechanism, at least in a democracy, cannot be stable if it rewards people in disproportion to what they believe they deserve',[5] he seems to acknowledge implicitly that people can be motivated by concerns other than a direct concern for their material interests. However, beyond expressing a suspicion that the cited belief may be an inevitable psychological byproduct of the institution of a labor market, he does not probe the potential of reasoning about desert or entitlements as itself a source of motivation. This is a bit puzzling, since he cites as definitive certain arguments by Rawls and others that an egalitarianism in direct opposition to the cited belief was 'not simply a "value judgment" that people might or might not have according to their taste, but rather a view of what social arrangements were right, that any rational, honest person had to accept' and he expects that 'through these academics, many more millions will eventually be influenced . . . .'[6] For Rawls, of course, a conception of justice has to be capable of achieving legitimacy – mutual, uncoerced acceptance as a basis for action – or it has to surrender any claim to validity.

A standard liberal argument that egalitarianism can achieve legitimacy invokes the idea of a 'moral division of labor' between institutions and individuals. Unlike a Benthamite scheme, a moral division of labor has individuals doing some of the moral work instead of its being left entirely to institutions. The idea is that a sense of justice can play an important motivational role in generating support for and compliance with egalitarian institutions, provided the latter are designed to provide sufficient scope for the pursuit of personal aims through system-conforming behavior.

Nagel investigates this idea at length and reaches pessimistic conclusions about the possibility of a non-utopian egalitarianism extending much beyond what is approximated and immune to public challenge in today's capitalist democracies: roughly, equal basic rights of citizenship, formal equality of opportunity, and insurance against the worst consequences of natural and social misfortune (through guarantees of disaster relief, unemployment compensation, access to health care, and the like).[7] Like Roemer's, Nagel's egalitarian ideal goes beyond this to regard as morally tainted any socially produced inequalities tied to variations in any factor for which individuals are not responsible, such as their socioeconomic class of origin or their innate abilities or talents. So if Nagel is right, the notion of legitimacy will not take us beyond what Roemer thinks is realizable by Benthamite methods, if indeed it can take us that far.

To secure legitimacy as Nagel sees it, we must find mutually acceptable ways for us to respond both to the egalitarian values we all must impartially acknowledge and to our respective personal concerns. That is, we must find an answer to the question, given that each of us not only acknowledges egalitarian values but also has his own life to lead, what can we all agree we should do? Finding an adequate answer requires imaginative social and economic modeling as well as ethics, since the livability of a morality of individual conduct as well as its ability to accommodate both personal and egalitarian concerns will depend on the institutional setting in which it is imbedded. For example, a limited morality of non-interference, respect for life, liberty and property, and duties of basic mutual aid can be an adequate individual morality only within a social system that itself does much more to satisfy egalitarian values. On the other hand, a social system cannot be justified simply by appeal to such values. It must be realizable and sustainable through deliberation and conduct it is reasonable to expect of individuals who have personal as well as egalitarian concerns. To ignore this requirement is to risk the utopianism of advocating a social ideal without a feasible underlying reasonable motivational psychology.

Nagel sees the charge of utopianism as hardest to deflect in the case of talents. Advantages due to talent, he says, come as a result of demand for scarce resources in a competitive labor market. The preservation of some form of labor market with economic incentives seems to be necessary for an adequate level of economic efficiency, productivity and growth. Social structure must therefore leave room for, and perhaps even encourage, the play of personal acquisitive motives in response to economic incentives, with its inevitable resulting inequalities. Complete elimination of inequalities due to talent thus seems to Nagel to be utopian in the extreme. The most that can be done is to impose structural limits on such inequalities that ensure that they work to everyone's benefit, especially to the benefit of those whose talents leave them with the lowest prospects. And even this idea, Nagel suggests, is utopian, because sustaining it requires a morally incoherent motivational psychology, one that would combine in one outlook both the attitude that inequalities due to talent should be minimized and the attitude that one is entitled to exploit one's talents in an effort to get as much out of the system as one can.

> An economically competitive egalitarian with the appropriate partition of motives is supposed to reflect, as he signs the astronomical check for his three-star meal, that although it's a shame that business talent such as his should command such rewards while others are scraping by, there is no help for it, since he and his peers have to be allowed to earn this kind of money if the economy is to function properly. A most unfortunate situation, really, but how lucky for him![8]

A moral division of labor is unworkable here. The idea of that strategy, roughly, is to effect a division of the self into public and private roles in such a way that the impartiality demanded of people in their private roles is minimized, and in those roles there is ample play for agent-centered prerogatives; the dominance of impartiality as a motive is restricted to public roles. For example, you can to a certain extent feel entitled to purchase extra education for your children while not feeling entitled to favor them through nepotism in some public capacity. You restrict your partiality to the private sphere. In your public status you are impartial, and this finds expression not only in your refraining from nepotism but also in your supporting measures that enhance equality of educational opportunities. Nagel claims that, while this can work to a certain extent with inequalities due to class, it is impossible to effect in the case of talent-based inequalities. You cannot, within an integrated moral outlook, feel entitled in your personal affairs to wring whatever superior advantages you can out of the system through aggressive use of your talents, while feeling disapproval as a citizen for any system that allows such activity to any degree more than necessary to benefit the least advantaged. How we decide to use our abilities has both public and personal significance, so both of these motives will come into play and oppose each other in such decisions.

G.A. Cohen would argue that this incoherence amounts to hypocrisy: if we are capable of deciding to make a given contribution without getting superior advantages in return, then we cannot reasonably expect others to accept our demand for those advantages as justified on the grounds that they are necessary to maximize benefit to the least advantaged.[9] Nagel would not call it hypocrisy, but rather an attempt to acknowledge certain realities about human nature, and the way it constrains motivational possibilities. But he would call it an unsuccessful attempt; the pervasiveness of personal motivation will destabilize any social commitment to make talent-based inequalities work to the benefit of the least advantaged. The personal acquisitiveness the system feeds on will tend to erode political support for the commitment among the better off. 'It's not like the case of people playing a strictly competitive sport under strict rules – when support for the rules is guaranteed by the fact that without them winning is meaningless.'[10] People's personal concerns make social and economic advantages meaningful, apart from any commitment to equality or legitimacy.

Have we reached an impasse? Benthamite proposals would face serious instabilities with respect to equality and moreover would not meet the socialist requirement of legitimacy. Thus if Nagel's investigations reveal the egalitarian limits of legitimacy, then socialism is indeed a utopian idea. However, if legitimacy might take a different form from the one envisaged by Nagel, a form more intimately bound up with rationality and equality, then such a conclusion is premature.

For Nagel, legitimacy is a matter of a convergence of different people's answers to the question of what they could reasonably agree to, given that they all have personal as well as egalitarian concerns that must find viable expression. This is a very specific understanding of the kinds of values that have to be accommodated and the kinds of motives that can be drawn upon. Individuals who relate to each other with legitimacy share a common framework of justification, and to that extent they relate to each other on the basis of shared reasons. Yet what is shared is a converged-upon sense of the reasonableness of specific assignments of relative weight or priority to the two kinds of concerns in various spheres of action. With or without legitimacy, the kinds of concerns remain the same. For Nagel, this is because their existence is rooted in a duality of standpoints fixed in each person's nature: the personal and the impersonal. Your personal standpoint takes into account who in particular you are. It thus enables you to identify reasons you have in virtue of your own features and circumstances – your subjective or agent-relative interests or values. On the other hand, you can also view the world in abstraction from your particular place in it; in abstraction, that is, from who in particular you are. To do this is to take up the impersonal standpoint. From this standpoint you can still consider your concerns, but not as your own particular concerns; rather, you consider them, as well as the concerns of others, simply as someone's concerns, without taking into account that you in particular are that person. When you do this, it becomes clear that some of these concerns still matter, and not just to the particular person whose concerns they are, but matter, period, since from the impersonal standpoint they matter to you no matter who you are. The impersonal standpoint thus discloses values that have a certain objectivity or intersubjective validity. Moreover, they are egalitarian values; from an impersonal standpoint everyone's life matters, and no one is more important than anyone else. On the other hand, from the personal standpoint each of us attaches special importance to his own particular concerns. The duality of standpoints within the self thus provides a source of two fixed kinds of concern, and the function of legitimacy, if it can be achieved, is simply to integrate them in the governance of action in a psychologically feasible and universally acceptable way.

On this view human nature determines certain forms of concern that serve as inputs to practical reasoning aimed at legitimacy. The most that such reasoning can do is to assign weights or priorities to these kinds of concern. The specifics of social structure – in particular, structures of deliberation – do not enter the determination of these kinds themselves. These are fixed by human nature. Also fixed are certain limits on the feasibility of relations of weight or priority that they can assume. In particular, the impersonal, egalitarian concerns cannot approximate complete dominance over personal concerns. Human nature requires that personal concerns play a strong and significant role in life. This is why economic gains by the better off remain meaningful apart from any commitment to equality and legitimacy. And this is why socialism is utopian. What Roemer calls the 'socialist person' would require a motivational system outside the bounds set by human nature on feasible integrations of the two kinds of concern, even allowing for legitimacy to make some difference.

But suppose that the significance of motivational concerns depends less on human nature and more on socially specific features of deliberation than this view allows. Then legitimacy might have a wider role in the determination of the forms of concern that have significance. Strangely, though Marx stressed something like this possibility, it has gone largely unexplored. When confronted with the charge of proposing the hopelessly utopian idea of a society of altruists, he replied that egoism and altruism are complementary, socially specific motivating attitudes rather than transsocially necessary expressions of human nature. He was adamant in his insistence that

> the communists do not put egoism against self-sacrifice or self-sacrifice against egoism, nor do they express this contradiction theoretically either in its sentimental or in its highflown ideological form; on the contrary, they demonstrate the material basis engendering it, with which it disappears of itself. The communists do not put to people the moral demand: love one another, do not be egoists, etc.; on the contrary, they are very well aware that egoism, just as much as self-sacrifice, *is* in definite circumstances a necessary form of the self-assertion of individuals. Hence, the communists by no means want . . . to do away with the 'private individual' for the sake of the 'general', self-sacrificing man.[11]

These remarks are in direct opposition to the foregoing idea of the socialist person, and they gesture at a different conception, one in which changes in social structure can release hitherto untapped forms of motivational potential. An investigation into the possibility of socialism that did not explore the viability of such a conception would be seriously incomplete.

If we think of practical rationality as a kind of deliberative control over action, then we can distinguish two ways in which agents might seek to meet its standards in multi-agent situations: independent agency and collective or joint agency. In independent agency, individuals engage in separate deliberations that exclusively concern their own respective actions. They treat the actions of others as events to be anticipated, matters of uncertainty their deliberation has to address, but not as matters they have any part in deciding. Nor do they conceive of others as playing an authoritative role in their own deliberations.

In collective agency, by contrast, it is common knowledge that everyone takes as a source of reasons for his individual action actual or possible public deliberation about the entire profile of actions. Agents treat the question of which profile will be realized as a matter under their joint deliberative authority. In collective agency there is thus a public commitment to possible reasoned consensus as a constraint on deliberation. It is common knowledge that everyone accepts the ideal of making their willingness to perform their respective individual actions depend on the acceptability to everyone of the profile as a whole.

Collective and independent agency can be distinguished in three significant ways. First, they solve different problems. When a decision problem is formulated, it divides features of the world into environmental variables, whose values have to be predicted or estimated as a basis of decision, decision variables, whose values are to be decided, and consequence variables, thought of as functions of environmental and decision variables. For an agent participating in collective agency, the actions of the other agents are thought of as decision variables rather than environmental variables, as is the case in independent agency. In this respect more of the world is brought within the scope of decision. Secondly, they take place under different intentions. In collective agency each agent acts under a collective intention – an intention to act jointly with the others by performing his individual action. Moreover, in fully realized collective agency it is not only true but common knowledge that all agents act on the basis of such intentions, and that these intentions have as a common object the realization of the entire profile of individual actions.[12] Thirdly, they are regulated by different self-conceptions. Rational collective deliberation is aimed at the construction of a common or joint practical orientation, one reflectively acceptable to all as a basis of joint action. When one deliberates as an independent agent, one is guided by a conception of oneself as having exclusive control over the alternatives one faces, as the sole deliberative authority. When one engages in collective deliberation, one conceives of oneself as accountable not only to oneself, but also to the other cooperating agents, understood as themselves similarly accountable to everyone in the group.[13]

Legitimacy understood as this type of collective rationality suggests a different potential for the ideal of legitimacy as a source of motivation. Its aim would not be to arrive at a generally acceptable allocation of given, independently significant attitudes of personal and impersonal concern. It would no doubt end up certifying certain matters as properly belonging to a personal sphere of decision, but the aims pursued within this sphere would be understood as depending on their legitimacy for their meaning and value, because in this sphere one would conceive of oneself as acting socially, even when exercising one's prerogatives. Under this ideal, personal economic gains would derive their value even to the gainer in part from their legitimacy. Nagel's rejected analogy with a fiercely competitive sport is more apt in this case.

Unlike conceptions that preserve the opposition between morality and self-interest by understanding legitimacy as appealing to standards of reasonableness separate from and taking priority over the demands of rationality (as when we say, 'What she's doing is quite rational, but she's not being reasonable'), this conception takes reasons of legitimacy as entering into the determination of what is rational. Deliberation aiming at rational collective agency seeks to arrive at a joint practical orientation that satisfies the standard formal requirements of rationality in a manner acceptable to each participant from the requisite point of view. This point of view differs from that of an independent agent pursuing his separately determinable values (whether these be disclosed by a personal or impersonal standpoint). It is rather that of one of a number of equally sovereign participants in a common endeavor. It is required not in virtue of a separate standard of reasonableness, but rather as the point of view appropriate for judging the rationality of joint action.[14] For this reason, Cohen's idea that 'people would mention norms of equality when asked to explain why they and those like them are willing to work for the pay they get' seems less utopian when interpreted within the framework of this conception of legitimacy.[15]

Personal gains at the expense of equality might be more difficult to justify under this conception – and have less motivating force – for another reason as well. Insofar as Roemer follows a Benthamite approach, he does not attempt to anchor his egalitarianism through its engagement with citizens' reason at all. For Nagel, egalitarianism has its origin in the impersonal standpoint but is certified as non-utopian and thus receives whatever final justification it has through its legitimacy, which is determined by the extent to which it can be endorsed as a way of life by the practical reason of each member of society. Legitimacy as consensual deliberative rationality could certify many forms of equality in this way as well. But for some forms there is an even tighter connection. The status of citizens as fully cosovereign cannot be achieved without equality of at least some rights, opportunities and resources. Such equality gets anchored as necessary for proper deliberation rather than merely certified as the outcome of such deliberation.[16] To the extent that this kind of legitimacy is required for meeting the challenge of utopianism, there is a much more intimate connection between socialist egalitarianism and the ideal of democracy than Roemer is inclined to endorse in his book. Rather than simply a means to equality, the ideal of democracy provides egalitarianism with its proper foundation.[17]

I have not shown that such an ideal can succeed in establishing as non-utopian a more democratic and egalitarian socialism than Roemer is prepared to defend. That cannot be done without an exploration of the possibility, rational accessibility and stability of principles and procedures that would both answer to and reproduce a concern for consensual deliberative control over economic affairs. I hope only to have made plausible that such an exploration is worth undertaking and indeed may provide the only hope for socialism or indeed any significant advances in equality, given the stability problems that Roemer's proposals would face and the limited potential of legitimacy as Nagel understands it.

Notes

1. John E. Roemer, *A Future for Socialism*, Cambridge, MA: Harvard University Press 1994.

2. John Stuart Mill, *Utilitarianism*, Indianapolis and Cambridge, MA: Hackett 1979, pp. 17–18.

3. Thomas Nagel, *Equality and Partiality*, New York and Oxford: Oxford University Press 1991, p. 55. Nagel cites Bentham's 'Outline of a Work Entitled Pauper Management Improved', in John Bowring, ed., *The Works of Jeremy Bentham* vol. 8, Edinburgh: Wm. Tait 1843; reprint edn New York: Russell & Russell 1962, pp. 380–81.

4. I offer an explication of this idea in 'Reification as Dependence on Extrinsic Information' (unpubl. MS).

5. Roemer, p. 119.

6. Ibid., Roemer, pp. 26–7.

7. Nagel, *Equality and Partiality*.

8. Nagel, p. 117.

9. G. A. Cohen, 'Incentives, Inequality and Community', in Grethe B. Peterson, ed., *The Tanner Lectures on Human Values* 13, Salt Lake City: University of Utah Press 1992, pp. 261–329.

10. Nagel, pp. 117–18.

11. Karl Marx and Friedrich Engels, *The German Ideology*, S. Ryazanskaya, ed., Moscow: Progress 1968, p. 272.

12. The action pair (x, y) would be such a common object of collective intention if agent 1 had the intention of jointly performing (x, y) with agent 2 by performing x while agent 2 had the intention of jointly performing (x, y) with agent 1 by performing y. In acting on these intentions the agents would assume it to be common knowledge that the pair is such a common object of collective intention. In fully realized collective agency this assumption would be correct. In treating a collective intention as an intention to act jointly with others by performing an individual action, I am in agreement with John R. Searle, 'Collective Intentions and Actions,' in Philip R. Cohen, Jerry Morgan and Martha E. Pollack, eds, *Intentions in Communication*, Cambridge, MA: MIT Press 1990, pp. 401–15.

13. In taking deliberation about joint action to stand under a requirement of inter-personal justifiability that does not constrain independent-agent deliberation, I am in agreement with Wilfrid Sellars, *Science and Metaphysics*, London: Routledge & Kegan Paul 1968; New York: Humanities Press 1968, ch. 7 and Margaret Gilbert, 'Walking Together: A Paradigmatic Social Phenomenon', *Midwest Studies in Philosophy* 15 (1990), pp. 1–14.

14. One might claim that a distinct standard of reasonableness is required to motivate people to formulate their problems as collective decision problems in the first place. But if independent agency can be expected to lead to reification, then an interest in deliber-ative control could close this motivational gap by itself. I explore this possibility in 'Reification as Dependence on Extrinsic Information'. The matter is complicated, since questions of attainability and stability have to be carefully distinguished.

15. Cohen, p. 317.

16. For some discussion of this idea, see Joshua Cohen, 'Deliberation and Democratic Legitimacy', in Alan Hamlin and Philip Pettit, eds, *The Good Polity: Normative Analysis of the State*, New York: Blackwell 1989, pp. 17–34; see especially pp. 28–30.

17. As a consequence, the principles of socialist egalitarianism might differ from those specified by Roemer. For example, I think that at least some of the socialist concern for self-realization is more properly interpreted as a concern for deliberative control and consequently as being met by society's commitment to legitimacy as collective rationality.

The Prospects for Coupon Socialism in Ex-Command Economies

15

Why Coupon Socialism Never Stood a Chance in Russia: The Political Conditions of Economic Transition

Michael Burawoy

John Roemer writes that the best chances for the adoption of coupon socialism are to be found in the former Soviet societies.

> The countries where the opportunity costs of adopting market socialism are the least are, I believe, those that have formed in Eastern/Central Europe and out of the Soviet Union since 1989. These countries face a momentous task of institution building, no matter what kind of market system they will have, and one could argue that the costs of designing stock market, a bank-centric monitoring system, and constitutions that adequately shelter economic institutions (banks, firms) from state interference would be no greater than the costs of building a capitalist system along Anglo-American lines. Indeed, [Corbett and Mayer] have argued that a monitoring system based on banks would be easier to build in the new republics than one based on decentralized market actors and the takeover process.[1]

Indeed, institutional changes in Russia do suggest a convergence with Roemer's market socialism:

1. The command economy with central allocation of resources has given way to a market economy.
2. There are commodity markets and labor markets.
3. Transactions between firms have largely been monetized and firms compete for profits.
4. All citizens were given coupons (vouchers) to the value of 10,000 roubles which they have used to invest in mutual funds or in the purchase of their own or other state enterprises.

5. The most popular form of privatization has been one in which employees assume 51 per cent ownership of their own enterprise.
6. There is no effective capital market so that firms have to raise capital through loans from banks. The government dissolved the old state banks and encouraged the growth of 'independent' and competing banks. Many are tied to conglomerates and thus can be likened to the Japanese 'main banks', which connect firms in a single industry.
7. The central bank monitors all banks to ensure their fiscal responsibility and has at its disposal wide-ranging sanctions: from levying fines, to increasing the reserve ratio (that banks have to deposit in the Central Bank) to the withdrawal of license.

However, the results of these moves toward coupon socialism are far from Roemer's anticipations. The economy has plunged into a nose dive, output has dropped, investment has fallen, the existing means of production are being run down, budget constraints continue to be soft, and inflation has averaged between 20 per cent and 30 per cent a month. Inequalities have widened with the differential chances to exploit market opportunities.

Why is there a gap between promise and reality? At the level of equality Roemer would argue that the Russians made the mistake of allowing trade in vouchers. In Roemer's scheme vouchers are not convertible. They can only be used for purchasing stocks and all transactions in vouchers are recorded. On death, a person's vouchers revert to the state. At the level of efficiency Roemer might argue, as he does for the curiously analogous situation in Yugoslavia in the 1970s and 1980s, that 'those in control of the state organs, national and republican, [were unwilling] to allow firms autonomy or to encourage competition.'[2] It is not an accident that the interference of political authorities, the political distribution of bank credits, and excessive printing of money to meet government budgetary deficits – in short, the rise of soft budget constraints – coincided with the disintegration of the party state. In Roemer's model of coupon socialism the state is *deus ex machina*, a solution more than a problem. It is an untheorized exogenous variable, called upon in voluntaristic manner to guarantee the political conditions of coupon socialism.

In this short comment I argue that such political conditions of coupon socialism are least likely to be realized in Russia today. I highlight the peculiar institutional foundations of the Russian market economy, both as a legacy of the past and of the dynamics of the transition itself. In brief, the disintegration of the party state strengthened certain features of the old economic order which subverted the intended effects of price liberalization, of the distribution of coupons, of privatization and of the rise of banks. The Russian state was unable to make these reforms work, which raises the question of what sort of state would be necessary to ensure an efficient market economy in Russia. More broadly we have to ask whether market socialism makes consistent demands on the form of state necessary to its functioning and, if so, what institutional forms might meet such requirements.

1 From Disintegration to Reform

Behind Roemer's claim that the chances for market socialism are greatest in former state socialist societies is the assumption, held by many economists and political scientists, that the collapse of the party state meant the collapse of the entire Soviet order, in particular its economy. The task, therefore, was to 'build' new institutions and 'design' a new market economy. This popular view has its origins in Sovietology's understanding of the Soviet Union as a society held together by the Party, so that when the Party disappears society crumbles. Nothing could be further from the truth.

The stereotype of the 'command economy' is one in which a planning center dictates to executing enterprises exactly what they shall produce, when and with what means. The center is the brain of society and when it dies the entire social body dies. This model was probably never operative but certainly in the post-Stalin period the relationship between planners and executors was a bargaining relationship in which firms' monopoly of knowledge allowed them considerable control over their own activities. Still, relations among enterprises were constricted, connected to one another like stations on an assembly line. When the center disintegrated enterprises spontaneously recreated their relations of interdependence.

Effectively, the withdrawal of the party led to the strengthening of monopoly tendencies of enterprises, and even more so of the conglomerates that organized individual industries. The party no longer constrained conglomerates and their member enterprises from exploiting their regional monopolies. Barter relations, which had always existed but under the surveillance of the party, suddenly expanded rapidly to the advantage of those who controlled scarce resources. The disappearance of the party not only affected relations between enterprises but also within the enterprise, where workers assumed even greater control over production than before. The short-age economy did not disappear with the disintegration of central planning but became even more erratic. This drew managers' energies even more toward garnering supplies rather controlling the shop floor, while uncertainty of inputs made worker autonomy and impro-visation even more imperative. At the same time a major instrument of managerial control over the shop floor, namely the party, evaporated. In other words, three features of the old order – monopoly, barter and worker control – all increased at the same time as and because of the disintegration of the party state.

The collapse of the party state and resilience of the Soviet economy were the backdrop for the reforms of the post-Soviet period, signaled by price liberalization in January 1992.[4] Price liberalization was to be followed by stabilization, by control over budget deficits and over inflation. Enterprises would have to face market competition and in-efficient ones would have to declare bankruptcy. The weakness of the state and the strength of the network of relations among enterprises subverted those intended consequences.

With the stabilization program in tatters, in the summer of 1992 the Russian government blithely moved ahead with its privatization scheme by distributing 10,000 rouble vouchers to all citizens. State property was effectively given away or auctioned off for token prices. At the same time, the Central Bank started to issue an ever-increasing volume of credits to enterprises at negative interest rates which further fuelled inflation. The failure of reform was seen as a failure of political will, attributed to the divisions between a market oriented executive and the still communist legislature, or to the Stalinist hangovers of the managerial class. In fact, these divisions were not the cause of paralysis but the consequence of the balance of power in the country: a reconstituted economy still dominated by the old apparatchiki and an ever weaker central state. To understand the failure of reform one has to explore further the changes occurring in this second phase of the transition.

2 Monetization of the Economy, Inter-enterprise Debt and Disintegration of Conglomerates

Monetization of the economy was one of the most startling changes. Beginning in the second half of 1992 and increasing in 1993, despite inflation rates of 20–30 per cent a month, barter relations between enterprises were replaced by monetary transactions. Enterprises that had a monopoly or near monopoly of needed goods could charge high prices and require immediate payment; those enterprises which produced goods in lesser demand found themselves in a much weaker position, unable to obtain immediate payment and thus entering into debt with suppliers.

Two consequences followed. First, enterprises became increasingly concerned about whether they could sell their goods, given the inflation and declining real budgets of families and firms. Many enterprises found themselves reducing output, introducing shorter working weeks and even closing down for extended periods. There has been a slow shift from a supply-constrained economy to a demand-constrained economy.

Second, enterprises continued to remain afloat despite indebtedness by borrowing from one another. Inter-enterprise arrears grew astronomically during 1992 and 1993 to the level of between 25 and 40 per cent of the GDP. Cancelling mutual debts in the summer of 1993 led to a fall in such debts to a seventh of their former value. These spontaneous credits were essentially interest-free loans in a time of rampant inflation. As a result enterprises could, first, avoid dealing with banks that were increasingly controlling their finances and, second, confuse attempts at estimating their book value, necessary for privatization. As I shall describe below, in addition to inter-enterprise borrowing, banks became involved in short-term lending to cover shortfalls in working capital. Enterprises were able to avoid bankruptcy even when they were heavily in debt. That is to say, soft budget constraints continued despite a movement from supply-side constraints to demand-side constraints, from a shortage to a surplus economy.

Another consequence of the monetization of the economy was the weakening of conglomerates. Individual enterprises could now sell their produce to whom they wanted at whatever price they could obtain and they could purchase inputs from whomever would supply them. In other words, conglomerates no longer had a monopoly of the distribution, neither of the products of enterprises nor of the supplies necessary for production. The most successful and profitable enterprises within conglomerates, whose resources had been drained off to subsidize less profitable enterprises, declared independence and hived off on their own. In such a case the conglomerate was left with the less lucrative remainder. Alternatively, a conglomerate would strike a preemptive deal with the more successful enterprises and abandon the rest to their own devices.

More generally, conglomerates, whose power was challenged by the disintegration of the old administered economy, reacted by creating their own banks and, through the dispensation of loans, could continue to control the transactions of enterprises. Behind many of the new banks was the power of the old conglomerates. In order to understand how these banks operated we must turn to a more detailed examination of the changes in the financial system.

3 The Rise of Banks and the Rationalization of Soft Budget Constraints

Under the Soviet order, there was an extensive banking system but it was one that passively recorded and expedited transactions that had already been completed in the material distribution of goods and services. The banking system was a massive accounting structure that helped in the formulation of plans and then tracked plan fulfillment on micro and a macro levels. Beginning in 1988 bank reforms shifted from the mono-bank system to one based on five specialized banks. These banks and their branches began to have greater discretion in giving out credits at the same time that planning was being decentralized and money was becoming of greater importance. Enterprises were subject to 'state orders' that in principle gave them some leeway to plot their own future if they could produce above the state requisitions.

Already conglomerates began to develop their own pocket banks into which they could funnel money which they could then use for other ends than the ones intended by central planners. In Russia's struggle against the Soviet Union, beginning in 1989, the Russian government encouraged the specialized banks to pursue a course independent of Russia. In particular, in 1990 legislation dissolved the state banking system. With the exception of the Savings Bank, banks had either to privatize or liquidate themselves. Most of the existing banks found sponsors so that they could continue their commercial activities. At the same time hundreds of new banks were created from scratch with funds from conglomerates. The Central Bank continued as a major source of government credits and as a regulatory body that monitored all banking transactions.

As the economy became monetized so the banks assumed new regulatory role in the economy. All enterprises had to have one and only one bank account and all non-cash transactions underwent a cumbersome transfer process from bank to bank through their correspondent accounts in the Central Bank. The old division and non-convertibility between cash and non-cash operations continued.

Not surprisingly, there are long delays in transactions between enterprises, which often redound to the benefit of banks who use the 'float' to extend their loan portfolios. Whereas banks previously represented clients in the payment and requisitioning of bills, now the responsibility lies with the client – except when they move into the red. In this case banks assume control of the client's finances, paying off their debts in a specified order, with government taxes and utilities being first.

The Central Bank regulates banks through prudential norms of capital adequacy, asset ratios and risk factors but, more importantly, through monitoring the balance of each bank's correspondent accounts. Since virtually all transactions go through the Central Bank, the latter can apprehend and punish banks which engaged in illegal activities or allowed their account to move into the red. The Central Bank can fine a bank, raise its reserve ratio or even close it down by rescinding its license.

In effect, the Central Bank compels banks to operate according to hard budget constraints and banks in their turn try to impose hard budget constraints on their clients. They lend out money to clients they trust who are often the sponsors of the bank itself. Enterprises become shareholders of one or more banks in order to obtain credits from those banks. In these very uncertain conditions insider lending is not only legal but becomes the norm. With inflation at 20–30 per cent a month, long-term loans were three months and were offered at negative interest rates, indexed to the interest rate of the Central Bank. In much of 1992 the Central Bank loans were officially at 80 per cent although many loans were offered at even lower rates. Even at these lower rates banks rarely used their money for long-term investment. As a result, businesses with rapid turnover (trading enterprises) were the only ones who could afford to take short-term, high-interest loans. Insofar as they protected their own profit margins and operated under hard budget constraints banks intensified the development of merchant rather than industrial capital.

Since their day-to-day existence was threatened, enterprises had short time horizons. They most urgently required loans, not so much for investment but for working capital. They could borrow money from one another, they could try to borrow from the banks, but a third road was to appeal directly to the regional government or Central Bank. If an enterprise could make a convincing case that without a loan they would be bankrupt and the local community would suffer, the regional government or the Central Bank found ways of issuing a loan. These credits were in effect distributed on the basis of political criteria. The regional government, that had installed itself in the old regional party headquarters, acted just like its predecessor, either dictating the distribution of loans to the Central Bank or finding resources from its own budget.

However, banks had to assume responsibility for any government loan given to its clients. For servicing the loan the bank received a mere 3 per cent. At such a rate (spread) not surprisingly banks were often unwilling to assume loans, even on behalf of their best clients, and a special bank (the biggest bank in the region which acted as pocket bank of the government) was used to channel the money to enterprises. Under orders from the regional government, the regional branch of the Central Bank was forced to relax its standards of fiscal liability.

This new economic order dominated by banks is in effect a rationalization of the system of soft budget constraints. The regional government and regional office of the Central Bank work together to guarantee the survival of all enterprises irrespective of their economic prospects. Instead of having to organize the delivery of needed supplies or machinery, the central organs simply distribute credits on the basis of need. In this way the central organs perpetuate the dependence of enterprises on themselves. As the head of the economic planning committee told us: 'Managers are simply not ready for reforms, we will have to keep on supporting them for some time.'

The argument can be extended to the relations between Moscow and the regions. Once economic transactions are monetized and the party state has disintegrated, the only way the central government can maintain control is through the extension of credit which comes at the expense of inflation and escalating budget deficits; in other words, at the expense of stabilization. Democracy, if it did nothing else, precluded dictatorship, and left the state reliant on fiscal levers for exercising control over the regions. From each (enterprise) according to its ability, to each according to its need becomes the recipe for perpetuating soft budget constraints and increasing budget deficits, inflation and a rising real cost of living.

4 Privatization, Trade and Worker Control

The irony is that soft budget constraints continue despite privatization. What form does privatization take? Following experiences in Eastern Europe the Russian government realized that few would be interested in buying even the best of Soviet enterprises. Locally, there was not the capital and internationally, foreign capital simply could not work in a context so uncertain and so dependent on personal contacts, bribes and racketeers. Foreign investors expected immediate returns and would only be likely to participate in joint ventures for the exploitation of natural resources. Even then, only the most unscrupulous of Western capitalists would risk investment, particularly when opportunities were rife in so many other countries where the rule of law obtained.

In the summer of 1992 the Russian government distributed 10,000 rouble vouchers to each Russian citizen, who could deposit them with a mutual fund or invest them directly in an enterprise. They could also buy and sell these vouchers, although their market value never reached their nominal value. Enterprises prepared their own privatization plans according to one of three models, the most popular of which was to sell 51 per cent of the shares to employees. The system of evaluating enterprises was arbitrary, often equivalent to the voucher-buying power of the employees and their families. In effect, 51 per cent ownership was given to enterprise employees. In this process managers would receive a higher per capita share of ownership than the average employee and the enterprise was effectively handed over to those who had run it before.

However, employees as stock owners could replace their managers and herein lay their power beyond the shop floor. They might rise in rebellion when managers were caught feathering their nest by selling off parts of the enterprise, making side agreements that benefited only themselves. In one case, in Vorkuta, the director of the largest and richest mine was caught distributing Volga cars to his friends in high places; cars that were bought out of the mine's revenues. Workers staged a rebellion, organized a strike and a sit-in underground, seized the managerial offices, threw out the director and installed their own. In the furniture factory, where I worked, falling wages, mismanagement and corruption charges were leveled at the director and his entourage. They were thrown out of office by the labor collective and elections produced a new manager. With the evacuation of the party, no body has emerged to mediate relations between workers and managers in such employee-owned firms.

Managers have been prepared to make concessions to the labor collective, trying to guarantee wages and resisting layoffs, but they have been unwilling to subject themselves to being overseen by the shareholders. Given the short-term strategies of many directors and their immediate assistants, this is not surprising. Rather than use profits to reinvest, managers seek to maximize immediate gains by

consuming their profits and cannibalizing their enterprises. In the
industries we studied, managers' main objective was, if at all possible,
to sell goods abroad at low prices and use the proceeds to buy foreign
consumer goods (or deposit unknown amounts in foreign banks) and
distribute these among employees at token prices. Natural resources,
oil, coal, wood, were flowing out of the country and Western
consumer goods were coming in, from trainers to televisions, from
Barbie dolls to fridges, from cigarettes to cars. Indeed, one of the most
popular businesses involved the reimportation of Russian manufac-
tured Lada cars, virtually unobtainable locally. Foreign cars were not
only more expensive but they also required spare parts unavailable
in Russia. Short time horizons have led to rapid disaccumulation
in industry, with some managers making windfall gains. In these
circumstances workers might have longer time horizons, concerned
to maintain enterprises in order to keep their jobs.

Plundering the country's resources has become part of the local
currency. The government gives out 'quotas' of oil, wood or coal to
local enterprises; that is, the right to export specified amounts of these
commodities. Quota in hand the enterprise goes to one of the firms
with a license to export which organizes the purchase of the raw
material at domestic prices and their export at international prices.
The difference is divided between the 'export' firm and the enterprise
which was given the 'quota'. Thus, when the local hockey team
needed money, the President of the Republic called the head of the
economic planning committee and instructed her to obtain a 'credit'
from the main bank which would receive a 'quota' in return. The
local pharmacies were continually being subsidized with quotas in
order to import badly needed medicines. On the other hand, the oil
industry complains that the government regulates its exports and at
the same time depresses the domestic price so that it is unprofitable
to extract.

Russia does have a market economy, enterprises are socially owned
and they even compete with one another, *but* that competition is
over capturing the proceeds from trade. We are back in an era of
mercantilism, in which exchange dominates production and the state
orchestrates trade, distributing export quotas, licenses and money
credit.

5 From an Overpoliticized Model of State Socialism to an Underpoliticized Model of Market Socialism

Roemer's claim that the opportunity costs of transition to market socialism are lowest in the Soviet Union and Eastern Europe rest on an overpoliticized conception of state socialism. It assumes that the disintegration of the party state entails the disintegration of the economy. The opposite is nearer the truth: the withering away of the party state led to the reconstitution of the economy and the emergence of a fragmented, anemic and ineffective liberal democracy, incapable of introducing a market economy with hard budget constraints. There is no market road to a market economy: it requires a strong centralized state that dictates the transition to economic actors.

This raises the question of the political conditions of market socialism, questions Roemer does not theorize. Let us first see how he understands politics under capitalism. He assumes that many of the public bads stem, not from the market, but from the concentration of ownership among a small group of people who wield disproportionate power over the state. These capitalists, therefore, effectively resist policies that, for example, protect the environment at the expense of profits. There is, however, an alternative view of the capitalist state in which big business wields much less influence. In this perspective the capitalist state has to be autonomous from the capitalist class in order to protect capitalism against capitalists. The state seeks the maximal expansion of capitalism to increase its own revenues. If the state is interested in the health of the capitalist system rather than the fate of individual capitalists, then there is no reason to believe that its policies will change substantially with the egalitarian distribution of ownership.

Change would seem a likely eventuality if, and only if, citizens, by virtue of their ownership, could and would direct the state to pursue anticapitalist policies. It assumes a democratic state that can be penetrated by citizens and citizens who would want to preserve the environment at the expense of their immediate income. It would assume a radical democracy; a democracy that was concerned with more than the expanded reproduction of capitalism.

Is such a radical democracy compatible with the imposition of hard budget constraints, a state that can remain impervious to pressures for differential distribution of loans, differential interest rates for sectors? Can one insulate radical democracy as the articulation of needs from the state assigned to implement those needs? Is the Taiwan state successful in dictating the trajectory of investment, because it is able to insulate itself from democratic pressures, because those pressures are in any case weak?

Roemer can maintain that the easiest transition to market socialism will be in the ex-socialist countries only if he can show: (1) how the disintegrated party state will be replaced by an authoritarian state, necessary to install a market economy with hard budget constraints; and (2) that this authoritarian state will wither away leaving a radical democracy behind. We are left with the old Leninist problematic: how can dictatorship give rise to democracy? Democracy is not simply an end in itself but a necessary means for the viability of market socialism. It, therefore, needs to be *theorized* as such. Moreover, the realization of the economic conditions of market socialism may be trivial compared to the *realization* of its political conditions.

Acknowledgment

This paper is based on research conducted with Pavel Krotov in Northern Russia, in the Republic of Komi, between January and July, 1993, and funded by grants from the John D. MacArthur Foundation and the National Science Foundation.

Notes

1. John E. Roemer, *A Future for Socialism*, Cambridge, MA: Harvard University Press 1994, pp. 126–7.
2. Ibid., p. 89.

16

The Prospects for Democratic Market Socialism in the East

Thomas E. Weisskopf

In *A Future for Socialism*, John Roemer cogently develops a model of democratic market socialism designed to overcome the limitations of past models of socialism – actual and theoretical – and to constitute an efficient and equitable alternative to capitalism. Toward the end of his book he suggests that 'the countries where the opportunity costs of adopting market socialism are the least are . . . those that have formed in Eastern/Central Europe and out of the Soviet Union since 1989'.[1] The perception that the prospects for some form of democratic market socialism are now brightest in the countries of the former 'second world' has indeed been widespread among advocates of a 'third way' between capitalism and Communist-Party-directed socialism.

Roemer offers some persuasive arguments in support of this perception.[2] With the collapse of the Communist Party (CP) state and the ubiquitous desire to establish a new market-oriented economic system, 'these countries face a momentous task of institution building, no matter what kind of market system they will have'. Each of the countries is engaged in a process of redistribution of rights to national property on a large scale; indeed in some countries (e.g., Russia and Czechoslovakia) ongoing programs of 'voucher privatization' of state enterprises are reminiscent of Roemer's 'coupon economy'.[3] In most cases the establishment of a new system of property rights is far from complete and thus potentially open to socialist as well as capitalist arrangements. Moreover, the growing inequalities and insecurities which have accompanied the growth of private enterprise in the new market environment have generated increasing popular antagonism, and this suggests that a political base could be formed in favor of a more socialist form of market economy.

In this paper I argue, to the contrary, that the prospects for developing a viable form of democratic market socialism out of the

wreckage of the CP-directed socialist economies are in fact very
poor, for both political and structural reasons. I begin in section 1 by
tracing briefly the history of market socialism in the East, with an
emphasis on recent developments. In section 2 I consider political
obstacles to the establishment of a market socialist system in the post-
communist nations. Then in section 3 I discuss some of the ways
in which the structural characteristics of post-communist societies
constitute an inhospitable environment for market socialism along
Roemerian lines. I conclude in section 4 by speculating on some
of the implications of my pessimistic appraisal of the prospects for
shaping a new and desirable form of socialism in the East.

1 The Evolution of Market Socialism

As far back as the 'New Economic Policy' initiated by Lenin in the
early 1920s to set the war-torn Soviet economy back on its feet, the
idea of combining markets with socialist forms of property ownership
and regulation has had considerable appeal for CP leaders. Indeed,
in most of the many historical instances in which a centralized CP-
dominated system – in the Soviet Union, Eastern Europe or the 'third
world' – encountered serious economic problems, reform efforts were
launched to reduce the degree of centralization and increase the scope
of markets.[4] These reform efforts rarely went as far as to create a
system that could be called 'market socialism'; though the experiences
of Yugoslavia since the early 1950s, Hungary since the late 1960s and
China, more recently, do warrant that label. In these cases, of course,
the CP maintained authoritarian political control and a substantial
degree of bureaucratic economic control as well. These examples
of market socialism were still a far cry from the kind of market
socialism proposed by Roemer and other advocates of a democratic
'third way'.

By the late 1980s CP-directed socialism in the Soviet Union and
Eastern Europe was creaking and crumbling. The growing economic
crisis was aggravated by the worldwide economic doldrums of the
1980s, but there could be little doubt that internal economic weaknesses were becoming increasingly serious. CP leaders were well
aware of the need for major economic and political reform if there
was to be a future for any kind of socialism in their countries. In
several of the East European nations, notably Poland and Hungary,
new decentralizing reforms were introduced; and in the Soviet Union,
CP General Secretary Mikhail Gorbachev launched his programs of

glasnost and *perestroika*, thereby initiating a process of growing marketization and decentralization of political and economic power which would accelerate with each passing year.

Not only were CP leaders increasingly interested in reforming their brand of socialism in a more capitalistic direction, but many leading dissidents in the East favored a 'third way' for their economies, if and when they would be liberated from the yoke of CP dictatorship. These dissidents sought to combine political democracy with an economic system that would combine the efficiency of market mechanisms with fulfillment of the humanitarian social goals that CP-directed socialism had honored much more fully in rhetoric than in reality. The idea of market socialism resonated well with such an agenda.

In some countries of the East dissidents found very appealing the notions of worker ownership and workplace democracy – elements of a variant of market socialism which, unlike Roemer's model, places strong emphasis on worker self-management. Thus, in Poland in the early 1980s, the Solidarity Movement embraced workers' control as an important element of its economic program; and in a number of countries (including the Soviet Union as well as Poland) CP regimes, under pressure from workers and reformers, began to confer greater power on enterprise-level workers' councils. As the momentum for economic reform accelerated in the late 1980s and early 1990s, worker ownership and control of enterprises increasingly appeared as a politically and economically promising alternative to conventional forms of capitalist ownership and control, especially for those who sought to transform state-dominated economies into something other than full-fledged capitalist systems.

In the early 1990s there was a flurry of interest in market socialism in the rapidly changing nations of the East. After the collapse in 1989 of the old-style hard-line CP regime of Erich Honecker in East Germany, a new generation of reformist leaders came to power (briefly) advocating a market socialist 'third way' for East Germany. In Czechoslovakia, Vaclav Havel and some of the intellectuals in his circle of Charter 77 dissidents sought to develop an alternative to what they viewed as the excessive individualism and rampant commercialism of Western capitalist economies. In the Soviet Union, Mikhail Gorbachev gathered around him economic advisers, such as Leonid Abalkin, who talked openly about converting the Soviet economy to a form of market socialism.

In general, support for some form of market socialism in the East came from professionals active in the reformist wing of the CP or from intellectuals prominent in the underground resistance to the CP.

But both of these bases of market-socialist support were soon to be overwhelmed in the political arena by the forces unleashed by the crumbling of CP authority. A new generation of political leaders and (Western-trained) economists rose to embrace market capitalism and the most rapid possible transition thereto, with strong support from the West and from indigenous entrepreneurs and speculators who had begun to do very well as their economic freedoms expanded. In many countries of the East the new breed of politicians and economists were welcomed, or at least tolerated, by a substantial fraction of the population eager for economic improvement and ready to believe in the miraculous powers of free enterprise and the market. Thus names such as Balcerowicz (in Poland), Klaus (in Czechoslovakia) and Gaidar (in Russia) came to the fore, embracing Thatcherite and Reaganite conceptions of capitalism as the wave of the future for their countries.

Many of the economists and other professionals who at one time had invested their hopes and energies in the promotion of market socialism (with or without worker self-management) now abandoned all interest in a third way. It turned out that for all but a committed minority, the embrace of market socialism in one form or another had merely represented a marriage of convenience based on the limits of the possible. Once the ideological barriers to full-fledged capitalism came tumbling down with the Berlin Wall, most intellectuals and professionals abandoned the project of reforming socialism and joined the movement to build a new capitalism in their nations.

To be sure, in some countries of the East, such as Romania and Ukraine, the thrust toward capitalism was much weaker, as con-servative nationalist leaders limited the pace of privatization and the scope of the transition to a market economy. But such go-slow approaches that arose after the collapse of hard-line communism had little or nothing to do with market socialism. Rather, they were rooted in the effort of much of the CP *nomenklatura* to maintain their privileged status in the old style rather than try to convert it into a favorable position in the new market economy.

By 1992, just a few years after the opportunities for market social-ism had seemed so bright, realistic political prospects for a 'third way' seemed to have vanished throughout the East. The Soviet Union had collapsed, and the Yeltsin–Gaidar team in Russia was firmly commit-ted to a rapid transition to capitalism. Two years of 'shock therapy' in Poland, begun by Balcerowicz in early 1990, had thrust the economy irreversibly onto the road to capitalism. Vaclav Klaus had supplanted Vaclav Havel as the dominant political personality in Czechoslovakia, becoming the darling of the World Bank and the IMF among political leaders in the East. In those Eastern nations yet to embark on a systematic transformation of their economies, the old socialist system was crumbling and a form of primitive capitalism was emerging in a chaotic manner, in the absence of any well-conceived or strongly supported alternative.

Since 1992 the political tides have again turned, though hardly as dramatically as they did in 1989. In elections in 1993 and 1994 (in Lithuania, Poland, Russia and Hungary) large numbers of voters turned against the most avid free-marketeers and the most enthusiastic pro-capitalists who initially rose to power in the wake of the demise of the CP. In a context of continuing economic dislocation, declining real incomes for the majority of the population, and increasingly conspicuous inequalities, many people turned to reformist elements of the old CP apparatus and other opposition groups in search of some protection from the ravages of the collapse of the old system and the transition to the new.

Yet the beneficiaries of this backlash against the 'big bang' strategy of transition to capitalism have not been advocates of market socialism. For the most part the gainers in the 1993 and 1994 elections have been politicians and parties also committed to a transition to capitalism, but a more gradual one in which more attention is paid to preserving employment and more public spending is devoted to social programs to cushion adverse effects of the economic changes on ordinary people. The programs of these parties have much more in common with social democracy than with market socialism.

A partial exception to the above generalization is the growing support evinced (in countries such as Poland and Russia, and now apparently also in Ukraine) for forms of employee ownership as a mechanism of privatization. Although firmly opposed by the first generation of post-communist leaders and economic decision makers, privatization schemes in which employees acquire a majority of the publicly held shares of corporatized former state enterprises have emerged as a popular means for removing these enterprises from government control. Such employee-majority-owned enterprises could conceivably provide the foundation for a worker self-managed variant of market socialism. In practice, however, employee majority ownership of former state enterprises has almost always meant undisputed managerial control.[5] Ostensibly employee-oriented privatization schemes have served much more as a vehicle for insider 'nomenklatura privatization' than as a basis for the establishment of industrial democracy. Indeed, they should be interpreted as part of the ongoing struggle over the private appropriation of formerly state property rights in the post-CP era rather than as part of a movement that has anything to do with democratic self-management or market socialism.[6]

In sum, the evidence is strong that the idea of market socialism, as a viable alternative option for economies of Eastern Europe and the former Soviet Union making the transition to a market economy, is dead. One may be able to identify a few countries of the East (Romania, Uzbekistan?) where the political leadership remains some-what skeptical of capitalism and might become interested in a genuine alternative. But these are countries in which the influence of old-style CP leaders remains very strong and in which democratic traditions are particularly underdeveloped; thus market socialism, should it ever be introduced, is highly unlikely to take a democratic form that would reflect the aspirations of its most committed devotees.

2 Obstacles to the Establishment of Democratic Market Socialism

What accounts for the failure of democratic market socialism to take root in the East? One obvious candidate for an explanation is the absence of a clear and well worked-out blueprint for such a system (Roemer's book, after all, only appeared in 1994!). But many of the general ideas underlying market socialism have been circulating for quite some time and, indeed, advocates of variants of such a system could be found in virtually every post-communist country. What needs to be explained is the evident difficulty of developing a strong constituency for democratic market socialism within the more open political arenas of the post-communist societies.

First of all, consider the advocates of market socialism themselves. They consist for the most part of well-educated professionals, government officials, skilled workers and labor leaders: but in every country of the East they constitute only a small minority of their peer group. Because of their small numbers (and lack of disproportionate resources), they are clearly not in a position to prevail in open political competition without a large and/or powerful set of political allies.

One might argue that market socialism has in fact a very large latent constituency in the poorer classes of society, for they stand to derive the greatest economic benefits from its redistributive impli-cations. Workers, moreover, might well be attracted to variants of market socialism involving substantial elements of worker self-management. But here another obstacle arises: the complexity of the concepts and mechanisms of democratic market socialism. It is not easy to explain in simple and compelling terms how a market socialist economy would work to benefit the majority, particularly in the case of the relatively sophisticated versions of market socialism, like Roemer's, that arguably offer the best prospects for combining economic efficiency with social justice. Nor is it easy to show how self-management will yield palpable gains for workers. It is far simpler to make a case for social democratic modifications of capitalism as a way of meeting the economic interests of the poor, or to interest workers in forms of employee ownership that are much closer to syndicalist capitalism than to market socialism.

The unfortunate fact is that the political prospects for market socialism tend to be brightest when authoritarian regimes in control of socialist economies begin to loosen up – when their leaders become receptive to experimentation designed to improve the nation's economic performance without compromising the leaders' overall political authority. Under these circumstances, the leaders provide some opportunities for intellectuals and professionals to devise the kind of decentralizing economic reforms (in the context of society-wide economic regulation) which characterize market socialism. This was the case in the few sustained historical examples of market socialism: Yugoslavia from the 1950s, Hungary from the late 1960s and China under Deng Xiao-Ping. Yet in none of these cases was an authoritarian regime prepared to allow the degree of political liberalization needed to undergird a democratic form of market socialism.

Once the preconditions for political democracy have been established with the collapse of authoritarian CP-dominated regimes, the impetus for market socialism tends to be lost for two reasons. First, many of those who supported it for pragmatic reasons jump ship and join the movement for full-fledged capitalism. Secondly, and even more important, the legacy of a discredited state apparatus looms as an enormous obstacle to popular support for a socio-economic system involving a critical role for the state.

This last point can hardly be overemphasized. Clearly the establishment and operation of a market-socialist economy involves a continuing role for the state and its officials, albeit one that is much more subtle, more indirect and more benign than running an administered socialist economy. Yet the state has been so discredited in the East by the history of CP bureaucratic domination that it can no longer plausibly present itself as a source of effective and beneficent social engineering. Popular cynicism about the role of government in the economy, in the wake of the manifestly self-serving, corrupt, and obtuse behavior of its representatives under CP regimes, is perfectly understandable; but it poses a huge obstacle to advocates of democratic market socialism in their efforts to rally support for their cause.

To be sure, many citizens of Eastern nations exposed to the inequalities and insecurities of a relatively unregulated market system in recent years have started to long for a return to greater order amid the unfamiliar and unsettling chaos. There is evidence of growing sympathy for a 'strong ruler' to set things right again. But this reaction can hardly be interpreted as a new sense of confidence in the ability of public officials to manage the economic affairs of a nation in a democratic framework. This kind of popular sentiment appears to point more surely toward an authoritarian form of capitalism than toward a democratic form of socialism.

3 The Inhospitable Environment for Market Socialism

Let us suppose now that the political obstacles to the establishment of a democratic market-socialist system can somehow be overcome. Is it plausible to suppose that such a system would survive and prosper in the environment of the post-communist societies of the East?

I believe that the answer is most probably negative, because the institutional and cultural context bequeathed by CP-directed socialist societies is in too many ways incompatible with the requirements for the successful operation of a democratic socialist market economy. Roemer is right that the failure of the Soviet-type system was not necessarily a failure of socialism; he makes a good case that socialism can work if it is embedded in (robust) democracy and markets rather than in authoritarianism and commands. But a society emerging from authoritarianism and commands is ill-equipped to make democracy and markets work effectively, and it is also ill-equipped to sustain the kind of sensitive state role in setting limits to the operation of free markets which represents the essence of the socialist project in a market environment.

That it will be very difficult to establish effective democracies in post-communist societies is a perfectly commonplace but no less valid observation. The *forms* of democracy can be and in most cases have been introduced in the East: more-or-less free elections, a relatively free press, political parties, etc. What is widely recognized to be lacking are the underlying *institutions* that sustain a vital democracy: strong organizations representing and serving various interest groups, reliable sources of information for citizens, opportunities for meaningful debate and discussion of issues. Also lacking and just as important are a social culture in which individuals believe they can make a difference and have some incentive to participate in political activity, and a political culture in which politicians are ready to negotiate and compromise in order to satisfy partially many interests rather than seek to impose totally a single interest. Because the CP monopolized the political arena so completely, suppressing most manifestations of 'civil society', the institutions and culture undergirding democracy must be built up virtually from scratch in the East. This is a time-consuming process, and it will take all the longer in the nations of the former Soviet Union which were dominated by the CP for 70 years than it will in those areas of Eastern Europe where CP dominance began only after World War II.

It will be just as difficult and time-consuming a process to develop an effective market system. To be sure, the market mentality (Adam Smith's 'propensity to truck and barter') never disappeared, even in the most rigidly administered economy under CP rule, and all kinds of markets have mushroomed in the East since the command system collapsed. But it is one thing for myriad transactions to take place between buyers and sellers; it is quite another for such transactions to work 'as if by invisible hand' to coordinate the independent actions of atomistic individuals to achieve a significant degree of overall economic efficiency.

To function effectively a market system must be embedded in a general culture of honesty and trust; it must also be embedded in institutions that limit problems of malfeasance and, more generally, the transactions costs of market operations.[7] What is needed is a comprehensive institutional structure of laws, regulations, and sanctions which undergird an ethic of personal reliability and responsibility. This in turn helps to channel people's self-seeking instincts into activities that create new wealth rather than simply redistributing old wealth.

Moreover, to be efficient a market system must also find ways to limit the incidence and avoid the negative consequences of 'market failures' arising from public goods, externalities, and other well known sources of divergence between private and social benefits and costs. Depending on the context, market failures may best be alleviated by the extension or redefinition of private property rights, by state regulation or intervention, or by voluntary mechanisms of

EQUAL SHARES

cooperation. But each of these kinds of solution depend on an appropriate institutional or cultural framework: institutions backing up property rights and/or state programs, or 'cultures of cooperation' of the kind that can be built up only through frequent and multiplex interactions among relatively equal members of a community (who can bring to bear reputation effects, informal sanctions, etc., to assure cooperation).[8]

In the absence of the appropriate institutions and culture, market participants will have to devote substantial resources to such non-productive activities as security and contract enforcement, rent-seeking activities will tend to displace productive activities, and private benefits and costs will depart significantly from social benefits and costs. This is precisely the case now in the East, in the wake of the collapse of CP-dominated structures of authority and discipline. New legal and regulatory institutions are woefully underdeveloped; extreme individualism, widespread distrust, and opportunism are rampant; and market failures are largely ignored. As a result, the costs and risks of doing honest business are very high, and the economic efficiency gains from a decentralized market system are very hard to realize.

The obstacles to effective democracy and markets in the East are just as sobering for the prospects of a democratic form of capitalism as they are for democratic market socialism; they suggest that the early hopes and expectations of many Western reformers for a rapid transition of the post-communist countries to a Western-style economic system were naive at best.[9] But there is good reason to suspect that conditions in the East are even less hospitable to democratic market socialism than to some forms of capitalism. This is because, first of all, democratic politics is considerably more important for the success of a democratic market-socialist system than it is for the success of a capitalist system; indeed, history provides many examples of capitalist economies which have prospered in the absence of democracy. Second, as compared with democratic forms of capitalism, democratic market socialism calls upon the state to play a particularly critical and sensitive role in order to serve distinctively socialist goals such as distributive justice.

To accomplish its tasks under democratic market socialism, the state must be strong enough to set and enforce rules and regulations regarding property rights and the operation of markets, in ways that are of course much less overbearing and intrusive than under CP-dominated socialism, but which are somewhat more extensive than under most forms of capitalism. The state must also be held accountable for its activities to the general citizenry. Yet the environment and the culture in which the state now operates in the East are unfavorable in both these respects.

For one thing, state authority at the national level has been greatly weakened since the collapse of the CP regimes. In most of the post-communist countries there has been substantial diffusion of political power to regions and localities; and there has been diffusion of effective economic power to former state enterprises (and/or monopolistic associations thereof) and to local government agencies. National governments are having a great deal of difficulty raising revenues, and they lack resources to undertake programs and even to enforce laws and regulations.

For another thing, all of the countries of the East face grave problems of accountability of the public sector. The legacy of corruption and opportunism among government bureaucrats, and the whole culture of soft budget constraints, has made it almost second nature for public officials to serve particular private rather than general public interests. Moreover, mechanisms and attitudes that would support effective monitoring of the actions of public officials are largely lacking. Throughout Eastern Europe and the former Soviet Union, the state is regarded (with considerable justification) as at best incompetent and at worst thoroughly corrupt.

Economic development and transformation in the East is therefore going to have to rely, by default, largely on initiatives from below. Because of the decline in the authority and legitimacy of the state, political leaders and national economic decision makers will have relatively little influence over the course of events. To the dismay of anyone desirous of rational, ordered and equitable change – including notably all advocates of market socialism – the countries of the East seem most likely to be in for a Hayekian process of spontaneous and chaotic change motivated largely by individual self-interest, constrained less by conscious social engineering than by the pressures of an increasingly powerful global capitalist economy.

4 Concluding Observations

My conclusions about the prospects for democratic market socialism in the East are very pessimistic indeed, especially for those (myself included) who believe in the kind of social rationality, responsibility and justice reflected in contemporary models of market socialism. The realities of the Eastern environment appear to be at least as inhospitable to the preferred models of the Left as they are to the preferred models of the Right. Indeed, because Roemerian and other contemporary models of market socialism involve more ambitious goals with respect to democratic decision making, they face even more daunting obstacles in the chaos of post-communist societies.

This pessimistic appraisal raises the question: under what conditions could democratic market socialism ever have been or still be expected to succeed, in the East or elsewhere?

I would argue that the prospects for a viable and democratic form of market socialism in the East would have been substantially greater had the effort to establish it occurred as part of a process of gradual transition from CP-directed socialism to a freer economic and political system, rather than in the wake of the collapse of the communist system. Forward-looking political leaders with substantial authority to bring about fundamental change, ready to listen to and act upon the advice of innovative social and economic reformers, and under strong pressure from an aroused and mobilized citizenry, could conceivably have initiated the kind of fundamental reforms that would introduce democratic and market and (truly) socialist institutions in a gradual, systematic and ultimately more effective way. In such a context the reform effort would not have had to contend with the degree of private cynicism and opportunism, and the extent of governmental corruption and impotence, which have plagued contemporary efforts to promote effective democracy, efficient markets and social justice.

Needless to say, this kind of scenario is enormously demanding and (even without the benefit of hindsight) could never have been considered a very strong historical possibility. Perhaps Czechoslovakia in the 'Prague Spring' of the 1960s offered the best historical opportunity for such a scenario to unfold. Had Soviet troops not put an end to the experiment, it is possible that a democratic and economically successful form of market socialism could have developed in this little country with relatively strong democratic, market and socialist traditions, poised between East and West. The Soviet Union under Gorbachev in the late 1980s might be considered another such historical opportunity; but the fact that Russia and the USSR have had such a long history of authoritarian and bureaucratic rule no doubt makes efforts at reform in a democratic market socialist direction all the more problematic. Yugoslavia, Hungary and China did of course develop forms of market socialism under more favorable conditions than now exist in the East; but these three historical examples lacked the critical ingredient of strong democratic traditions and pressures.

I would therefore suggest that, if democratic market socialism is to have a future anywhere, it is most likely to be in those parts of the world where democratic and market institutions and cultures have already been well established. Here the critical missing ingredient is the socialist commitment to greater egalitarianism (and more profound democracy). To be sure, recent political and economic trends in the developed capitalist countries of the world do not suggest any movement in this direction – quite the contrary. Political circumstances have a way of changing over time, however, and they surely change more readily than institutions and culture. It seems to me, therefore, that the long-run prospects for democratic market socialism are best where history has prepared at least some of the institutional and cultural grounds for its successful operation.

Notes

1. John E. Roemer *A Future for Socialism*, Cambridge, MA: Harvard University Press 1994, pp. 126–7.

2. Ibid., pp. 127–30.

3. It should be stressed, however, that these voucher privatization programs differ from Roemer's coupon plan in a number of respects; most importantly, the vouchers, as well as any enterprise shares obtained for them, are fully negotiable.

4. Reform efforts in 'actually existing socialism' are amply documented in a vast literature; for a particularly instructive source, see Wlodzimierz Brus and Kazimierz Laski, *From Marx to the Market*, Oxford: Clarendon Press 1989.

5. For an informative account of this phenomenon in the case of privatization in Russia see Joseph Blasi, 'Privatized Enterprises in Russia: Organizational Trends and Problems', draft paper, Russian Privatization Center (Moscow) 1994.

6. When I presented to a conference in Moscow a paper advocating the transformation of state-owned enterprises into democratic self-managed firms, the labor-oriented participants showed little interest in the provisions for one-person-one-vote workplace democracy; their main concern was to assure that enterprise assets would remain under the control of insiders – including management as well as the leadership of workers' organizations – rather than be open to acquisition by outsiders. For more detail see Thomas E. Weisskopf, 'Democratic Self-Management: An Alternative Approach to Economic Transformation in the Former Soviet Union', in Bertram Silverman, Murray Yanowich and Robert Vogt, eds, *Double Shift: Transforming Work in Post-Socialist and Post-Industrial Societies*, Armonk, NY: M. E. Sharpe 1993.

7. I am drawing here on a very useful analysis of the embeddedness of successful market systems by Mark Granovetter, 'Economic Action and Social Structure: The Problem of Embeddedness', *American Journal of Sociology* 91, No. 3, pp. 481–510.

8. For an instructive account of the role of cultures in cooperation in market economies see Mieke Meurs's essay in this volume, chapter 6.

9. In a few exceptional cases, perhaps the Czech Republic, Slovenia and Estonia, these hopes may not prove to have been so unfounded. But these exceptions can be attributed in considerable part to the small populations and favorable geographical locations (vis-à-vis the West) of the countries involved.